Praise for
The Ones Who Hit the Hardest

"As a thick slice of football history, *The Ones Who Hit the Hardest* is a winning touchdown, and that's all it really needs to be."
—*Pittsburgh Post-Gazette*

"A lyrical volume that is as much a social history of Pittsburgh in the 1970s as a chronicle of the Steelers' early glory years." —*The Wall Street Journal*

"A simply standout addition to the rich lore of the Steelers."
—Behind the Steel Curtain (official Steelers fan site)

"Exciting, informative reading for NFL fans with an interest in the league's history." —*Booklist*

"Head to your local bookstore and score a copy of *The Ones Who Hit the Hardest*. You won't be sorry." —*Maxim*

"Chad Millman and Shawn Coyne have crafted a well-researched, nicely paced history of the Steelers franchise and the team's heated rivalry with the Cowboys, but fans of any NFL team will enjoy this book."
—NPR's *Only A Game*

"Chad Millman and Shawn Coyne have written a terrific book forged in grit, soul, perseverance, and faith. This was America in 1978, when the Pittsburgh steel mills were shutting down. Meanwhile, in Dallas, the banks were still burning money. Super Bowl XIII was my first to cover as a newspaperman, and it was the best ever. Millman and Coyne have brought the event to life, with all of its remarkable contrasts, like never before."
—Jim Dent, author of *The Junction Boys* and *Twelve Mighty Orphans*

"This is a gripping portrait not just of a football team, but of the city that team fought for. It's all here—from the Cowboys and Steelers slugging it out on the field to the steelworkers clawing out an existence as their livelihood slipped away." —Tom Callahan, author of *Johnny U*

Chad Millman is a senior deputy editor for *ESPN The Magazine* and is the author of numerous books, including the *New York Times* bestseller *Iceman: My Fighting Life*. He lives in New Jersey with his wife and two sons.

Shawn Coyne is a former editor and publisher who has overseen numerous bestsellers, including *Favre*, *Payton*, *Taylor*, and *Namath*. A native of Pittsburgh, he lives in New York.

THE ONES WHO HIT
THE HARDEST

THE STEELERS,
THE COWBOYS,
THE '70S,
AND THE FIGHT
FOR AMERICA'S SOUL

CHAD MILLMAN and SHAWN COYNE

GOTHAM BOOKS

GOTHAM BOOKS
Published by Penguin Group (USA) Inc.
375 Hudson Street, New York, New York 10014, U.S.A.

Penguin Group (Canada), 90 Eglinton Avenue East, Suite 700, Toronto, Ontario M4P 2Y3, Canada
(a division of Pearson Penguin Canada Inc.) · Penguin Books Ltd, 80 Strand, London WC2R 0RL,
England · Penguin Ireland, 25 St Stephen's Green, Dublin 2, Ireland (a division of Penguin Books
Ltd) · Penguin Group (Australia), 250 Camberwell Road, Camberwell, Victoria 3124, Australia (a
division of Pearson Australia Group Pty Ltd) · Penguin Books India Pvt Ltd, 11 Community Centre,
Panchsheel Park, New Delhi–110 017, India · Penguin Group (NZ), 67 Apollo Drive, Rosedale,
Auckland 0632, New Zealand (a division of Pearson New Zealand Ltd) · Penguin Books (South
Africa) (Pty) Ltd, 24 Sturdee Avenue, Rosebank, Johannesburg 2196, South Africa

Penguin Books Ltd, Registered Offices: 80 Strand, London WC2R 0RL, England

Published by Gotham Books, a member of Penguin Group (USA) Inc.

Previously published as a Gotham Books hardcover edition

First trade paperback printing, September 2011

2   4   6   8   10   9   7   5   3   1

Gotham Books and the skyscraper logo are trademarks of Penguin Group (USA) Inc.

The Library of Congress Cataloging-in-Publication Data has been applied for

ISBN: 978-1-592-40665-4

Printed in the United States of America
Set in Minion Pro • Designed by Julie Schroeder

To Stacy, Zac, Owen, Bibb, Bleecker, Waverly, and Crosby.
They earned it.

CONTENTS

I believe the game is designed to reward
the ones who hit the hardest.
If you can't take it, you shouldn't play.

JACK LAMBERT

PROLOGUE

ON FRIDAY, JANUARY 17, 1969, THE FORTY-TWO-YEAR-OLD COM-missioner of the National Football League checked into a Jacksonville hotel. Forewarned that a charismatic, game-changing quarterback was in town for an all-star football game, hotel security was doing its best to hold fans at bay. But the commissioner couldn't help but notice the bevy of young women in the hotel's lobby and lounge, waiting expectantly for the star to make his entrance. This wasn't the kind of crowd Pete Rozelle was used to. Red-faced men in fedoras were more his speed. He settled into his suite, ordered a rusty nail and a bowl of nuts from room service and waited, just like the others, for the guy the kids were calling Broadway Joe.

Five days earlier, Joe Namath had led the New York Jets to victory over the Baltimore Colts in Super Bowl III. Rozelle had read William N. Wallace's column for *The New York Times* the morning after the game:

> Because of what Joe Namath accomplished in the Super Bowl yesterday, pro football will never quite be the same again . . . The reason for having such games, these Super Bowls, is so that once in a long while the impossible can happen . . . if it could never happen, the great talent of Joe Willie Namath would be pumping gas in Beaver Falls without rhyme or reason.

Namath won with deception, handing the ball off when the Colts expected pass, and passing when the Colts were thinking run. When he threw the ball, it wasn't to Don Maynard, one of the top wideouts in pro football, but to a little known possession receiver named George Sauer Jr. He called the Jets plays brilliantly and, despite a stirring effort by legendary Colts quarterback Johnny Unitas, Baltimore played the patsy. Namath even guaranteed a Jets win days before kickoff. And his ability to back up his claim—seemingly singlehandedly—broke every tenet of proper pro football behavior.

But what made Rozelle wince the most was what happened after the game. As Namath left the field, filmed for posterity in heroic slow motion by NFL Films, he threw up his right index finger, signaling *I'm Number One*. Namath was the exact opposite of what Rozelle wanted from his league and his players—he was a bigger story than the game itself.

Rozelle firmly believed that professional football was America's favorite sport because it appealed to what the new president of the United States, Richard Nixon, defined as the "silent majority"—working men and their families. "They give steel to the backbone of America. They are good people, they are decent people; they work, they save, and they pay their taxes, and they care," Nixon decreed. Working men belonged to a union and drove the economic engine that made the United States the envy of the world. They wore hard hats—steelworkers, autoworkers, construction workers, meat packers, mechanics, and tradesmen. They'd fought hard to gain middle-class status and they resented the entitled youth culture that was tearing the country apart. They liked to place friendly wagers on games and chased shots of whiskey with their city's hometown beer. These men loved professional football because most of them had played the game once upon a time themselves and found it to be an apt metaphor for the hard and honest lives they lived.

Rozelle understood that the National Football League had deep roots in America's industrial cities—Green Bay, Chicago, Detroit, Cleveland, Baltimore, Pittsburgh, Philadelphia, New York. With their flattop haircuts and high-top black shoes, NFL players were the sons of workers who didn't draw attention to themselves. Like their fathers, they knew how fragile a job was and the importance of getting on with the men they worked with, especially those who paid their wages. The NFL owners and coaches were paternal authoritarians. To play football was to be a tool of the establishment, and the hierarchy of the game mirrored the traditional social structure of the culture. There was a top, and there was a bottom. The power flowed from owner to general manager to coaches. And on the bottom were the players. They kept their mouths shut and sacrificed for the good of the team.

Joe Namath should have fit right in. He was born and raised in western Pennsylvania, the son of a steelworker at the Babcock and Wilcox works in Beaver Falls. His father, John, took young Joe through the mill when he was eleven so he could feel the searing heat, choke on the dust and fumes, and shudder under the constant grind and crash of the machinery. He got the message—make something of yourself so you don't have to come here for the rest of your life.

Namath grew up looking for an edge—something to keep him from walking through the B&W gates the day after he graduated high school. He found it at a pool hall called The Blue Room. At fifteen he walked into the joint and lost his mother's grocery money. From then on, Namath would be the hustler, not the hustled. He put on a seemingly effortless cool—sitting cross-legged and wearing sunglasses for the baseball team photo, smoking and drinking with male and female acquaintances from the Blue Room—while working tirelessly to perfect his athletic skills. Joe Namath acted as if he didn't need anyone. As quarterback, he led Beaver Falls High to a Western Pennsylvania Interscholastic Athletic League (WPIAL) championship. As a left fielder, he led the baseball team to one, too. Then he went off to play for Bear Bryant at the University of Alabama.

He led Alabama to a national championship in 1964 (sportswriters awarded the prize prior to bowl games in '64) and into the Orange Bowl against Texas. His popularity was such that NBC bought the rights to that game for $600,000 and introduced the U.S. to prime-time football. It didn't matter that Namath, who had been plagued by knee woes since his junior year, wouldn't start because of injured ligaments. Twenty-five million people still tuned in, hoping to see him get in the game. And of course he did, coming off the bench and leading the Crimson Tide back from a 21–7 deficit to a nail-biting 21–17 loss. He was named Most Valuable Player, but was too busy to pick up the trophy. Joe Namath was on his way to Miami to sign the most lucrative contract in the history of professional sports.

By 1969, the son of a steelworker from western Pennsylvania was the biggest name in football. That much Pete Rozelle was happy about, as happy as he was when the face of the game had been Johnny Unitas, another son of the Pittsburgh area. But the similarities between these two icons ended with geography. Unitas wore his hair in a crew cut. Namath grew his out. Unitas was clean-shaven. Namath wore a Fu Manchu. Unitas had a family and was a discreet drinker. Namath got hammered publicly and chased women. Unitas owned a stake in a beer distributor in Baltimore. Namath owned his own bar on the trendy Upper East Side of Manhattan called Bachelors III.

It was the bar that proved the tipping point for Pete Rozelle. A Lucchese family capo named Carmine Tramunti, a Colombo family hit man named Carmine "Junior" Persico, and a Gambino soldier named Dave Iacovetti were all regulars. The hallway leading to the restrooms was lined with pay phones where bets were placed by Bachelors III clientele. For Rozelle, Namath's association with these elements tarnished the reputation of the league and would eventually alienate its blue-collar fans. And Namath's signature on the standard player's contract gave Rozelle the authority to make him sell his stake in the bar.

Namath was due to play in the AFL All-Star Game scheduled for that coming Sunday at the Gator Bowl. Out of respect, Pete Rozelle flew to Jacksonville to tell him to sell immediately, before the newspapers found out that Rozelle was making Namath do it. They would have a drink in Rozelle's suite, work it out, and Rozelle would be back in New York the next day. No need to air dirty laundry in public.

But Namath, the biggest sports star in the world, never returned the commissioner of the National Football League's call.

FIRST QUARTER

1

FOR AS LONG AS ART ROONEY HAD OWNED THE PITTSBURGH Steelers—thirty-six mostly winless years by the time January 1969 rolled around—their offices had been housed in hotels. These were the perfect locations for the affable Rooney, who liked to pad around the lobbies in his stocking feet, chomping on cigars made in Pennsylvania Amish country, talking to porters, shoe-shine men, guests, clerks, and local politicos. As a well-connected city ward boss, as the owner of a pro franchise, as a man who had turned his ability to pick winners at the track into a horse-racing empire that included thoroughbreds and tracks around the country, Rooney was as powerful a presence in Pittsburgh as any Carnegie or Mellon, only more approachable. To priest, pauper, or Pittsburgh scion, Rooney's office door, like the hotels he worked in, was always open.

In the early days, he settled in at the Fort Pitt Hotel, where his ground-floor suite had windows facing the street. Friends who hung around for late-night poker games appreciated that they could climb through the windows to leave instead of taking the longer, more public way through the lobby. In the late 1940s, Rooney moved the Steelers home base to the fourth floor of a respectable office building. But that location didn't last. One of his top players was afraid he'd forget he was so high up and, after a too-late night spent chatting with Rooney, accidentally walk out the window. So Rooney moved to the Roosevelt, at the corner of Sixth Street and Penn Avenue. The office was on the ground floor, but it didn't have any windows. Everyone would have to leave through the ornately designed English Tudor lobby.

The only thing more important to Rooney than being on the ground floor was always being able to make phone calls. When he needed to hear what was happening with his horses, or get down a bet on a pony, it had to happen as quickly as possible. Business depended on it. If one of his five sons tied up the lines for too long he'd scream at them, "Go find a pay phone." Once, when he was trying to call his wife and kept getting a busy signal, he sent a telegram to his house, asking her to hang up.

Rooney breathed the working-class ethos that defined his town; no matter how influential he became, he still lived like a real burgher, like the son of a saloonkeeper he had always been. He and his wife, Kathleen, raised their boys in the two-story, redbrick Victorian house on the rapidly deteriorating north side of town where he grew up. Even in the late 1960s, as increasing television revenue lined the pockets of NFL owners, Rooney still walked to work almost every day. And on the days he took a car, it was one of his sons picking him up, not a chauffeur, and in an Imperial, not a limo.

Rooney had bought the Steelers at the height of the Depression for $2,500, money earned by betting on horses and promoting local fighters. For the franchise's first thirteen seasons, he dipped into his own pocket to keep it alive. During the leanest times, he resorted to desperate measures to fill out the roster. "They had a league rule that teams had to have eighteen guys dressed and the ref would count the guys on your bench," says Art Rooney Jr., the second of Rooney's sons, who was a longtime Steelers scout. "My grandfather had a brewery with a lot of fat guys, and they would dress these guys and put 'em on the sideline. But no one had any intention of playing them."

Still, Rooney Sr. ran his team as if it were a city trust, not something he owned outright. The Steelers were Pittsburgh, the nickname chosen by fans in a contest. The team practiced in South Park, an Allegheny County–owned field normally used for fairs and stock shows, where anyone could watch. Rooney, a man who *Time* magazine once wrote "looked like a football," knew he was the owner, but he just thought of himself as the guy lucky enough to pay the bills.

As the decades turned and his influence increased, Rooney persisted in reaching out to the community, to forge the bonds that come from close contact. He became ubiquitous at funerals of old friends from his neighborhood. Young family members of the deceased would elbow each other, whispering, "There's the Chief," the nickname he'd picked up over the years. Then, as Rooney walked to the coffin to pay his respects, he'd slip the gawking kids tickets to a game.

Early on, the Steelers were so bad—the team had only eight winning seasons in its first thirty-six years of existence—that fans sometimes challenged the players to fights in bars. But there was a you-can't-blame-the-old-man attitude among the locals. Rooney's decency was undeniable, his mistakes born from good intentions. Even he didn't try to hide the stink on his teams. When the Steelers got new uniforms in the late 1960s but still continued to suffer, Rooney couldn't help but comment that his team looked like "the same old Steelers."

All of his coaches, no matter how badly their teams performed, no matter how badly they behaved, were treated by Rooney as geniuses. And when they walked through the doors of his ground-floor office at the Roosevelt Hotel they were greeted with the warmth of a blast furnace. He'd ask about the team and its progress, but his was a hands-off approach to ownership. He did not interfere with personnel decisions.

During training camp in 1955, the three youngest of his five sons, Tim and the twins, John and Pat, watched practice every day. The Steelers had three veteran quarterbacks in camp—Jim Finks, Ted Marchibroda, and Vic Eaton—and one rookie who barely got any reps, a spindly local kid named Johnny Unitas. The old pros called Unitas "Clem Kadiddlehopper" after the hick played by Red Skelton on his famous TV show at the time.

But the Rooney boys would stay after practice with Unitas and run routes for him. They were amazed by the strength of his arm and the precision of his passes. They couldn't believe he wasn't getting more of an opportunity from the Steelers coach, Walt Kiesling. Tim wrote the Chief a twenty-two-page letter, begging him to tell Kiesling that Unitas deserved a chance, that he was better than any other quarterback the Steelers had on the roster. The Chief shook his head—his boys were often given less than the full complement of his kindness—crumpled up the letter and tossed it into the trash. "I like John, too," he said. "But Kies is the coach, let him do his job." And so the great Johnny Unitas would be cut by the Pittsburgh Steelers.

By the end of the 1968 season, the team that had lost so often for so many years had hit rock bottom. Bill Austin, a disciple of legendary Packers coach Vince Lombardi hired solely because the great coach gave Austin a sterling recommendation, led the Steelers to eleven wins in three seasons, including just two in 1968, and was let go. And Dan Rooney, Art's oldest son, who had been taking on more of the team's management responsibilities, was charged with filling the job.

While the Chief was big and broad and lived for late nights around the poker table, Dan cut a lither figure and operated cautiously. "The Rooneys were gregarious," wrote Art Jr. in his autobiography. "Except Dan." The Chief was a horseplayer who made his choices on instinct. Dan was a college-educated accounting major who was preternaturally mature. In high school he had traveled with the team on East Coast trips, getting help from the players with his homework. During summer vacations from Duquesne University he worked training camps and negotiated Steelers player contracts. By the time he was thirty-seven, he and his wife had nine kids and The Chief had ceded day-to-day operations of the Steelers to him. He didn't have time for whimsy. While his father sometimes treated owning the Steelers as an amusing hobby, Dan considered the team to be nothing less than his life's work. And he wouldn't leave any decision to chance, especially when given the opportunity to find the team's next head coach in 1969.

Dan Rooney's first choice for the job was Penn State head coach Joe Paterno, whose team had just gone undefeated and won the Orange Bowl.

But Paterno wasn't swayed by the NFL. Truth was, his Nittany Lions team was probably better than anything the Steelers could put on the field. That year. Or most years prior.

So Rooney continued to survey the league. He spoke to owners and head coaches about assistants on their staffs. He read team media guide coaching bios, searching for an overlooked genius. One name kept coming up in conversation, one bio looked better than all the rest: Chuck Noll's.

Noll had been a player in the NFL for seven years and an assistant for eight more. His pedigree was unmatched: He played for Cleveland and Paul Brown, the coach who wrote the NFL's first playbook; he was hired as an assistant in San Diego by Sid Gillman, father of the NFL's modern offense; he went on to be the top defensive assistant in Baltimore to Don Shula, a wunderkind coach who led the Colts to the NFL title game when he was just thirty-four. As a player Noll had been an undersized guard and linebacker who made up for his lack of size by focusing on the nuances of the game's fundamentals. He insisted that those who played for him did the same. For the thirty-seven-year-old Noll, the beauty of the game was in its precision and detail. He didn't play it to get famous, but to study it. And he didn't coach it for the glory of winning, but for the mental challenge of perfecting it. Sunday was for the players, their final exam. Monday through Friday was for him.

But outside of coaching circles few people knew of Noll. He was studious and dry-witted, not the most alluring traits to owners with bad teams who needed a fresh face to sell tickets. And, in January 1969, Noll was perhaps best known as the architect of the defense that had somehow just lost Super Bowl III to Namath and the Jets.

The day after that game, at the urging of Shula, Dan Rooney and Noll sat together for the first time. "We met for two hours," Rooney wrote in his autobiography. "Noll's general knowledge of football and his specific knowledge of the Steelers strengths, weaknesses, and potential struck me as extraordinary. I mean, it's the day after the Super Bowl, with all the attendant hype, hoopla, and pressure, and he's telling me things about our offense and defense I thought only our coaches would know."

Still, Rooney wouldn't settle for the first guy with a strong reference from a powerful coach. The Steelers had been down that road before. He did his own accounting of candidates, speaking with other assistants and scouring the college ranks for potential head coaching gems. He'd end up interviewing ten coaches. But he kept in contact with Noll on the phone. They were similar in so many ways: They were the same age, both had been overshadowed by dominating personalities, both were confident but self-effacing; it never occurred to them they had anything to prove to anyone. "Dan kept saying, 'Chuck is one of us,'" says Art Rooney Jr. "But Chuck wasn't like a Rooney at all. He was really one of Dan."

Several days after that first interview Rooney and Noll met again, this time at the Roosevelt Hotel. The Chief was there. So was Art Jr., then the Steelers head of scouting. They talked for several hours, discussing personnel philosophy, coaching strategy, expectations. Noll spoke as he always did, assured without being emphatic, respectful without being a yes-man. He answered questions as if he had been thinking about how he'd run a franchise for his entire life. He had the countenance of someone who'd been there, as he talked less about winning than about building.

Soon after Noll left Pittsburgh that day, Dan Rooney decided to hire him. And he didn't want to wait to spread the news. He hastily arranged a press conference at the Roosevelt and said, "When I first talked to Noll after the Super Bowl game, I thought he was young for the job. But when we brought him to Pittsburgh he sold himself to us . . . we have some good personnel and expect to draft a few more good prospects. We just need someone who can put it together."

It had all the grand expectations that come with a team's rebirth. Only one thing was missing: the new coach.

Noll was still in Baltimore, packing his boxes, making his plans.

2

VIOLENCE HAS BEEN A PART OF PITTSBURGH FROM THE VERY beginning.

During the French and Indian War in the mid-1700s, a young general named George Washington recognized how valuable the location, at the intersection of the Monongahela, Allegheny, and Ohio Rivers, could be. A four-year battle of attrition ensued, with Washington winning and one of his officers burning the French compounds to the ground. Washington and his men built a new fortress and called it Fort Pitt, in honor of the British Secretary of State William Pitt. They named the land between the three rivers Pittsborough.

But when the war ended, the real dirty work began. Just across from Fort Pitt was a thousand-foot peak the locals called "Coal Hill." It proved to be an entry into a massive coal seam that ran from Maryland, through West Virginia, and into western Pennsylvania. With coal across the river, Fort Pitt and the borough's early settlers had easy access to fuel. Laborers who mined the hills poured into the city by the thousands. By the early nineteenth century, as the American economy began its long ascent to prominence, Pittsburgh, with locally manufactured goods that could readily move north, south, east, and west, became the focal point for U.S. industry.

It was a city that worked, more than anything else, and it attracted a certain breed of laborer. These men expected life to be a physical trial, and the mines at Karen, Maple Creek, Ellsworth, and Beck's Run made their expectations pale to reality. Biographer James Parton once described

Pittsburgh as "hell with the lid off." But it was British novelist Anthony Trollope who captured the ambiguity of the industrial enclave best:

> Pittsburgh, without exception, is the blackest place I ever saw. . . . I was never more in love with smoke and dirt than when I stood there and watched the darkness of night close in upon the floating soot which hovered over the housetops of the city.

Coal wasn't Pittsburgh's only natural resource. Iron ore was also discovered in the area in the late 1700s. Local industrialists, constantly refining the way they mined and distributed their coal, quickly realized that with the ore, the abundance of coal, and the ever-present oxygen in the air, they had all three materials needed to make steel. Soon thereafter, a lucrative new production pipeline blossomed, with forges growing in number along the banks of the Allegheny and Monongahela rivers.

Making steel is, and always has been, an explosive process. It requires mixing large percentages of iron with small percentages of carbon derived from a specific type of coal, called coke, under extreme heat. The first stage requires the construction of the appropriately named "blast furnace." At the top of an imposing cylinder (some as high as thirty stories) is the feeder hole where the iron ore and coke are dumped. The coke falls hundreds of feet and packs the teardrop-shaped bottom, where it is heated until it glows cherry red. The bottom of the teardrop furnace has two holes. One is filled by a straw-like hollow tube, and another larger "tapping" hole is closed with a heat-resistant ceramic. Iron ore is added from the top as the coke heats. Once the iron ore/coke mixture temperature has risen to 1,200 degrees Fahrenheit, a blast of hot air is pushed through the straw and into the boiling liquid.

The oxygen in the air reacts with the fluid and an explosion results—similar to the pop you hear when a gas stove is lit, only a quantum-size louder. The 3,000 degrees of heat generated from the explosion causes the carbon from the coke to bind with iron from the iron ore. The resulting compound from the blast is the first stage in making steel. It's called pig iron. Once the pig iron has formed, the ceramic in the tapping hole at the bottom of the blast furnace is knocked out, allowing the molten iron to flow into holding railroad cars. After the blast furnace has been drained, the tap hole is plugged and the process starts anew. A single batch is called a "heat."

But pig iron has too much carbon in the compound and must be heated again and manipulated to convert it into steel. The first technology used to get the excess carbon out of the pig iron was called puddling, and it required a certain breed of man to execute it. Puddlers tended large furnaces (seven feet high and six feet wide and deep) with two chambers. One chamber held fuel and was religiously tended by helpers. The second chamber held five to six hundred pounds of pig iron delivered from the blast furnace. The pig iron would melt and the puddler and his helpers would take turns stirring the boil. The heat was so overbearing and the work so heavy and intense that each man could only work the iron for ten or twelve minutes at a time. Once they finished their "spell" they went outside to sit on a bench and recover, sweat-soaked and exhausted. They were required to do six rounds of puddling (also called heats) in a ten-hour shift—stirring 2,500 pounds per man per day. What made the puddlers invaluable was their experience, knowing how much to work the pig iron and when just enough carbon had been burned out to become steel. Once a heat of steel was produced, it went on to be shaped into various products. This process is called "rolling."

The "rougher" guided the red-hot steel into the first set of rolling presses. At the end of the roller was a "catcher" who guided the billet back through the press, where it would be caught again by another catcher and fed into a second roller, until eventually the still-hot steel was turned into a rail, beam, wire, or nail. It would be cooled and stacked in cavernous warehouses where it awaited sale.

For the men who toiled in Pittsburgh's early mills—mostly made up of the first trickle of European immigrants (Germans, English, Irish, Welsh, and Scots)—social status was skill dependent. You either worked at the "back" or the "front" of the mill. While the puddlers were at the front and maintained a level of autonomy, the back workers were a dime a dozen. They did the work that mules or horses would have done, but no animals would get anywhere near a blast furnace. Top fillers shoveled loads of iron ore and coke into wheelbarrows. Then they pushed them up a steep incline to the feeder hole at the top of the furnace. With a wind shift, the exhaust from the molten furnace below blew noxious fumes (including odorless but deadly carbon monoxide) into their faces. One mill owner described the ultimate top loaders as "Gorilla Men."

Because it was necessary to maintain temperatures of 1,500 degrees Fahrenheit, the blast furnace was a twenty-four-hour-a-day, three-hundred-sixty-five-day-a-year enterprise. It was just too cost prohibitive to turn it off for eight hours and then start it up the next morning. So the blast burned brightly from dawn to dusk and back again, with men working twelve-hour shifts. The night-shift switchover, called "the long turn," was particularly brutal. The day shift would change to night by arriving on a Sunday at 6:00 A.M. They'd work twenty-four hours, rest twelve, and then start the night shift at 6:00 P.M. on Monday. Every other Sunday was a day off.

The overbearing noise from the explosions, tappings, and train cars carrying raw materials and moving out pig iron made communication between the men extremely difficult. Injuries, maiming, and death were commonplace. With each explosive blast came a shower of sparks, soot, and slag shards—crust from impurities in the mix. Men who slipped on the incline would fall into the furnace and instantly incinerate.

By the last decades of the nineteenth century, the Gorilla Men were phased out by skip hoists that took large buckets of raw materials automatically to the feeder hole.

And technology made the puddlers obsolete, too. The Bessemer process, an extremely compact furnace that did the puddlers' work, came online at Andrew Carnegie's Edgar Thompson Works in 1875. It burned out precise amounts of carbon from much larger batches of molten pig iron without "stirring" and did it in a fraction of the time it took a puddler to do a heat. Now the distinction between front and back workers was meaningless. As blast furnaces grew ever larger to service the Bessemers, bigger cranes were built to handle bigger loads of steel. Massive ladles were designed to collect and pour the steel from the Bessemers into ingot molds. Larger ingots went to ever more sophisticated rolling mills. Every one of these departments scaled to its limits—blast furnace, steel works, rolling mills. Tending the monstrous machine required ever more manpower to keep it online.

By the mid-1800s, Pittsburgh, called the "Iron City" in national magazines, had 939 factories, which employed more than 10,000 workers and used 400 steam engines to haul an annual consumption of 880,000 tons of coal, 127,000 tons of iron ore, and $12 million (equivalent to $50 million today) worth of goods out of the city. In steam tonnage, Pittsburgh was the third-busiest port in the nation behind New York City and New Orleans, all with a population of just under 50,000.

But even as money rolled in and steel mills modernized, the conditions were still life threatening. Accidental spills of molten iron and steel were commonplace. Navigating the blast furnace and Bessemer (and later open hearth and basic oxygen furnace) floors without incident required intense concentration. Men were burned day in and day out by the sparks created during an oxygen blow. The noise was overbearing, and communication usually required the use of hand signals. Most steelworkers suffered from acute hearing loss. Malfunctioning skip hoists showered iron ore and coke onto the blast furnace floor. Limbs were caught between swinging ingots and rail cars. The air was filled with soot, ash, and hazardous gases that often overwhelmed and asphyxiated workers on the floor. Hands were severed in rolling machines.

Every shift that a steelworker worked increased his odds of dying at the mill.

3

WHEN CHUCK NOLL WAS A ROOKIE WITH THE CLEVELAND Browns, in 1953, a reporter looking to make conversation asked him if he had a girlfriend. Noll's response: "First I've got to make good. Then maybe I can get serious about girls."

It was typical Noll. He always had a plan, an if-then strategy tucked in his back pocket for easy reference. His ideas were never fanciful, never full of dreamy prose; no one would ever make one great and glorious leap to the moon listening to him talk. But they'd know the first step they needed to take, and the next and the next, until, suddenly, they were floating amongst the stars. He could make the most complicated journey seem as simple as a walk to the store, if you followed his rules. And the first lesson was always the same: work hard, work right.

He'd learned that playing high school football at Benedictine High in Cleveland, as part of a team that won the school its first city title. Noll was poor growing up, and he was small. But to be a boy living in Ohio in the 1940s and '50s was to dream of playing football. And not just for anyone, but for Paul Brown. Noll wanted that for himself, and so did another Ohio kid his age, Don Shula.

As the coach at Ohio State, Brown led the Buckeyes to the 1942 national championship. He joined the Browns after the war and, utilizing forward passing schemes and the skills of quarterback Otto Graham, Brown's teams went to ten straight championship games, winning three of them. Because Brown's teams were so good, and because he was so revered, the entire state seemed to become a breeding ground of acolyte coaches who followed the Paul Brown way.

That meant studying the best technique and being smarter, not just better, than your opponent. In Brown's football the angle at which some-one was tackled was taken as seriously as how hard the tackle was. The cerebral, slightly built Noll understood that a running back planting his foot two inches inside a hash mark, rather than at the mark, was the dif-ference between hitting a hole at full speed and being forced to stop and start again.

Noll played offensive tackle in high school. But in college, at Dayton, he switched to linebacker, where he played well enough that Brown drafted him in the twenty-first round. The match between pupil and teacher was perfect. Noll played both ways, linebacker on defense and "messenger guard" on offense. Every other play, he and the other guard switched off, relaying plays in from the sideline. "After a while," Brown once said, "Chuck could have called the plays himself without any help from the bench. He was that kind of student."

Noll was always asking Paul Brown, "Why, why, why?" And he wasn't just curious about football, either. He went to law school during the off-season. And sold insurance. And worked at a trucking firm. And studied wine and classical music and how to tend roses and how to fly airplanes. He lived his life the way he approached football: Knowledge was the ulti-mate prize.

After seven NFL seasons, Noll retired from the Browns. He was healthy, but he wanted to coach, and he was hired by Sid Gillman to handle the defense for the AFL's Chargers. Gillman revolutionized NFL offense with his precision passing game. His players ran exacting routes, dissecting the field into finely calibrated geometric angles, the distances they covered perfectly timed to how many steps the quarterback dropped back. Today it's called the West Coast offense, and its timing patterns are a staple in every NFL team's game plan.

But Gillman also believed in learning the tics and tells of opponents, basing his schemes on how a defensive back turned his shoulders or what kind of depth a linebacker used in coverage. And the only way to figure that out was by painstaking film study. Gillman used so much film that he was one of the first coaches to hire full-time cameramen. Each of his assistants was required to splice together their own reels, specific to their coaching assignments, and then break down the opponent's schemes for their boss. It could take hours of manual labor to cut and analyze a single set of downs. Most coaches hated it. Except for Noll. He had studied film as a player—but what Gillman offered was a master class in editing, in using the tools that were being offered to their greatest advantage. He'd spend hours in the darkness, taping together pieces of film, running projectors back and forth. This was where he'd find the answers. It was hard for Noll to turn it off, to stop himself from sharing what he learned, even when it earned him derision. Fellow assistants called him "The Pope," "Knute Knowledge" and "Knowledge Noll."

When Shula, another ex–Paul Brown player, hired Noll to run his defense for the Colts in 1966, he knew all this. And Noll didn't shy away from sharing opinions with his much-revered boss. Heated arguments could erupt on the proper alignments of defensive backs, or just about anything else. In those moments, they weren't expert tacticians steeped in the theories of Paul Brown. They weren't boss and employee. They were just a couple of football-obsessed kids from Cleveland having a spirited debate.

4

THE PRIMARY ACTION OF FOOTBALL—TAKING A BALL ACROSS an opponent's designated line of defense—is as old as community. Historians describe a medieval game that matched one small village against another in bloody conflict. An inflated pig's bladder served as the ball, and with no rules beyond "no murder or manslaughter," no limits on the number of players and plenty of liquid courage on hand, the game called "Mob Football" evolved across Europe. Ironically, it was played on Shrove Tuesday, the day before Ash Wednesday, which was dedicated to preparations for confession and penance and one of the few days in the year when working men were given the day off. The game turned so vicious that royal decrees eventually banned the "hustling over large balls." But the competition's popularity proved unrelenting.

In the mid-nineteenth century, American football rose from this primal tradition and took hold at eastern college campuses. With plenty of leisure time on their hands, the gentlemen of Harvard, Yale, Dartmouth, Princeton, Rutgers, and Brown played games like "Bloody Monday," "Ballown," and "Old Division Football," all of which derived from Mob Football. The injuries sustained and the brutality of the contests brought bans from Yale and Harvard in the 1860s. But not before the game had migrated into the eastern prep schools, where "townies" were brought in as last-minute ringers.

Variations of the game evolved, and standardized rules came with them as interest grew. Postgraduate gentlemen's clubs and athletic associations began fielding teams to draw new members, and inevitably, the first "professional" football player took the field on a November afternoon in 1892, in Pittsburgh.

The city had embraced the rugged game in full measure. For most, to live and work in Pittsburgh was to stoically endure, and no game required more physical endurance than football. Local teams organized. Mine and mill workers joined the company-sponsored teams and went to watch their sons play sandlot ball in the spare moments they had between their shifts. The Monaca Scholastics, Garfield Eagles, McKeesport Union Clothier, Homestead Library and Athletic Club, Latrobe Athletic Association, North Side All Stars, Butler Cubs, Bloomfield Rams (the team that Johnny Unitas would lead after being cut from the Steelers), the Allegheny Athletic Association (AAA), and the Pittsburgh Athletic Association (PAA) were just a few of the local teams. And it was the bitter rivalry between these last two squads that ushered in the professional era.

After a disappointing tie on Columbus Day 1892, the two teams mobilized all of their resources for the rematch scheduled for November 12. Recreation Park on the North Side (the land on the northern shore of the Allegheny River) was commandeered for the game. Both teams scoured the county and country to find the best ringers. The AAA's leader, O.D. Thompson, went as far as tracking down a former All-America guard from Yale named William "Pudge" Heffelfinger, who was working as a railroad clerk in Chicago. Thompson played at Yale with Walter Camp—who became known as "The Father of Football" for rewriting much of the sport's rulebook as the coach at Yale and Stanford—and followed his alma mater's team religiously. But he did not reach Heffelfinger first. The PAA had already offered Heffelfinger $250 to play for them. The first professional player attracted a bidding war, resulting in the AAA's paying $500 (the equivalent of $12,000 in today's currency) and $25 for his traveling expenses. Heffelfinger delivered a victory for AAA when he forced a fumble and ran the ball back for the only touchdown of the day.

Ten years of successful barnstorming teams later, a new professional football league emerged. The original National Football League was made up of just three teams, two from Philadelphia and one from Pittsburgh. The Pittsburgh Stars won the first NFL championship and a team sponsored by the Franklin Athletic Club in Philadelphia made up of both cities' finest players won the second, but the league folded after only two seasons.

Other pro football leagues organized in Illinois, Ohio, Pennsylvania, and New York, but they remained insular and provincial. Crowds came for games that determined area bragging rights. Interstate exhibitions did not draw nearly as many fans. But by 1920, a critical mass of interest in college football—the University of Pittsburgh Panthers won three national championships—attracted the attention of the founders of the American Professional Football Association, what we know today as the NFL.

The men that founded the franchises were favored sons of their city, often playing on or coaching the team themselves. The Bears' George Halas, the son of Hungarian immigrants who settled in Chicago, was one of the original founders. Curly Lambeau, a shipping clerk for a meatpacking company, was the brawn and the brains of Green Bay's Packers, who joined the NFL in 1921. New York's Tim Mara was a brilliant bookmaker who, in 1925, had the vision to see that the bedrock of one of the largest cities in the world was the factory workers and longshoreman who would embrace a rough game. Pro football wasn't for the 21 Club crowd—it engaged the working class, and Mara bet that selling to the man on the subway would be far more lucrative than selling to the man in the limousine.

In 1933, Pennsylvania added two teams to the mix. Rooney, who had been a local legend as a jock, playing barnstorming baseball and making the U.S. Olympic boxing team in 1920, founded Pittsburgh's entry. In Philadelphia, Bert Bell formed the Eagles with a couple of college football teammates from the University of Pennsylvania. He'd become the NFL's second commissioner. Twenty-six years later Bell would collapse after a massive heart attack while watching his Eagles score the winning touchdown against Pittsburgh. Fittingly, he was pronounced dead in the stands at Philadelphia's Franklin Field.

In 1934, George Richards, who had built Detroit's most popular radio station, took over the Lions and bankrolled his team through economic hardship. Lambeau, Halas, Richards, Rooney, Bell, and Mara defined themselves as citizens of their respective cities, and in the first thirty years of the league they fielded teams more out of responsibility than for a return on their investment.

In 1952, the revenues for the entire NFL were $8,327,000, with a net profit for all the teams of $236,000, a meager 2.84 percent margin. The thought of folding a team, however, was anathema. A good year was breaking even, a great year a single-digit profit. But by the mid 1950s, everything changed.

The economy and the population boomed after World War II. Under Franklin Roosevelt's leadership, trade unions made inroads in every major manufacturing industry, fighting to get workers larger wages and benefits and better working conditions. The working class now had leisure time to watch and the money to buy a television, ushering in an entirely new revenue stream for the NFL. Some teams, like the Los Angeles Rams and the Washington Redskins, were able to negotiate television coverage for every game they played, while most others sold them piecemeal to local channels.

But no matter how the deals were done, everyone would soon realize that TV would change the game.

5

EVENTUALLY, NOLL DID INTRODUCE HIMSELF TO THE PITTS-
burgh press. This was a grizzled group, having lived through black winters
where coal dust blocked out the sun and blanketed streets in midnight-
colored ash. They were used to losing seasons and gruff coaches. While
asking Noll a question, one of the reporters ticked off the names of the
local teams, one by one—Steelers, Pitt, Pirates, Penguins—and commented
that Pittsburgh was a "city of losers."

"We'll change history," Noll said. "Losing has nothing to do with
geography." Noll was hired just ten days before the NFL draft, and the
Steelers, winners of two games and in need of a roster overhaul, had the
fourth overall pick.

Most coaches, then and now, treat the draft as a combination of toy-
store raid and having to face a firing squad. They have the most talented
young football players available to them. They test them, study them, en-
vision how they'd fit in their scheme and how they'll mesh with veterans.
In less lucid moments, late on a sleepless night, they think about how a
player will credit them for making it to the Hall of Fame. Choose right
and the coach will be hailed as a genius, or at least win some games. Choose
wrong and, well, in a game that relies on talent, those with none to coach
will be lost.

But for Noll, the draft was nothing less than the first step in executing a grand human experiment. He had sold the Rooneys on a theory that
the only way to build a team was through the prudent choosing of young

talent. He promised that he would mold them into the players he wanted them to be, full-speed extensions of him on the field. Technically sound, smart. It's seems obvious, sure, but in fact football coaches are a notoriously myopic bunch. Rookies are raw, they make mistakes, they lose you games. Veterans know how to win—that's how the axiom had always gone. And coaches don't want to risk their futures by training some green player so he can be better for the next guy roaming the sidelines.

Buddy Parker, an irascible Texan who won back-to-back NFL titles with the Lions in 1952 and 1953, was the Steelers coach from 1957 to 1965. He despised young players, and he'd give away top-round picks for fading veterans nearly every year. In 1958, it was two first-rounders for thirty-two-year-old quarterback Bobby Layne, a fellow Texan recovering from a badly broken leg who had been Parker's quarterback with the Lions. In 1961 Parker traded the team's first five draft choices. "Pittsburgh was the last spot for a lot of veteran and older players who really were on the downside of their careers," says former Steelers player and coach Dick Hoak. "I was drafted in the seventh round in 1961, and I was our second pick."

While the moves helped Parker lead the Steelers to their best run ever—four of his eight teams finished with winning records—they destroyed the franchise's future. In 1964, a year removed from finishing the season one win from playing in the NFL title game, the Steelers went 5-9. During training camp the next year they lost four straight exhibition games. And practices were akin to high school scrimmages. Parker saw how bad the talent was—the aging team he had cobbled together—and quit. He told the Chief, "I can't win with this bunch of stiffs."

Three years later, nothing had changed. But from the moment they first met, Noll presented the Rooneys with a solution. "He pointed out that the Steelers had traded away their future," Dan Rooney wrote. "He thought the way to build a championship team was through the draft. Get young, raw talent, then teach them the fundamentals of the game. Above all he counseled patience. He knew it would take some time to rebuild the team and instill in the players a winning attitude."

It was a plan that seemed so logical, so simple, that if they allowed him to follow it, they'd all one day see the football equivalent of a man strolling on the moon—the Steelers would be respectable. Maybe they'd even win.

6

THE ORIGIN OF U.S. TRADE UNIONS BEGINS WITH THE PUD-
dlers. They thought of themselves as part of a higher class than the blast-
furnace and rolling-mill workers, and they came together to formalize
their prejudices. What set them above the laborers was their knowledge
of how long it took to heat and squeeze pig iron into steel. It gave them
power. The supply was always behind demand. Mill owners loathed the
reality that if the puddlers walked off the job, production would come to
a screeching halt.

In 1849, a group of Pittsburgh puddlers did just that. They turned off
their furnaces and demanded better working conditions and higher
wages. It was the first strike in steel industry history, starting in May and
lasting nearly six months. But the puddlers did not come out on top. Because those on strike didn't have the full cooperation of every puddler in
the industry, replacement workers were hired, wages were cut, and the
troublemakers who left the job were blacklisted. Full power would only
come when all of the puddlers stuck together.

Soon the "Iron City Forge of the Sons of Vulcan" was organized in a
hotel bar on Diamond Street in 1858, and the puddler's life improved im-
measurably. The union forced the big steelmakers to increase wages during the demand boom from the Civil War. But when the Bessemer process
came to the United States at the Edgar Thompson Works in 1875, the puddlers' days were numbered. The small forges, and the skilled craftsmen
needed to run them, fell by the wayside as steel became a larger, more
automated business. Upton Sinclair's *The Jungle* describes the Bessemer
best as, "Three giant caldrons, big enough for all the devils of hell to brew

their broth in, full of something white and blinding, bubbling and splashing, roaring as if volcanoes were blowing through it—one had to shout to be heard in the place. Liquid fire would leap from these caldrons and scatter like bombs below . . . and suddenly without an instant's warning, one of the giant kettles began to tilt and topple, flinging out a jet of hissing roaring flame . . ." Puddlers now manned the hellish kettles, their expertise superfluous. The Sons of Vulcan scrambled to merge with the blast-furnace and rolling-mill laborers to form the Amalgamated Association of Iron and Steel Workers union.

With the early work done by the Sons of Vulcan, Amalgamated contracts were honored throughout the industry. But in the last decade of the nineteenth century, Andrew Carnegie put Henry Clay Frick in charge of the Homestead Steel Works. Frick had no love of the union—wage increases came straight out of profits—and he was determined to tear it apart. With the Amalgamated contract due to expire at the end of June 1892, Frick demanded a new deal that called for a 22 percent decrease in wages. If the Amalgamated did not agree to his terms, he would no longer recognize its power. He'd simply hire nonunion workers to take Amalgamated jobs. When the Amalgamated refused, Frick called for the construction of a ten-foot fence around the Homestead Works to be topped with barbed wire. He had sniper towers erected to further discourage anyone from entering the mill. Once the fence and towers were complete, Frick locked out all of the union workers and fired them.

Frick had already advertised for replacement workers in newspapers around the country. With a prearranged Pittsburgh police escort and a barge full of Pinkerton detectives as rear-guard security, the new workers were to be protected while they entered the mill. They never made it.

A bloody revolt ensued between three hundred Pinkertons and four thousand Amalgamated strikers, resulting in the deaths of two Pinkertons and four union members and dozens of other casualties. The state militia was called in to seize Homestead on July 7, 1892, in what became a standoff, with striking workers on one side and government troops protecting Carnegie Steel on the other. The Amalgamated had stopped replacement workers from entering the mill and now wanted an audience with Carnegie Steel to hammer out a deal. But even after being stabbed by a radical anarchist at his company office, Frick refused to negotiate. Unable to support their families, many strikers were slowly starving to death. They snuck back into the mill and worked under Frick's terms. A year later, when every other steel manufacturer joined Carnegie Steel in its refusal to recognize the union, the Amalgamated's membership dropped to fifty-three members.

For the next forty years, the Amalgamated struggled. Calls for national steel strikes in 1901, 1919, and 1936 failed. Strikers were beaten and some killed. Big Steel would not negotiate an across-the-board contract for every worker on its payroll, nor would it improve working conditions or work hours.

7

IN 1952, A GROUP OF TEXAS BUSINESSMEN LED BY BROTHERS Giles and Connell Miller, heirs of a Dallas textile fortune, bid on the failed New York Yanks football franchise. The Yanks owner, Ted Collins, had lost one and a half million dollars in a failed attempt to compete with the Giants for New York allegiance. Collins sold the team back to the NFL, and while a group from Baltimore also bid for the franchise, Dallas won the day with a vote of 11–1 by the NFL owners. The lone dissent was Art Rooney, who believed that Baltimore was a better home for the team. With three African-American players on the Yanks, Rooney suspected that the South's deeply ingrained racism would keep fans from Dallas's Cotton Bowl on Sunday. Rooney proved prescient. After just five games, the Texans couldn't make their payroll. They gave the team back to the NFL and the Texans finished 1-11, their sole win coming on Thanksgiving Day against the Chicago Bears at their "home" stadium—the Rubber Bowl in Akron, Ohio. At the end of the season, Baltimore, led by another textile millionaire, Carroll Rosenbloom, was awarded the remains of the Dallas Texans, and the Baltimore Colts began play in 1953.

At the end of the decade, Rosenbloom's Colts would win the 1958 NFL Championship against the New York Giants. Considered the "Greatest Game Ever Played"—more for the impact made by NBC's live coverage of the sudden-death overtime victory than the level of play—the Colts' championship proved to be spectacular entertainment for homebound husbands on Sunday afternoon. Even with a New York metropolitan area blackout (Yankee Stadium had not sold out), forty-five million people watched with racing hearts as Johnny Unitas moved the Colts seventy-three yards to set up a tying field goal with seven seconds left in the game. Then he matched that drive with an eighty-yard march, capped by the winning touchdown on the Colts' first series of overtime, cementing his legacy. The Pittsburgh kid who wasn't good enough for the Steelers— no matter how much the Chief's youngest boys tried to tell their father otherwise—was the greatest clutch quarterback of a generation.

The coaches on the field that day, Weeb Ewbank (head coach of the Colts), Vince Lombardi (offensive coordinator of the Giants), and a mild-mannered former defensive back named Tom Landry (defensive coordinator of the Giants) weren't too bad, either. They'd go on to assemble the winners of four of the first five Super Bowls (Lombardi's Packers, Ewbank's Jets, Landry's Cowboys) and coach players who defined football as physical (Green Bay's power sweep), emotional (Broadway Joe's guarantee), and precise (the Cowboys Flex defense).

A twenty-six-year-old Texan named Lamar Hunt watched the 1958 NFL championship game in a Houston hotel room. The beneficiary of an extraordinary fortune from his father, billionaire oilman H. L. Hunt, he was just two years out of SMU with a geology degree and zero interest in joining the family business. A young entrepreneur with deep pockets whose previous venture (a miniature golf franchising idea) didn't quite pan out, he was looking to be part of what the people his age called "show business."

An avid sports fan, Hunt was in Houston to attend the Southwest Conference Holiday Basketball Tournament at Rice Gymnasium, but he decided to skip the second round of games to watch the NFL championship. Seeing Unitas's surgical aerial assault on the tired Giants defense convinced Hunt that not only was professional football the future of American sports, it was the future of American entertainment. He later recalled thinking, "Well, that's it. This sport really has everything. And it televises well."

Hunt quickly applied for a Dallas expansion franchise with the NFL. But with the failure of the first version of the Texans still heavy in the minds of the owners, along with the concern that adding franchises could weaken the core structure of the twelve-team league—and their pocketbooks—Hunt was denied.

He then tried to buy an existing franchise—the Chicago Cardinals—with the intent of moving the team south. Hunt got on a jet and flew to Miami to work out a deal with the Cardinals owner Walter Wolfner, who had married widow Violet Bidwell and got her deceased husband's team in the deal. Wolfner got right to the point. There was another oilman in Houston named Bud Adams who wanted to buy. There were people in Denver (Robert Howsman) and in Minneapolis (Max Winter) who wanted the Cardinals, too. He even heard about another guy in Dallas who had been trying to get a franchise for years. Get in line.

Young Hunt wasn't interested in waiting his turn. He knew what he wanted and he had the money to buy it. On the American Airlines flight home, he asked a stewardess for some stationery. If there were other up-and-coming businessmen like him who were refused professional football franchises from the NFL, there must be enough of a demand to create another league. When he got off the flight in Dallas, he had a rough outline for a new American Football League that included the number of teams for the first year, how the new league's draft would be handled, how revenues would be split, and a list of men to approach to invest. Over the next several months, he continued to flesh out his plans and wait out the Cardinals' decision. By the end of spring, it became clear the Cardinals had no intention of selling—instead, the team moved to St. Louis, Wolfner's hometown, in 1960. No matter. Hunt called Bud Adams and had an oilman-to-oilman conversation. Hunt flew south, ate a steak with him, and shook hands. When he left Houston, he had Adams's commitment to join the new league.

While Hunt approached all of the other jilted wannabe NFL owners around the country, starting with those who had been interested in the Cardinals, NFL commissioner Bert Bell was dealing with the fallout from threats by U.S. Senate reformer Estes Kefauver. Kefauver, famous for his investigations into organized crime, wanted legislation to ensure that the major sports leagues were treated under the same antitrust laws as the oil and steel industries. NFL violations were numerous, its draft of college players being the most obvious transgression. The draft gave the rights to college players to one and only one franchise, effectively eliminating any competitive bidding for their skills.

Bell, aware of Hunt's plans for the AFL, asked for the upstart's help. Could he announce Hunt's new league while testifying in the Senate in July? If Bell could prove that another league was soon to start up, then he could argue that college players would have more than one employment opportunity and could therefore leverage one league against another in order to get their fair market price. Hunt did not fail to see the irony in Bell's request. The NFL had barred him from joining their business and now they wanted to use him to defend their unregulated monopoly.

But Hunt, who could appreciate the power of the media to prime public demand, gave Bell the go-ahead. *The New York Times* headline read, "Bell tells Congressional Hearing new Pro Football League Is Being Formed." And the story went on to report that "Bell said the new teams would definitely constitute a new major league and not a minor one . . . [He] did not identify the promoters of the new league except as 'people from Texas.' He told reporters later he was not at liberty to divulge their names but hinted that they were 'oil men.'"

The announcement was picked up by wire services across the country along with the possible cities being discussed as franchise awardees—Dallas, Denver, Minneapolis, Houston, Los Angeles, New York, Boston, and Buffalo. By announcing the league Bell gave it immediate legitimacy. Hunt now had not only the leverage to get his American Football League off the ground at the local stadium box office level, but even more critically he would have it later on with Madison Avenue. The buzz began to reach NFL players. Cleveland head coach Paul Brown tried to cut off any curiosity. At his 1959 training camp he told his players, "There's a new league starting. Don't pay any attention to it. It's not going to succeed. It's a bunch of sons of rich guys who don't know anything about football."

But having dodged Congress in July, the NFL owners, who had struggled for decades to get pro football profitable, knew that a bunch of sons of rich guys could become a real problem. The NFL owners did not have the deep pockets that the younger AFL generation had. So they took their message to the public to undercut the AFL at the box office. Bell spoke for the self-appointed guardians of the game: "I told Hunt that money is not the most important thing in starting a football team, it's the operation of the sport." The subtext was anything but subtle. Beware of spoiled rich kids tampering with the blue-collar game.

Then "Papa Bear" George Halas took matters into his own hands. Halas—the league's sole remaining founding owner—back-channeled a proposition to Hunt and Houston's Bud Adams in August. Abandon your new league, and we'll give you NFL franchises. Halas was as old as Hunt's and Adam's fathers, and he expected them to get in line and apprentice. Their money, Halas hinted, would not buy them immediate equality in the NFL. But if they hired the right football people they could one day field respectable teams and move into the old boys' club of owners.

Hunt and Adams, however, didn't want to play by those rules, and declined Halas's offer. Days later, on August 29, Halas and Art Rooney held a press conference in Houston to announce they were recommending that NFL franchises be awarded to Dallas and Houston. Bids from sources with "virtually unlimited financial resources" were forthcoming.

8

NOLL HAD BUILT HIS REPUTATION AS A DEFENSIVE COACH. When the Chargers won the AFL title in 1963, Noll's unit allowed the fewest points in the league. In 1968, Noll's last year with the Colts, Baltimore allowed just 144 points the entire fourteen-game season, then an NFL record. For all his exposure to Brown and Gillman and their offensive innovations, the defensive aspects of the game came more naturally to him. A good defense was steadfast and strong and straightforward, dominating in a physical and merciless way. Offense could be messy and tricky, full of mistakes that made the ball tumble to and fro, taking the coach's stomach for a ride along with it. For Noll, like Brown before him, football's greatness appeared in the finest details, the inches won in the trenches, not the bundles of yards gained by the fleetest feet or the strongest arms. But mostly, to play great defense was practical, and there is logic and beauty in pragmatism. Logic was Noll's muse.

"I knew what you had to do to win. Number one, you had to not lose," Noll said. "That means you have to play good defense. And you wanted an offense that didn't get your defense in trouble. We have to play good defense and not make mistakes on offense—even if we have to run the ball on every down and punt."

Noll liked to see the whole board when he coached, not just the pieces in front of him. That meant it wasn't enough just to scout future prospects, grade his own players, or study opponents' tendencies. Talent alone couldn't dictate what his game plan looked like or what kind of players he wanted. The NFL rules were just as important, and he scrutinized them like the lawyer he was, looking for the smallest advantages that could help him build the most efficient team. And in the late 1960s and early 1970s, pro football favored brute strength, especially at the point of attack along the line of scrimmage. "At the time the edge went to defensive linemen," Noll said. "Rushing the passer a lineman could come in and slap you up the side of your head, grab your jersey, grab your shoulder pads and go right past you. Offensive linemen had their hands in front of them, and that was what they called protecting."

It made sense then that, with his own team, Noll decided his first move would be to draft a defensive player, one who could dominate the line of scrimmage. And he had a guy in mind. A defensive tackle who played for tiny North Texas in Denton, a school thirty minutes northwest of Dallas, named Joe Greene.

Each assistant on Don Shula's staff was responsible for making trips to see prospects during the off-season. They divided the country into territories, like salesmen peddling palm oil, and Noll's included Texas. For three springs he made sure to stop in Denton, where he watched the 6'4", 275-pound Greene destroy his teammates in practices. Greene crackled with intensity, barely able to hide his competitiveness. Pride seemed to be his sole motivation. Noll spent time with Greene after practice, listening as the player told him how badly he wanted to make it in the pros. The energy was still there while he spoke, but he was softer standing still. Whatever anger he played with disappeared after the whistle.

When Greene went off to classes, Noll sat with North Texas coaches and watched film of Greene from the previous season. These sessions were always when Noll decided a player's worth. Spinning the reels back and forth, checking how their shoulders lined up when making a tackle or if their feet ever stopped moving or how they absorbed and then shed blocks. More importantly, he could slow the film down and see what the player was looking at, track the cues he was following. It told Noll everything he needed to know about instincts and vision.

Watching Greene in those dark rooms, all the energy Noll saw during their conversations was converted into kinetics. Greene uncoiled his body within fractions of a second after the ball was snapped and then blew the middle of the offensive line into three separate pieces. He was a human bomb.

In three seasons at North Texas, Greene's teams went 23-5-1 and held opponents to less than two yards per rush. After his senior year in 1968 he was named a consensus All-American. When Noll was coaching for the Colts, who were fresh off a Super Bowl appearance and drafting late in the first round, he knew there was no way a talent like Greene would last. But now that he was the boss of the Steelers, drafting Greene was a real possibility.

There was only one problem: Defensive tackles from lesser-known colleges in Texas don't exactly motivate the fan base in northeastern industrial towns, especially when the team has won just eleven games in the previous three seasons. And that's especially true when the team is in desperate need of a quarterback. During the Bill Austin era, the Steelers used headliners such as Kent Nix and Bill Nelsen, who often had a hard time distinguishing between their teammates and opponents. Meanwhile, one of the most famous college players in the country at the time was a quarterback named Terry Hanratty. He played for Notre Dame. He was a two-time All-American. He had led the Irish to a national title and had been on the cover of *Time* and *Sports Illustrated*, in which he was called the "New Legend at Notre Dame." But Hanratty, like the people of Pittsburgh, was unassuming and unimpressed with himself, no matter how well he played. When he broke some team records that were still held by George Gipp (of "win one for the Gipper" fame) his response in the press conference afterward was, "I feel like I've broken my mother's most expensive set of china." His attitude made sense: Hanratty happened to be from Butler, Pennsylvania, which is just outside Pittsburgh. If there was ever going to be an elixir that pleased Steelers fans, it was Hanratty. Remembered Rooney Jr.: "They wanted him, clamored for him."

No one would have blamed the Steelers for choosing Hanratty with their top pick. Especially since most of the team's scouts were less convinced of Greene's future greatness than their new boss. Their scouting reports on Greene read like this: "Puts on weight, tendency to loaf." "Physically he has it all, mentally he is disappointing . . . will need a heavy hand but he can play." "I would question taking him in the first round as he could turn out to be a big dog."

One guy, however, who didn't worry about Greene was Rooney Jr. "He was a third-down guy all right," he said. "But that was the only down he had to play. He was a guy who just completely dominated guys when he wanted to."

While Dan and Art Sr. were anxious about the hiring of Noll for all the reasons bosses are usually nervous about a new hire—Will he do well? Will he embarrass us? Will we look like fools for handing him the job?— Art Jr.'s anxiety came from an entirely different place. He was the complete opposite of older brother Dan. He was big and loud and disarmingly honest, even when it came to how people perceived him. He was the first to admit how much he benefited from being a namesake of Art Rooney. "I knew whenever I sat in a room folks looked at me like I was the rich kid who got a job with the team because of my dad," he says.

He was the Rooney son who looked most like his father, a little rounder in the middle, a little more skin hanging from his face, a pair of thick, black-rimmed glasses resting on his nose, just like his dad. He idolized his father, who never swore, treated people fairly, and stayed honest in businesses—horse racing, pro football, real estate—where honest men were usually run out.

But it was complicated being the son of Art Rooney, too. "No one ever called him Chief to his face," says Art Jr. "We called him Dad or Mr. Rooney or Your Majesty or something."

The Chief was gone a lot when his boys were growing up. And he was harder on them than anyone in his orbit. Art Sr. provided all of his kids with jobs throughout his empire—but in exchange for this benefits package, they were his whipping boys. He called Art Jr. fatso and would ride him when he saw him chewing tobacco.

When Art Jr. graduated from college, he first tried to create his own path. Kind of. Rather than work for the Steelers, he asked his father to pull strings and get him into Georgetown Law School. When Art decided law school wasn't for him and he wanted to be an actor, Art Sr. set him up in New York while his son studied at the Actors Studio. And when Art decided to stop acting and join the Steelers, he got a job in the scouting department. "It was perfect," he says. "If the Chief yelled at me I went to scout for two weeks. I felt bad for Dan. He had to see the Chief every day. And when they argued he'd use numbers and the Chief would get perplexed."

He lived a life of constantly proving himself, being underestimated. During the season he was on the road practically seven days a week, scouting from the West Coast to the East Coast, flying in prop planes through freezing rain, convinced he was going to leave his wife a widow and his kids fatherless just so he could get to Ames or Tuscaloosa or Provo to see the next great offensive guard. The problem was, he had joined the Steelers during the reign of Buddy Parker, who had as much use for the kind of information Art Jr. dug up as a priest in the seminary. As soon as Art Jr. was convinced he'd found the next great prospect, it seemed Parker was trading away the draft choice. No matter how much he advocated building on young talent, picking the best available athlete in the draft, his advice was ignored. He had begged his dad and Dan to let him manage the scouting department without any interference from coaches, and they'd brushed him off. "Just get it through your head that we are going to do things my way," his dad would tell him.

When Art Jr. heard his father and brother were interviewing Noll at the Roosevelt Hotel one afternoon—he'd been left out of the loop and heard about it from his assistant—he burst into the Chief's conference room. He introduced himself, and then sat quietly while his brother and father chatted with their potential new coach. But after a few minutes, he couldn't contain himself.

"Coach," he blurted out, "how do you feel about building a team and maintaining a team through the draft?"

He could feel his father glaring at him through his inch-thick glasses. Dan frowned in disgust.

"Well," Noll said, "when I was with Sid Gillman we developed a lot of good players who came to us in the draft. I don't see a problem with doing that in Pittsburgh. You only have to be patient."

This was what Art Jr. had wanted to hear. He knew his father and brother would never let him run the scouting department independent of the coach. But he at least wanted to know that the coach believed in scouting. When Noll was hired soon after that, Art Jr. was determined to prove his worth, all over again.

The night before the draft, on the eighth floor of the Roosevelt Hotel, where the Steelers had their draft war room, Art Jr. was working through draft lists with his staff. Every prospect's name was written on a big board, with vital information beneath it. As their rankings changed, the names had to be rewritten in their new spot. It was mind-numbing work, easy to make mistakes. And it put Art Jr. on edge with his staff. If someone's name was spelled incorrectly or put in the wrong spot, he grew more irate. "The first thing Noll will see when he walks into this room are those charts," he yelled that night. "If he sees a lot of mistakes, our credibility will be shot."

Very late the night before the draft, Art Jr., Noll, and Dan sat in Art Jr.'s office, going over a list of prospects. Greene was at the top of Noll's. And, despite protests from his staff, Art Jr. had him there, too. They briefly talked about Hanratty, the local kid turned Notre Dame superstar, and the Steelers' need for a quarterback. "But I don't think we can afford to take one," Noll said. "We need too much help in other areas." They all agreed that building the defensive line was the best way to rebuild this team.

Still, Art Jr. wanted to impress. On January 28, the morning of the draft, he was in the war room by 6:00 A.M., two hours before everyone else was set to arrive. He ordered coffee, tea, doughnuts, and rolls, items that every scout needed to survive the day. He checked the phone lines to New York, where the draft was being held and his brother Tim was located. He wiped his brow and checked his board and made sure names were spelled right.

When Noll arrived he said nothing, and changed nothing. He and Art Jr. talked about the press that was lurking inside the room and the ground rules they followed to maintain access. Then, at exactly 8:00 A.M., NFL commissioner Pete Rozelle announced the first pick of the 1968 draft: "Buffalo . . . First choice in the first round . . . O. J. Simpson, running back from USC."

With the second pick Atlanta chose Notre Dame tackle George Kunz. And picking third the Eagles took Purdue running back Leroy Keyes. In the Steelers war room there was a hush. Art Jr. looked across the table at Noll and asked him, "Greene?" Noll said, "Let's go for him." Dan then picked up the phone, called Tim standing by in New York, and said one word, "Greene." The next sound they heard was Rozelle, at the podium: "Pittsburgh . . . Fourth choice in the first round . . . Joe Greene, defensive tackle from North Texas."

The press in the room grumbled. Reporters wanted a name brand to sell some papers. They wanted to build excitement around the moribund franchise that had, in their eyes, yet again, botched the one way to get better: making good draft picks. They would, in fact, get their local-kid-made-good story when the Steelers picked Hanratty in the second round. "In doing so we deviated from our plans," wrote Art Jr. in his book. "He was not the best athlete available. We took him for one reason: pressure from our fans."

But that wasn't good enough to please the reporters who were trying to please those fans. They chose not to focus on the fact that every other team in the NFL had passed on Hanratty in the first round as well. Instead one reporter took to the streets and randomly asked local fans if they had ever heard of Joe Greene. No one said yes. The headline the next day read simply: JOE WHO?

Joe Greene felt as bad about going to Pittsburgh as fans did about him coming there. He was a small-town Texas kid who had grown up a Cowboys fan. After he got the call from Noll, he looked through the sports books lining his shelves and the magazines in his room trying to find one positive thing written about Pittsburgh or the Steelers. He found nothing. "I was sad," he says. "I wished I hadn't been drafted at all. I didn't know anything other than they were in the Steel City and it was old and smoky from the mills."

And the headline in the *Pittsburgh Post-Gazette*—"Joe Who?"—made things even worse. What Noll had liked most about Greene, more than his unmatched size and speed, was his pride. He was a nasty, ill-tempered competitor. Losing burned him from the inside out, like an ulcer. When he was embarrassed on the field and felt as though his pride had been damaged, he lashed out at whoever was causing the pain. Teammates suffered in practice with a club move to the head; opponents felt a swift punch to the stomach. Greene was, well, mean. So mean that the green-clad North Texas football team, historically called the Eagles, became known as the Mean Green during his tenure. The name stuck. For player and school.

Greene had plenty of reasons to be angry growing up in Temple, Texas, a hundred miles south of Dallas. When he was ten, his father left his family ("Just went somewhere," Greene said), leaving Joe to comfort his mom and three younger siblings. She worked as a maid while Joe was the after-school watchdog at home. But money was always tight, and the Greenes often found themselves forced to move from one run-down home to another.

When he was older, to help out at home, he occasionally spent weekends working menial labor jobs, usually picking cotton beside grown men who were trying to support their families on a dollar or two an hour. He was already the biggest kid in his class, but these experiences aged him, stealing a part of his adolescence. He wouldn't live his life like this, he thought to himself. He'd never let it get this bad for him, for his family. "When I was twelve I told myself I would never go back to the fields," he said. "I had a burning desire to be a success at something." Every slight he ever felt on the playing field—from a coach, from a teammate—was construed as his not being good enough. Every punch he threw because some offensive lineman was holding him came from a fear of being embarrassed, of not being able to do his job and being told it was time for him to go back and work with those men.

Because he was so big, and because he so rarely smiled, kids his age were scared of him. He was a man among ten-year-olds, brooding, hulking, and moody to those around him. He was a bully by decree, not actions; someone who looked tough, and therefore *was* tough. Years later, after he was drafted, there were rumors that he was actually six years older than his official age. No one could be that big and that strong and that young.

People's perception of him made him feel isolated, like an outcast, and imbued him with a sensitivity, a shyness, that would last a lifetime. Not even football spared him. "I went out for football because I was one of the biggest kids and the head coach taught me math and the assistant was teaching me geography so they were all over me to play," Greene says. "Most of the guys in school, if you weren't in the band, you played sports, and even the kids in the band had to play. Guys marched in the band in their football uniform. In central Texas that happened a lot.

"When I started playing in high school, I was scolded by an older player for not being aggressive and for getting blocked. He was a linebacker and I was getting knocked back into him and that was a big time no-no."

Greene weighed 203 pounds as a high school freshman. The next season, having grown to 235, he moved to middle linebacker, and was so ferocious that he was kicked out of every single game. His junior year, he was booted from nine more. By his senior year, he was a 250-pound linebacker with a rep as a wild man. Once, after losing a home game, Greene saw a bunch of the players from the other team at a local restaurant. The star quarterback was eating an ice cream cone, which Greene promptly shoved in his face. He then heard a bunch of players sitting on the bus who had seen what he'd done yelling his name. So he ran through the front door of the bus, ready to take on everyone, only to watch the entire team jump out the emergency door in the back.

None of the fans in Pittsburgh knew these stories yet. They didn't know that this big man burned hotter than molten steel. They didn't know that he feared losing the way most people fear poverty. They didn't know that he understood what every blue-collar mill worker felt every time he walked into the foundry, because he'd stood there, too, just a guy punching a clock looking for a paycheck. And losing meant doing it again. He had no intention of doing that.

That's who Joe was.

9

LAMAR HUNT WASN'T THE ONLY SON OF A MULTIMILLION-aire oilman in Dallas who wanted a new toy. Clint Murchison Jr. (pronounced Murk-a-son) had been after an NFL franchise for close to a decade. Like Hunt, who was a third-string end at SMU, Murchison, a scrawny halfback in prep school, had a love of the game but played it with little distinction. And like Hunt, he was convinced that Dallas would support a professional football team. After trying to buy the original Texans before their insolvency in 1952, the San Francisco 49ers in 1955, and George Preston Marshall's Washington Redskins in 1958, Clint Jr. was not about to be denied an expansion franchise.

When Hunt and Adams refused to abort the AFL, Murchison pursued Halas until he agreed to recommend that he be given the honor of paying $600,000 for the rights to the Dallas team. Halas assured him that formal approval would not be a problem at the annual owners meeting in January 1960.

Halas had also secured an ownership group from Houston, but this time Bud Adams outflanked him. The hometown son locked up Jeppesen Stadium for his Oilers. The only other pro football–worthy Houston stadium was at Rice University. And, in October, Rice made a surprising announcement that it would not lease the stadium for professional football use. The AFL won round two. The NFL would not play in Houston.

October 1959 dealt a serious blow to the NFL, when Bell, the former Eagles owners and current league commissioner, was felled by a heart attack while watching the Steelers-Eagles game. Red Smith wrote, "It was like Caruso dying in the third act of *Pagliacci*." At the most crucial time in its history, when the NFL needed its steady and respected consigliere to broker a truce with the young turks of the AFL, he was gone. It had been Bell who calmed the waters by saying there was easily enough talent to go around for both leagues. The owners stuck NFL treasurer Austin Gunsel in the chair until they could sort out the best choice at their meeting in January 1960.

With Bell gone and no one left to hold him back, Halas went for the jugular. The AFL had just secured its eighth and final franchise when Billy Sullivan in Boston locked down financing for his Patriots. And the AFL had scheduled its first player draft. The owners planned to meet at the Cedric Adams Hotel in Minneapolis at the end of November. As the group came together for dinner the night before the draft, Harry Wismer (the New York Titans owner) arrived with news. "This is the last supper! And he's Judas!" He pointed a newspaper at Max Winter, the owner of the AFL's Minnesota franchise. Winter confessed that he had accepted an offer from George Halas to join the NFL.

With the exception of the hyperbolic and underfinanced Wismer, the AFL's owners were the next generation of American businessmen. Among its members were the sons of many of the country's most successful industrialists and forward-thinking entrepreneurs—jet-setters unburdened by provincial loyalties. They looked at the game as a national enterprise rather than a local responsibility. They were in it for the business.

Barron Hilton, the son of hotelier Conrad Hilton, started up the Los Angeles franchise. He named them the Chargers, after a new business that he and his father were in, the Carte Blanche charge card. Within a year, he found a better market and picked up and moved the team to San Diego. Ralph C. Wilson Jr., the son of a successful insurance broker who diversified and scaled his father's business to great success, owned the Buffalo Bills. When the Oakland franchise was in financial trouble, Wilson lent the team $400,000 to keep it and the AFL viable.

Even with the loss of the Minnesota franchise, Lamar Hunt and Bud Adams were not about to panic. With Hilton intent on finding a West

Coast rival for his Chargers, Hunt encouraged him to reach out to Oakland real estate magnate Chet Soda to replace Minnesota with Oakland. And Bud Adams did his part by drafting the Heisman Trophy winner for 1959, Billy Cannon of LSU.

The NFL's Los Angeles Rams held the number-one draft pick and were intent on signing Cannon before the AFL. The general manager of the Rams, Pete Rozelle, quietly worked out a deal with Cannon that called for a $10,000 signing bonus and a salary of $15,000 per year for three years. Because Cannon had been rebuffing his overtures, Adams suspected that the Rams had gotten to him before he could. When he finally reached Cannon, he learned that not only had the Rams and Cannon negotiated, he had in fact signed a contract. So Adams doubled the NFL offer.

LSU was the defending national champion in 1959 and was poised to play Mississippi in the Sugar Bowl on New Year's Day 1960. As soon as the last second ticked off the clock, Cannon met an Oiler representative under the goalposts and signed a contract worth $110,000. When Rozelle and the Rams challenged the signing, it became clear that they had broken a cardinal rule—college players were forbidden to sign pro contracts while still playing in the NCAA. The dispute went to court and the judge ruled in Houston's favor. The war between the AFL and the NFL was in full swing before the new league got one play off from scrimmage.

Rozelle's audacity throughout the Cannon controversy—even with the ultimate failure of the scheme—proved compelling to the NFL owners. They needed a bold leader, capable of beating the AFL youth movement. When he attended the NFL owners meeting in Miami just three weeks later, in January 1960, the thirty-three-year-old Rams general manager got an offer he never expected: He was elected commissioner of the NFL.

10

MEN LIKE I. W. ABEL GREW UP WATCHING THEIR FATHERS come home mornings and evenings dirty, hoarse, and bleary-eyed. Their bodies deteriorated from the inside out with each passing year as their lungs filled with coal dust and ash. Many were so severely burned in accidents that instant incineration would have been a mercy. There was no such thing as workman's compensation or disability pay or company-sponsored life insurance. If you got hurt, too bad. There was no shortage of men who would take your place.

Abel was born in Ohio in 1908, and by the time he was seventeen, he was firing kilns, often working twelve hours a day, seven days a week, for just sixteen cents an hour. A yeoman laborer who went from mill to mill in search of the highest wages, Abel got a good look at the toll that working in an inferno took on the men on the floor. He'd see the older workers and pray he didn't end up like them. One day he stopped praying and did something about it.

At the Timken Roller Bearing mill in Canton, Ohio, Abel led wildcat strikes (those not approved by the Amalgamated leadership) to get better working conditions. Abel's militancy attracted the attention of Phillip Murray, the leader of the new Steelworkers Organizing Committee. Murray took Abel under his wing and encouraged him to establish Canton's Steel Workers Local 1123.

When Congress passed the National Labor Relations Act in 1935, limiting an employer's ability to retaliate against workers who joined a union, engaged in collective bargaining, or went on strike, the Steelworkers Organizing Committee finally convinced U.S. Steel to sign a union contract. The smaller steel companies refused to follow suit. The SWOC called for a national strike to get all steelmakers to comply. This is when Abel came into his own, proving that he could galvanize his fellow union members. After he organized and led forty-two wildcat strikes, Murray pulled him into the national leadership. The strikes persisted for four years, amidst violence—the Memorial Day massacre in Chicago left ten dead and thirty wounded strikers—and resistance from steel companies. In 1941, the SWOC finally prevailed. "Little Steel" agreed to the same contract as "Big Steel."

The SWOC changed its name to the United Steelworkers of America in 1942 and Murray rented a shabby office in Pittsburgh's Grant Building. As one of the leading figures in the movement, Abel climbed the union ranks and was elected secretary-treasurer of the USWA on the ballot with presidential candidate David J. McDonald in 1952. The USWA continued to face recalcitrant steel manufacturers, and was compelled to strike in 1952 and 1959 to raise wages and working standards. The strikes were brutal on steel-working families, and as secretary-treasurer, Abel got the brunt of the misery. The USWA did not have a strike fund in those days, and Abel's hands were tied when the wives of steelworkers, their husbands too proud, pleaded for financial relief. He couldn't authorize it even in the most extreme cases. If he had, there would have been a run on the building. He never forgot.

By the mid-1960s, despite his long tenure, McDonald was losing his grip on the members. He drank often, joined the fanciest clubs in Pittsburgh—clubs that steelworkers built but could never afford. He bought high-end toys and had a reputation for being vain and self-centered. There wasn't a press conference or broadcast that he didn't seem to appear in.

Abel, meanwhile, was constantly working the rank and file, traveling all over North America, meeting with local union officers and listening to their members' gravest concerns. He also became skeptical of the deals that McDonald bragged about making. When McDonald came up for reelection in 1965, Abel ran against him. In a bitter campaign, Abel accused McDonald of "tuxedo unionism" and having "utter contempt" for the rank and file. McDonald, with his air of superiority, said Abel was nothing more than a bookkeeper. But with the help of thousands of disgruntled steelworkers his own age, Abel squeaked out a victory by a margin of 10,000 votes out of 600,000 cast.

II

ON MARCH 16, 1963, A GROUP LED BY A FORMER AGENT AT THE Music Corporation of America completed the purchase of New York's AFL franchise, the New York Titans. The Gotham Football Club paid $1,000,000 for the bankrupt franchise, far above its market value, but the club's leader, David Abraham "Sonny" Werblin, knew the draw and potential for professional football.

Werblin had been a brilliant talent agent who served as president of television for Lew Wasserman's MCA. He made his fortune selling MCA-produced shows to networks. In fact, NBC ceded their entire prime-time schedule to Werblin and MCA in 1957. NBC's president Robert Kintner famously declared at the programming meeting, "Sonny, look at the schedule for the next season; here are the empty slots—you fill them."

Sonny sold television shows by selling stars—Frank Sinatra, Dean Martin, Jackie Gleason, Andy Williams, Eddie Fisher, Ed Sullivan, Jack Benny, Phil Silvers, Abbott and Costello, Ozzie Nelson, and a movie actor named Ronald Reagan. If you had the stars, the deals and audiences would follow.

The 1958 NFL championship ratings did not go unnoticed by Werblin. While the scoreboard said Colts versus Giants, Werblin saw it as the steely-eyed, blue-collar Johnny Unitas versus the metropolitan heartthrob Frank Gifford. There was a reason why viewers in Idaho, Iowa, Tennessee, and every other state tuned in. It wasn't because they cared about the cities represented or even the teams. It was the men on the field.

The forty-five million people who watched the game comprised 25 percent of the U.S. population in 1960. Madison Avenue now had the opportunity to speak directly to the demographic they coveted most, and the one that was the hardest to reach: the male aged 18 to 45. These men were or soon would be heads of households who bought cars, beer, cigarettes, razors, and aftershave. John DeLorean, then general manager of the Chevrolet Division of General Motors, said it best: "You know you're not reaching Maudie Frickert; you're reaching men, the guys who are making the decision to buy a car."

Werblin followed the startup AFL closely. With Bert Bell's announcement of the new league at the congressional hearings, founder Lamar Hunt negotiated a $2 million deal with ABC in June 1960 to carry the brand-new league. By 1962, the AFL hit critical mass. Fifty-six million viewers watched the double-overtime AFL championship between Hunt's Dallas Texans and Bud Adams's Houston Oilers.

The NFL followed up with its own $4.65 million TV deal with CBS in 1962. Meanwhile Werblin's life at MCA hit a crossroads. The Justice Department forced MCA to make a choice between its core agency business or television production. Production won and Werblin lost his stars. Football beckoned.

The NFL's old-school football-as-civic-enterprise setup was ridiculous to Werblin. Football wasn't about rivalries, or about keeping the hometown fans happy; it was entertainment. "A million dollar set [the Titans] is worthless if you put a $2,000 actor in the main role," he once said. "To me building a football team is like building a show. You can't go at it little by little. You have to go all out all the way. And professional football has become one of the great entertainment mediums in the United States."

With his purchase of the Titans, Werblin now had the stage. He just had to put on the right show. His first order of business was to change the name of the team, to get it far away from Wismer's "Titans" name, which was just a lame copycat of the Mara family's "Giants." Werblin's franchise wouldn't be an homage to the NFL. The "Jets" would be fresh, modern, and cool—just like the jet-set owners of the league.

Armed with more television money—in 1964, Werblin worked behind the scenes to secure an unprecedented $36 million deal for the AFL on NBC—the AFL franchises went to war with the NFL, outspending them to get the best college players. Werblin was not just on the lookout for talented athletes. He wanted a star.

Joe Namath was everything he could ask for. Werblin gave him a game-changing contract worth more than $400,000 in 1965 (as much as many teams' entire payroll) and got tens of millions of dollars of publicity for the Jets in the bargain. (Namath actually had a four-year deal worth $25,000 per season, plus $200,000 worth of annuities that did not pay out for years, and salaries for his family.)

As soon as he joined the team, Namath did exactly what Werblin expected. And what he wanted. The star QB missed curfews. He wore white shoes when everyone else wore black. But he was a warrior, too. He played hurt and at times brilliantly. Football's core audience didn't like Joe as a person, but respected him as a player. Meanwhile, a brand-new audience looked at Joe as the rebel against the system, an individual stuck in a crew-cut collective. Joe made a fortune, lived a life out of *Playboy* magazine, and rubbed it in the establishment's face.

Namath sold out Shea Stadium and every stadium on the road, too. He became bigger than the game he played, and every other professional football player wanted what Joe had—the money and the power to behave any way he wanted to. With Joe Willie Namath, the professional football hierarchy was on the precipice of revolution. As New York Jets defensive lineman Gerry Philbin explained it, "There was one set of rules for the team and another for Joe."

12

BY THE SPRING OF 1969, NOLL STILL HAD YET TO MEET WITH
his team. And those he had met, like Pro Bowl linebacker Andy Russell,
didn't exactly get a warm embrace from the coach. "I met him at his office
and we sat down to watch film and the first thing he said to me was, 'I
don't like the way you play,'" says Russell. "He thought I had bad form,
was undisciplined and took too many chances. And I was one of our better players. I had just made the Pro Bowl."

Dick Hoak had made the Pro Bowl in 1968, too. "Not long after he
was hired I went in to meet him. He didn't even have his whole staff hired
yet," Hoak says. "He tried to explain what we were going to do offensively.
He talked about running this and that. He had a plan, you could tell he
did. We were going to build through the draft and quit trading these
choices. You could tell it was going to be hard."

Hoak was a Pittsburgh kid who had starred as a two-way player for
Penn State in the late 1950s. He had learned to play football from his two
brothers, who were more than a decade older than he was, by watching
them play in the park across the street from his house. When his oldest
brother broke his arm, the Hoak boys' mom forbade him from playing
football. But the slightly built Dick was too nifty, too fleet-footed, and too
smart on the field to ever take a clean hit. He had an uncanny sense for
how a play would develop. His mom never had to worry about him.

The Hoaks were a mill family. Charles and Donald, the oldest brothers, both spent time working in a rubber factory making tires. Hoak's
father worked in mills, too, making grenades and shells during the war
and then picking up work wherever he could when it was over. After

Dick's senior year in high school, his father never found steady work again—the family got by with help from Dick's brothers. Dick didn't intend on doing hard labor; he wanted to teach and coach. He had the perfect temperament for it—never too impressed with his accomplishments; never too disappointed with failure. Even when he was drafted by the Steelers in 1961, it wasn't cause for celebration. After talking it over with his parents he called the Pittsburgh scout and said, "Okay, I might as well try it." All Hoak asked was that the team help him finish school at Penn State, where he was six credits shy of graduating. The team Hoak joined was, by the barest definition, a pro team. It played in the NFL. He got paid. They had uniforms. But in so many ways, this was a minor-league outfit. Those uniforms? Well, sometimes the helmets were different colors. The team was essentially homeless, playing its home games at the University of Pittsburgh's Pitt Stadium, and at Forbes Field, where the Pirates roamed. And while fans loved the fact that the Steelers practiced in the public spaces at South Park—there were times that Frisbee-throwing fans and players had to watch out for each other—the players deplored it. When it rained, water drained to the middle of the field, making it impossible to practice. On those days, they moved indoors, to a barn where they kept police horses and manure piled high on the ground.

When it wasn't raining, the players had to walk the field themselves to remove rocks and debris. When coaches sent the team on endurance runs for training, the players had to run a course that traveled in a circle through the nearby woods. Veterans would stop just inside the shade and make the rookies finish the circuit. They'd smoke some cigarettes, rest on the rocks, and then pick up with the crowd of newbies as they circled back.

After the run, or lack thereof, they retired to the locker room in the basement of an old building on the grounds. Each player got a nail for his clothes. Hot water for showers after practice wasn't an option. Two of the showers didn't work at all, which meant the entire team shared only four. The toilets didn't have any seats. "You go from college, playing in a huge stadium and perfect practice fields," says Russell, who starred at Missouri. "And all of a sudden you're in Pittsburgh, practicing in South Park and playing in a tiny stadium. Well, it's hard."

Noll didn't care. Playing for him would be harder. Hoak knew it the first time they met. And Noll confirmed it when the team finally got together on the field at South Park for a spring practice. "Chuck came in and said, 'Some of you aren't good enough to play,'" remembers Hoak. "It was nothing personal, he was going to be honest, you either produced or you weren't going to be there. He was not a rah-rah guy, not a guy that gave a lot of speeches. He felt you were in the pros and you had to produce. He basically said, 'You are a man now and I will not lie or treat you like kids—if you have a problem you can see me, my door is open.'

"But I don't know how many of us walked in."

That included the cornerstone of his franchise, Joe Greene. Before training camp started Greene decided to hold out. Simpson held out in Buffalo. Leroy Keyes, drafted third overall by the Eagles, held out. So Greene did, too. Something no Steeler had ever done before. At one point Greene became so frustrated with the negotiations that he told a Pittsburgh reporter, "I'd rather play for ten dollars a game in the minor leagues than back down any further in the money I'm asking."

It was pride. With Greene it always was. But once he signed—reportedly a three-year deal worth $200,000—he learned how quickly the Rooneys separated their business from their feelings. The guy who gave Greene a ride to camp was Dan Rooney.

That made Greene feel welcome, but when he got to camp his teammates saw him as the big-money rook driven to camp by the owner. Plus he was overweight. Fat and late and loaded. The veteran Steelers, struggling through their first few days with a new coach, were just aggravated enough to give Greene a lesson.

Noll, and most coaches, started training camp with the Oklahoma drill. There is no more physical—or violent—exercise in all of football. From a three point-stance a defensive player goes face-to-face with an offensive lineman. At the snap, the defender must engage the lineman, shed the block and then tackle a running back, who gets a seven-yard head start. "To make that play you have to be strong enough to lose the blocker so you can get a good lock on that running back," says Russell. "And you are at a disadvantage because the blocker knows the count."

Noll and his coaches loved the Oklahoma drill. Right away, from the first minute of camp, they knew who was full of tenacity at the point of attack, and who would rather be fishing. The players loved it, too, because it told them who was a target and who was legit. They were about to find out with Greene. "Ray Mansfield was first," Russell remembers. Mansfield was the Steelers longtime starting center. He was the son of a man who laid concrete for a living and had the ears of his teammates. If a player asked a teammate to go out drinking for the night, it was Mansfield. If there was someone who needed to say something when teammates were slacking, it was Mansfield. If there was someone who needed to get chippy and a little dirty with opponents, it was Mansfield. He loved the physical nature of football, embracing the violence in a way that was different, more comfortable, than other players, who accepted it as a job hazard.

He was one of the players most looking forward to hazing Greene. "So Ray was first. And Joe just threw him like a rag doll. Pushed him away with his left arm. Then he used his right arm to crush the back," says Russell. "I was standing there with some other guys and we just looked at each other."

"He beat the crap out of every one of the offensive linemen," remembers Hoak. "We had two defensive tackles, Kenny Kortas and Frank Parker, and they were watching Joe and they just looked at each other and said, 'Well, we might as well pack our bags.' They had never seen anything like that."

Years later, Russell would tell Rooney that was the day everything changed for the Steelers. That one drill. It established Greene as the meanest, maddest, baddest player on the team. After that, he'd rip into teammates he felt were giving less than full effort in practice. His disgust with losing, his fear of going back to Texas with nothing, didn't infiltrate the Steelers. It swallowed them whole. "He was the single most important player in the history of our success," Russell says.

This training camp was about setting a foundation, and that's what Noll preached, as much as he talked about winning a title. Immediately the veterans knew he was different than the Bill Austins and Buddy Parkers they had played for. He didn't yell for the sake of yelling; didn't punish just to punish. There was more method than madness.

If the veterans hadn't gotten that message when Noll told them how bad they were in the spring, they got it their first day in training camp. Practice jerseys didn't have numbers. They were black and they were gold. Last year's starters were this year's numberless, faceless bodies. Coaches wouldn't have any preconceived notions about anyone. Talent would rule the day.

Joe Greene dazzled in this environment. So did another rookie, defensive end L. C. Greenwood, drafted in the tenth round from Arkansas A M & N. Greenwood was tall and lanky and weighed fifty pounds less than Greene. But, when he played alongside the mammoth number-one pick in practice, he exploded off the line. Every lesson learned seemed to make him faster.

That first training camp was more like Football 101 than a masters class. Noll taught blocking and tackling and three-point stances. He stood next to players like Russell, one of the few vets other teams would like to have, and showed him where to put his hands and how wide his stance should be. He emphasized the importance of knowing your opponent, and how proper technique, not brute strength, was the key to winning a game. "He was like, 'I want your right foot two inches outside of your opponent's foot, I want you to reach with your right hand,'" Russell said in Dan Rooney's autobiography.

But Noll knew how far to push. He was there to make the Steelers better football players, not be their father. Gone were the petty rules players hated. No more dress codes. Being clean-shaven didn't matter. Noll looked the other way when Mansfield snuck players out of the dorms for a late-night beer. He even let reporters stay in the dorms, partly so they'd talk to players instead of bothering him. Noll didn't do these things to win hearts and minds; none of these rules helped improve performance. But to players they showed consistency, that Noll meant what he said when he'd treat them like men. It was his job to teach them and their job to act like professionals. Moves like this helped them believe in his process.

And then, by some miracle, in front of more than 50,000 expectant fans at Pitt Stadium on the first weekend of the 1969 season, the Steelers beat the Lions 16–13. It was exactly the kind of game Noll predicted his team would play: ugly, defensive, close. The first five scores through three quarters were field goals, with the Steelers ahead 9–6 in the fourth. Then a Lions go-ahead touchdown was answered by a Steelers game-winning drive that ended with just less than three minutes left. The Lions were a legit team—they would finish the season 9-4-1. The win buoyed the first-year coach and the franchise he was trying to make believe in him.

And that was as good as it got all season long.

The next week, playing the Eagles in Philly at Franklin Field, the Steelers were euphoric when they went up 13–0 in the first quarter. But by halftime, they were down 17–13. And midway through the third, the score was 31–13. They ended up losing by two touchdowns. The next week they scored first again, against the Cardinals, only to give up twenty in the second quarter in another loss. The week after that? A three-point loss to the Giants. And two weeks later? A one-touchdown loss to the Redskins.

The Steelers were showing all the growing pains of a young team learning a new system. They'd execute early, then fall back on bad habits when challenged by opponents. The team wasn't good enough yet to win on skill alone. And the players could see in the box scores that they were at their best, they were winning, when they played the way Noll taught them to play. But that was always early in a game, before fatigue set in and before opponents began to dictate how Pittsburgh's game plan would have to change. It was frustrating, the way a toddler feels when he's just learning how to walk. And there were times when it boiled over.

In November, playing in Chicago against the league's only winless team, the Steelers were blown out 38–7. The game was over from the moment it started, with the Bears jumping out ahead 16–0 and going into the fourth quarter up 38–0. At the time, the acknowledged toughest player in the NFL was Bears middle linebacker Dick Butkus. He was surly and nasty and hit with the intensity of a man looking for a meal. Win or lose, Butkus had the respect, and fear, of the league. "And on this day, he was just destroying us," remembers Russell.

Butkus wasn't satisfied beating up on the Steelers offense. He played special teams, too, and on one play he clocked L. C. Greenwood near the Steelers side of the field. That was too much for Joe Greene. He ran after Butkus, pulling him off the ground by his shoulder pads until the two were face mask to face mask. He was screaming at Butkus, who screamed back as loud as he could. Greene was in a rage—his team was being humiliated, his friend had just been leveled—so he pulled his helmet off and cocked his arm, as if he was going to hammer it over Butkus's head. "Then I heard Andy Russell yell, 'Whoa, daddy,'" Greene says. "So I hesitated." When he did, Butkus turned around and ran back to his sideline.

Two weeks later in Minnesota, Greene was still simmering. In the fourth quarter the Vikings scored twenty-one unanswered points, turning their easy win into a thirty-eight-point blowout. Greene was called for a late hit in front of the Vikings bench, which was on the same side of the field as the Steelers. As he got up, the Vikings star defensive linemen, Carl Eller and Alan Page, started taunting him. Greene didn't bother turning around. Instead he went to the Steelers training table, grabbed a pair of scissors and then ran after Eller and Page. His teammates stopped him. But his coach never said a word. "I don't know if anyone would have tolerated my behavior the way Chuck did," Greene once told NFL Films.

"What he saw was a raw kid who was immature, and he didn't quash that enthusiasm. He let me get it out and then he let me mold it in a positive way."

At the end of the year, despite the losses and the frustration, all of the Steelers sensed that they were better than what the team's record showed. Only once that season did Noll berate the team in the film room, and that was after the season-opening win over the Lions. Every loss was followed by instruction more than criticism. If a player made a mistake he would stop the projector and ask, "What did you see on that play? Tell me why you made the decision you made."

"He never lost us," says Russell. "He never said anything that didn't make sense. He said, 'You are going to get worse before you get better.' And we did. He said, 'I am going to teach you how to play this game.' And he did."

"What made him special was that he was so consistent in terms of his focus and in terms of what was viable and real as far as achieving our ultimate goal of winning the Super Bowl," says Greene. "He was not deterred by anything not going in our direction. And he didn't jump around from one idea to the next, jumping all over us one day and then the next day telling us everything was great."

Because it wasn't. But Noll could tell it was getting better.

SECOND QUARTER

1969–1972

13

A THIRD-GENERATION TEXAN AND A FOURTH-GENERATION American, Clinton Williams Murchison was born in 1895, seventy-five miles southeast of Dallas in Athens, Texas. The son of a dry-goods magnate turned banker, he was raised with privileges but behaved like a ranch-raised cowboy. With a wild streak and a remarkable head for figures, Murchison began training for his life's work at the age of nine. The big Texas cattle ranches were in the western part of the state, but livestock trading was ever present in Athens' corrals and wagon yards. At the first clang of the school bell, Clint was out the door, racing downtown to watch and listen to the cowboys trading and haggling over their stock. He was fascinated by the men who could outwit their ignorant prey, trading their weak horse or calf for another man's prize possessions. "If you have to get a calf's price down to eight dollars so you can sell it at ten dollars . . . you learn about people," Murchison once said.

Murchison's horse-trading was the perfect training for the events that followed on January 10, 1901. A thousand feet beneath a hillock named Spindletop, just two counties south of Athens, lay the largest oil field in North America. An oil well, financed by a couple of easterners interloping on the Texas fields, spewed petroleum one hundred feet in the air. It was a bona fide gusher. Before long, Spindletop was producing more crude than every U.S. oil well that had ever been tapped. Combined.

The big initial Texas oil fortunes were won by outsiders, led by Pittsburgher James Guffey, who owned the lease for the Spindletop well. When he sold the rights to his well to the European oil company Royal Dutch Shell, it was touted by newspapers across the country as the deal of the century. Then, with a rep for prospecting and a streak of luck, Guffey earned the backing of one of Pittsburgh's richest families, the Mellons, and moved south to the Gulf Coast field region. He struck oil again. The Mellons called the new company Gulf Oil and set up corporate headquarters in Pittsburgh.

The one conspicuous absentee from the rush was John D. Rockefeller's Standard Oil. The Texas state legislature had long sought to dismantle Standard, and as one of the company's spokesmen put it, "We're out . . . After the way Mr. Rockefeller has been treated by the state of Texas, he'll never put another dime in Texas." But Rockefeller was no fool. While he may not have put another dime in, he continued to take a lot out through his relationships with the railroads and his stranglehold on the majority of petroleum refineries.

Texas was not about to let the north carpetbag its natural resources. Texas's state senators and representatives passed a series of laws that prohibited vertical integration of the oil business. Oil prospectors were not allowed to refine the oil. Oil pipeline companies couldn't become barrel manufacturers, and up the chain it went. The fallout left the big eastern companies with the work of oil (piping, refining, transporting, etc.) and the native Texans with the fun—leasing land with potential oil reserves, drilling, and then selling the leases to the big companies after the wells came in.

The oil business, like every Texas commodity, boiled down to horse-trading. And like the cowboys he had learned from in Athens, Clint Murchison and a small band of other individual Texas speculators proved to be outrageously successful traders. Oil leasing worked like this. A landowner with acreage bordering an oil-producing field would sell the rights to sink wells on his property for a fee plus a percentage of the profits from the oil taken from his land. Men like Clint Murchison and his best friend Sid Richardson would move from town to town and buy up lease rights to drill on the thousands of acres of untested land. The trick was to spend little for the rights to land that had not yet come in, hire a wildcatter to dig a well, find the oil, and then sell the pumping rights to the land for multiples of what you paid for it.

What made Murchison was that he didn't just profit from lease transactions, he retained a percentage of profits from future wells, too. He'd buy 95 percent of a lease for $1,000 (5 percent would be retained by the owner of the land) and then sell 80 percent of the rights to a big oil company for $100,000. Not only would he reap a $99,000 profit from the transaction, he would also then own 15 percent of the underground oil for as long as it produced. The hard work of the oil-lease market favored the quick-footed and savvy individual over big business. And the Murchison family bank gave Clint a head start. He could leverage credit to buy more leases that would produce oil, which he could put up as collateral to find more credit. His financing by finagling strategy made him outrageously rich. By 1957, *The New York Times* estimated his wealth at $400 million and named him one of the seventy richest men in America.

For Clint Sr., "money was like manure—you got to spread it around to make things grow." This philosophy became the guiding principle for his relationship with his three sons, John, Clint Jr., and Burk Murchison. After eleven-year-old Burk died of pneumonia, Clint Sr. took a deeper interest in John and Clint Jr. He vowed to give them a leg up, like he'd gotten, when they began their inevitable business careers. After John graduated from Yale and Clint Jr. from MIT with an advanced degree from Duke, Clint Sr. brought them back to Dallas to give them their head start. In 1949, he handed them the reins to a $75 million company he had built for them called Murchison Brothers, a conglomerate holding company with majority stakes in twenty different businesses.

John and Clint Jr. proved as resourceful as their father. Nicknamed "Vice and Versa" because of their opposite approach to the world (John conservative, Clint Jr. aggressive), Clint Sr. used to say, "One of my boys won't make up his mind at all. The other makes it up too fast." The combination was lightning in a bottle. They leveraged Murchison Brothers and doubled its holdings in just ten years. While Clint Jr. found the opportunities to buy, sell, and invest, John oversaw the deal points. Between them they had interests in more than a hundred companies in construction, insurance, banking, hotels, oil, gas, and even book publishing. Their biggest deal, outdueling a Woolworth heir to take control of one of Wall Street's most influential holding companies, landed them on the cover of *Time* magazine. At the time, the only other Texas businessman awarded such an honor had been their father.

The rush of a business deal intoxicated Clint Jr., but once the transaction was done, he had little interest in the paperwork. He'd tire of the details until the next opportunity arose and the process would begin anew. His brother, John, would let off steam by flying to a ski mountain that the brothers had bought in Vail, Colorado, but Clint Jr. didn't want to relax. He wanted to be entertained.

And there was one thing that would always keep his interest.

14

AFTER WINNING THEIR FIRST GAME OF 1969, THE STEELERS lost the next 13, finishing 1-13. The Bears, with their win over Pittsburgh, matched that record. The futility of the two teams meant a coin flip for the number-one overall choice in the 1970 draft. On January 9, two days before the Minnesota Vikings and Kansas City Chiefs played in Super Bowl IV, execs from both teams met NFL Commissioner Pete Rozelle at the Fairmont Hotel in New York. In his pocket, Rozelle carried a 1921 silver dollar.

No matter who won the toss, there was only one player that any scout worth his suitcase considered taking with that top spot: Terry Bradshaw.

Bradshaw was a burly, cocksure, church-going blond from Shreveport, Louisiana, with a right arm made of gunpowder. Pop, pop, pop—the ball came out of his hand with a vapor trail behind it, traveling fifty yards on a straight line. He knew this was his gift. "Some families inherit intelligence, some get good looks," Bradshaw wrote in his autobiography *It's Only a Game*. "We got right arms."

He was the son of a welder who loved football. And with his three brothers and sometimes even his mom, Bradshaw would play football in his backyard. He had been practicing the game from the time he was four years old, throwing wadded-up pieces of paper as far across the living room as they would go. He eventually graduated to footballs. He'd get a new one every year for Christmas and would polish it with brown shoe polish to help it stay fresh. Lying on his bed at night he'd toss the ball into the air until it made a soft thud against his bedroom ceiling, where it would leave a slight brown smudge. Bradshaw played with the ball so often—in the rain, in the sun—that it would expand and snap the laces before the next Christmas came around again. So he'd take out his shoelaces to tie the ball back together again.

But Bradshaw, at heart, was a country kid. Every summer he and his brothers stayed with his grandparents at their forty-acre farm in Hall Summit, which was "25 miles and 50 years," Bradshaw wrote, from Shreveport. He learned how to pick cotton and cantaloupe and watermelons; how to stretch out animal skins so the eye sockets stayed round when drying out; how to fix a prolapsed uterus in a cow and how to make buttermilk and paste. Dresses were made from flour sacks, biscuits were made from scratch, transportation was a couple of Clydesdales hooked up to a wagon, and Saturday nights were for going into town to get haircuts and listen to the Grand Ole Opry. And the bathroom? That was a two-hole outhouse filled with horseflies the size of thoroughbreds and situated way on the other side of a briar patch.

Being outside was the perfect release for Bradshaw, a rambunctious kid who struggled in the classroom. Years later, he'd write that he suffered from attention deficit disorder. But at the time he was just a boy who couldn't sit still in class, who failed the tests he actually did sit through, and who constantly wondered why everyone thought he was so dumb, especially when he knew he could eventually figure everything out. He just didn't learn the way so many kids in his class did. He learned by doing, by freewheeling his way through a situation and reacting. In a classroom—forced to study by rote, to follow the plan laid out for him by a teacher and not the path his head was telling him to take—he had to suppress all that energy.

That's why he was never more confident than when he was outside, playing a game, letting his physical skills dictate how life in that moment would unfold. His instincts were his most trusted guide. That's why, when he was a junior in high school and backing up a high school All-American, he never stopped believing it was his destiny to be a professional football player. What else could he possibly do?

When Bradshaw finally got a chance to play his senior year, he unleashed three years of pent-up energy on his opponents. He flung the ball around like he'd been doing in his bedroom since he was seven years old: with precision and joy. If the coach called a run, Bradshaw might decide to pass anyway. The coach would never bench the guy who just threw a touchdown pass, he reasoned, and Bradshaw always assumed he'd throw a touchdown pass. In ways he'd never be in the classroom, he was unafraid of consequences, of failure. Nothing about the game he played was dependent upon study. It was all so easy. In his only season as a starter, Bradshaw led Woodlawn High School to the state championship game, where it lost by a field goal.

He received scholarship offers from Baylor. And from Louisiana State. And letters from nearly two hundred other schools. As a javelin thrower he set a then national high school record of more than 245 feet, which earned him calls from schools in Europe who wanted him on their track teams.

Every Louisiana high school kid's dream was to play for LSU. Not Bradshaw. The quarterback he'd played behind in high school was already in Baton Rouge, and he was sitting on the bench. Bradshaw figured that if the guy he couldn't beat out in high school wasn't playing, what chance did he have? But rather than disappoint all the folks in Shreveport who wanted to see him as a Tiger, Bradshaw, as he wrote in *It's Only a Game,* purposely failed the LSU entrance exam. "I am not claiming I could have passed that test easily if I had wanted to go to LSU," he wrote. "I know I didn't study for it, I didn't care about it and I definitely didn't want to go to LSU."

For all his big-time talent, Bradshaw was a small-town country kid. The slower the pace, the more comfortable he felt. So instead of LSU or Baylor or any of the showpiece football schools that recruited him, he settled on tiny, unheralded Louisiana Tech in Ruston, where his talents for sitting on the bench were more appreciated than his golden arm. For two years he backed up the starter, again waiting his turn, still believing he was a future NFL star. He sat until early in his junior season, when the number-one QB was knocked out of a game and Bradshaw finally got his shot. By the end of the season, little Louisiana Tech was 9-2 and Bradshaw, now 6'3" and 210 pounds, led the nation in combined rushing and passing yardage. He was, as he always expected to be, a prospect.

In Bradshaw's senior year, NFL scouts packed their bags and hopped on puddle-jumpers and unfolded their maps, looking for Ruston and the kid they had heard was a sure thing. Scouts are a dedicated bunch. They carried their own lightbulbs in case motel bulbs were too dim for them to read their reports. Sometimes they drove more than fifty thousand miles a year. This is how scouts lived and dreamed: The harder the prospect was to scout, and the more difficult he was to find, the better he must be.

Anyone could tout the star at Notre Dame or USC. But an eyewitness account of transcendence, tucked away in the woods, was gold to a scout. It's how he made his bones. And none of them could go back to their coaches and owners without having laid eyes on the country-strong kid in Ruston. When Art Rooney Jr. went down there he interviewed everyone from the student manager to the quarterbacks coach. "And everything I had seen, everything I had heard, made me a full-throated member of the chorus, singing Bradshaw's praises," he wrote in his autobiography. His biggest worry was that other scouts would come away from Ruston feeling the same way he did.

They did.

Bradshaw looked as good during his senior year as he had the year before. Slinging the ball through defenses that were now geared to stop him alone, he still threw for nearly 2,500 yards. His stats would have been even better, but in most games, Louisiana Tech was so far ahead that he was pulled to make sure he stayed healthy. The scouting service BLESTO, made up of a group of teams who filed scouting reports for the entire league so travel expenses could be shared, had him ranked number one out of a thousand prospects.

But it wasn't until it was clear that the hapless Steelers would have a shot at choosing Bradshaw that Noll made a trip to the Senior Bowl to visit this prospect for the first time. The word of his scouts wasn't good enough. "He was a doubting Thomas, he had to see to believe," wrote Rooney Jr. "Noll could be maddening."

As is still the tradition, NFL coaches took over each Senior Bowl squad, and Bradshaw's was coached by Don Shula. "We'll see how he picks up teaching," Noll told his scouts before the trip. This was, of course, paramount to Noll. It wasn't that he didn't believe his scouts when they said that Bradshaw had otherworldly talent. He trusted their instincts on dozens of prospects he never saw. But this was his potential quarterback, his extension on the field. A million-dollar arm didn't mean anything if the guy using it had a ten-cent head.

Noll was impressed when Bradshaw ran a 4.7 forty-yard dash. And he nodded in approval when Bradshaw completed 17 of 31 passes for 267 yards and two touchdowns to win the Senior Bowl MVP. He might have even chuckled at the way Bradshaw was so excited to play that he went the entire game without buckling his chin strap. But what sealed it for Noll was the IQ test—twenty-five math questions, twenty-five verbal—he gave Bradshaw. The kid who purposely failed his entrance exam into LSU did well enough to please one of the most cerebral coaches in the NFL.

Now he only hoped he could get him, because there was still the matter of that coin flip. Art Rooney, an old gambler imbued with all the superstition that comes from a life spent at the track, had a theory about coin flips: Always let the other guy call it. It put the pressure on him. Gambler's logic. Problem was, Dan was representing the Steelers at the Fairmont Hotel in New York, where the flip was happening. And Art never told his son his theory. "Pete shows us the coin, both sides, and he says, 'Okay, Dan, do you want to call it?'" Dan Rooney once remembered. "I said, 'No, let him call it.'"

The Bears rep called heads. It was tails. Rozelle picked up the coin and handed it to Rooney. And when Rooney and Noll took their wives out to dinner to celebrate having the number-one choice, the owner gave the coach that 1921 silver dollar. The coach subsequently turned that dollar into a franchise quarterback. "The night before 1970 draft, we were upstairs in Dan Rooney's office and the personnel people and Chuck were talking because the Cardinals had made us an offer, seven players, for the right to the first choice," says Joe Gordon, the Steelers longtime PR rep. "But Chuck was adamant that we not do it. He said, 'That was just more mediocrity—it wasn't going to get us any closer to a championship. It might have helped us win a couple more games, but not in the long run.'"

Meanwhile, down in Louisiana, Bradshaw was realizing a lifelong dream. Johnny Unitas had told him he was expecting big things. So had Y. A. Tittle. Don Shula said he was willing to trade six draft picks to get him. But Bradshaw was going to Pittsburgh. When asked how he felt, he replied, "Thrilled. I wanted to go with a loser."

He got his wish.

15

BUYING INTO THE NFL WAS NO BARGAIN. THERE WAS THE $600,000 Murchison shelled out for the rights to the Dallas franchise. And there was the low-man-on-the-totem-pole treatment from his fellow owners. They insisted that Murchison's new team begin play immediately, to compete with Hunt's AFL franchise. Established too late to participate in the 1960 draft, Murchison's new team would be built solely from cast-offs the other NFL teams didn't want.

But Murchison didn't care. Chicago Bears owner George Halas had already recommended a close friend—and former boss of NFL commissioner Pete Rozelle—to help Murchison run the new Dallas franchise. Texas Schramm Jr.—named after his Texan father, but raised in Los Angeles—entered professional football as the head of publicity for the Los Angeles Rams in 1947. A graduate of the University of Texas with a degree in journalism, he'd often write and edit different Rams coverage stories for L.A.'s five competing newspapers. Pro football was of such ancillary interest at the time that not one of the papers had a writer on staff to cover it.

Schramm was like a carnival barker—selling his team to the public—and the work paid off in larger crowds and a local television deal. Soon after joining the team, Schramm was named the Rams GM and became the right-hand man to the mercurial Rams owner, Dan Reeves. He hired an old friend, Tex Maule, to shore up the PR department and eventually put a fresh-faced PR apprentice, Pete Rozelle, on staff. (Maule would go on to become the lead pro football writer at a startup magazine called *Sports Illustrated*.)

Reeves, the son of privilege, had dreamed of owning a football team. After buying the Rams in 1941, he stayed out late in L.A. talking football with whoever would listen and fired coaches as frequently as he changed shirts. He was intimately involved in managing the day-to-day activities of the team, and Schramm realized that no matter how creative he was, the team would never truly be his. He was an employee, and he had ambition for more. When he resigned in 1957 to take a job at CBS Sports, Pete Rozelle took his place.

For three years, Schramm learned the television business, negotiating CBS's contracts with the NFL to broadcast the games. He stayed close with the owners, and one of them, George Halas, sensed that Schramm missed the concentrated, full-bore effort it took to run a football team. When Clint Murchison Jr. asked Halas whom he should hire to put together his new football team, Halas gave him one name. "Tex." Murchison loved the symmetry.

And Schramm loved Murchison's management strategy. During their first meeting, he looked Murchison straight in the eye and said, "The only person the players should be responsible to is the coach, and the only person the coach is responsible to is the general manager." The Murchison family bought new toys all the time. But they didn't put them together. They hired someone else to do that. In an extraordinary acknowledgment of his power, Murchison agreed to let Schramm attend all league meetings and vote for the Cowboy franchise.

Schramm got right to work. He hired a Texas-born head coach, Tom Landry, a full month before the Cowboys became an official NFL franchise. A colleague of New York Giants offensive coordinator Vince Lombardi, Landry headed up the Giants' game-changing defense. A former all-pro defensive back, Landry had an exceptional strategic and tactical mind. While he acknowledged the necessity of being fundamentally flawless with superior blocking and tackling (the Lombardi credo), he also anticipated the day when physical excellence would not be enough. Beating your opponent with your mind would be the margin of victory in the future. With expert forethought and planning, a team that created a strategic advantage (a system that would adapt to the tactical strengths of an opponent) would be able to outflank a better team and win. He had already turned theory into practice when he devised the run-stopping 4-3 defensive scheme for the Giants, which made the middle linebacker the central figure. With four down linemen engaging the offensive line, the unblocked middle linebacker would scan the offensive backfield and meet the running back at the line of scrimmage. With Landry's innovation, the Giants had the best defense in the NFL in both 1958 and 1959. With the Cowboys, Schramm was giving Landry the chance to mold a champion in his own image.

Gil Brandt, a former scout for the Los Angeles Rams during Schramm's tenure, was hired to sort out player personnel and negotiate contracts. A former children's portrait photographer in Milwaukee, Brandt was affable, an enthusiast. He liked to be liked. As a Big Ten scout for Schramm at the Rams, he had developed a network of college and high school coaches who would evaluate talent and send him detailed reports. Jack Elway, father of legendary quarterback John Elway, used to scout for Brandt in Washington State. Brandt would go to the annual college all-star game and throw a big party for the college coaches, their assistants, and his scouts to make sure that his men got preferential treatment on campus. He was also the master of the birthday card for any coach's kid that came along with free Dallas Cowboy paraphernalia.

Brandt's network was rich and deep, almost too deep, because he and Schramm found the player data that came in to be overwhelming. Schramm thought about how best to sift the data into a definitive and clean recommendation. After watching an IBM computer tabulate and update the results of the 1960 Winter Olympics in Squaw Valley, Schramm contacted IBM to do something similar for the Cowboys' scouting problem. They put him in touch with a lead scientist at one of their subsidiaries, Service Bureau Corporation in Palo Alto, California. Indian-born Salam Quereishi, who would today be called a software programmer, answered the call. Despite serious language barriers—with accompanying red-faced Schramm exasperation, Quereishi and Schramm devised a brilliant evaluation process to find the best prospects for the Cowboy system. Fifteen different categories defined each player. He would be given a numeric grade between 1 and 9, with 3 being average. Schramm understood that performance at the professional level was so competitive that a small edge separated outstanding from extraordinary. With five levels of above average, he demanded that scouts think harder about what truly made each player special.

After four years and millions of dollars invested in the system, Schramm's computer finally went online just before the 1964 college draft. In a dramatic culmination of money, time, and systematic management, the IBM 7090/7094 spit out the fifteen best professional prospects in that year's draft. It did not select the Heisman Trophy winner, John Huarte from Notre Dame, or his runner-up, Jerry Rhome from Tulsa. The first name on the list was Alabama quarterback Joe Namath. Huarte and Rhome would never become pro football stars. Namath would become, well, Namath. Schramm's computer was right on the money. And in that first draft, it helped the Cowboys select three Hall of Famers: Mel Renfro, Bob Hayes, and Roger Staubach.

With its space-age computer system, the Dallas Cowboys' system became the most efficient, regimented, and machine-like operation in professional football. Schramm was the central power, the big brother whom Landry and Brandt would bring in when they disagreed. The former PR man ran the day-to-day and made it his mission to sell the franchise to the people of Dallas and, ultimately, to the entire country. A bit over six feet tall, he was a burly, thick-necked presence, jowly and chubby-cheeked. His thinning hair, cold-eyed squint, and pursed expression put people on edge. For good reason. He had a very short fuse and would turn red with rage whenever things didn't go his or the Cowboys way. But he also liked to share time and a glass of whiskey and conversation. When he needed to be, he was very charming. One Cowboy once described him as "dishonest, sick, and demented," to which Schramm responded, "He got two out of three."

Perfectly in tune with the city's status as home to the freewheeling ten-gallon-hat millionaire, Schramm took a page from Stanley Marcus of Dallas's retail mecca, Neiman Marcus, and up-marketed the Cowboys to Dallas's nouveau riche. Most NFL teams kept their offices in the bowels of their stadiums or in beat-up office space in town. But in 1966, with Murchison's blank check, Schramm oversaw the build-out of the new Cowboy headquarters on the North Central Expressway. On the eleventh floor of a modern fifteen-story tower built and owned by Murchison, the office space was the most expensively constructed in Dallas. Schramm loaded it with terrazzo and Italian marble and state-of-the-art sunscreens. The message to the city and the country was that the Cowboys organization was new and fresh, far different from the dusty and generic industrial teams.

The Cowboy uniform also evolved. The helmets went from white, which had a tendency to get scuffed and dirty, to silver. The lone star became more clearly defined with an additional border detail. The pants morphed from traditional white to better-stain-hiding metallic blue. And their home uniforms, instead of featuring a signature color, were white. The silver sheen of their helmets reflected class and wealth, and the purity of their uniform reinforced the image. The Cowboys conjured adventure and success. They were the good guys, and win or lose, in the long run, their rightful place was at the top.

Schramm also anointed himself a league counselor to his former protégé, Rozelle. Other franchise owners referred to him in private as "Mr. Vice-Commissioner." His primary concern was competition with the AFL. Convinced that the salary wars between the two would increase the pay scale of players and further threaten the Cowboys' bottom line (of which Murchison gave him a vested interest in the form of ownership options), Schramm, along with Rozelle, made plans to negotiate a merger. Merger had been discussed several times in previous years, but the terms the NFL imposed on the upstarts never got any meaningful discussion off the ground. The NFL wanted to move the Jets and the Raiders out of New York and Oakland, and they were asking for $50 million for reparations. But after the riches handed out to college players at the AFL and NFL draft, Schramm thought the timing couldn't be more perfect. First, Rozelle secured informal approval from Congress that the merger wouldn't violate any antitrust laws (he promised Louisiana Senator Russell Long and Representative Hale Boggs a New Orleans expansion franchise). Then Schramm was tasked with working it out with Hunt.

The two met in secret at the Texas Ranger statue at Love Field airport in Dallas. Hunt agreed with Schramm about the impending doom that both leagues would confront if players' salaries continued to escalate. Hunt also agreed that the two leagues together would create something much more powerful than apart. Ever since the AFL's coming of age in 1962 with its fifty million–plus championship viewers, the networks and the public had clamored for a true championship that would pit the AFL winner against the NFL winner. Plus the television package that the combined league would be able to demand could take professional football to a whole new level. In further talks at Hunt's home, they ironed out the AFL reparations and whittled the number down to $18 million.

The final sticking point was the NFL's requirement that the AFL's Raiders and Jets relocate. Giants owner Wellington Mara finally caved on the issue. Kicking Joe Namath out of New York would not enamor him to New York's pro football fan base. "If I try to get the Jets moved," he said, "I'll be crucified." Schramm found the perfect solution. Eight million of the $18 million in payments would go to San Francisco, and $10 million would go to the Giants.

In June 1966, Hunt, Schramm, and Rozelle held a press conference and announced the merger. The leagues would have a common draft of college players beginning in 1966. And by the 1970 regular season, all ten AFL teams would integrate with the sixteen NFL franchises and begin interleague play. At the end of the 1966 season, a professional championship game would be played between the champion of the AFL and the champion of the NFL at a neutral site. This was the announcement that pro football fans had been awaiting for six years.

Just six years into his reign as GM of the Cowboys, Schramm negotiated on behalf of NFL owners who'd held franchises for more than forty years, and he delivered one of the best deals in the history of the league.

Rozelle rewarded Schramm with the most influential committee positions—head of the NFL's competition committee, which changes the rules of the game when it deems necessary, and executive and president of the NFL Executive Committee, which negotiates league-wide contracts with the NFL Players Association.

But as a former CBS Sports executive, Schramm's greatest influence was on establishing the Cowboys as a broadcasting brand. He had connections and worked tirelessly to get his team as much national television exposure as possible. The Cowboys joined the Detroit Lions as hosts of an annual Thanksgiving game, and he successfully lobbied for preferential scheduling and in-depth coverage on NFL pregame shows. The Cowboy game became the predominant late-afternoon game, televised nationally as the second game of NFL doubleheader coverage after the local teams played at one o'clock. Schramm made the Cowboys the first to fund a weekly newspaper dedicated to all things Cowboys, and he always picked up the tab for the local press, on the road and off.

On the field, the cobbled-together 1960 Cowboys had an ignominious start, going winless in their opening season. In fact, it wasn't until they faced the feckless Steelers in the first game of the 1961 season that they got into the win column. But Landry, like Noll, had plans and patience and surety of purpose. His team lacked a potent running threat. His raw offensive line, duct-taped together from past-their-prime veterans, was not the surest protector of his bright young quarterback Don Meredith. Landry knew that his best offense would be to confuse the opposition's defense. He needed to create a split second of uncertainty to give his team an edge.

So he created multiple offensive formations and had his skill players roam back and forth along the line of scrimmage before the snap. But his greatest and most lasting innovation had nothing to do with play sets. It was nothing more than a show, but one that dazzled the crowd and bedeviled the defense. Just before snapping the ball, the Cowboys offensive line would, in unison, do a stand-up, get-down herky jerk. It was a last-second reset—and it completely erased any keys a defensive lineman might have been zeroing in on. The team might have stunk those first few years, but it was entertaining. By 1962, the stand-up, get-down gimmick was the pistol start for an offensive scheme that scored the second-most points in the NFL.

The Cowboys had been potent enough that, in 1963, Lamar Hunt moved the AFL's Dallas Texans to Kansas City. The Cotton Bowl, the South Dallas stadium home to both teams, was half filled or less for both the Texans and the Cowboys, despite substantial marketing efforts. Hunt was losing close to $1 million a year; Murchison's losses averaged $500,000. But Hunt was trying to do more than make a team go, he was building a league. And he knew two franchises in Dallas couldn't last. In Kansas City, Hunt's Chiefs became a powerhouse of his emerging business.

Murchison, meanwhile, shrugged off his losses. He was rumored to be worth north of $800 million. He saw the team as a plaything, not a source of income. But now, as the only game in town, his team's audience began to grow, with attendance rising steadily from an average of 27,417 in the first year to 67,625 in 1966. It helped that, with Landry's improving offense, the team got better year after year, winning four games in '63, five in '64, and seven in '65.

By 1966, with shrewd drafting and consistent, mechanized "system" coaching—a philosophy that demands player adherence to game plans, not game plans devised to accommodate player strengths and weaknesses—the Cowboys won ten games and found themselves playing Landry's old colleague Vince Lombardi and the Green Bay Packers at their home stadium, South Dallas's Cotton Bowl, for the NFL Championship. The winner would go on to the first Super Bowl between the two professional leagues. It was a fluke, really. The Cowboys had only one starter over thirty—linebacker Chuck Howley—and no one considered them to be among the league's first-class teams. And yet, playing Lombardi's fundamentally perfect machine of a team, they stayed close, losing by just a touchdown after Meredith's last-ditch effort was intercepted in the end zone.

In 1967, the Cowboys got back to the NFL Championship. But this time they played at Green Bay's Lambeau Field. It was -13 degrees outside, and in a game that would be dubbed "The Ice Bowl," the Cowboys trailed 14–10 in the fourth. That's when Landry risked a fumbling, bumbling end to the game by calling a halfback option, hoping his players' frozen fingers could hold on to the ball through the trick play. It worked. Halfback Dan Reeves threw a fifty-yard pass to wideout Lance Rentzel, and the Cowboys led 17–14.

But the Cowboys defense couldn't hold the lead. With sixteen seconds left, Packers quarterback Bart Starr snuck across the goal line for the winning score. On the trip back to Dallas, Rentzel later said, "not one word was spoken the entire flight."

The Cowboys continued to dominate in the regular season, winning their division each year while posting a combined 23-4-1 record in 1968 and 1969. But again, in the playoffs, they stumbled, losing twice to the Cleveland Browns in the first round. Schramm, Brandt, and especially Landry obsessed. A former employee of NFL films recalled, "Landry came in for something or other, and all of a sudden he just started talking about those two losses. He really wasn't talking to me—anyone would have done—it was just something he had to say. He said, 'It's a lack of character, in the team and in myself. We just don't have what it takes. Maybe we never will. Maybe I never will.'"

16

FOR ALL HIS EXPERIENCE COMING UP AS A RABBLE ROUSER in the mills; for all the hand-to-hand combat he did negotiating with steel company bosses and union leaders, I. W. Abel had the countenance of your favorite grandfather. He preferred dark suits and gold-rimmed glasses. USWA members lovingly referred to him as Abe. He was stocky, white-haired and, in public at least, remarkably shy.

His greatest gift was his patience, developed over years of hardscrabble negotiations. From his burning-shoe-leather years in the mills, he learned as much about people as he knew about metal. Together, those two traits taught him how to find common ground. "Collective bargaining is pretty much of a crisis business," he once said. "You have to have patience and you have to be tolerant. You have to be a fair fisherman. You have to sit back and wait for a bite."

In 1968 Abel negotiated the biggest wage and benefit increase in USWA history—a 16.3 percent increase over three years. Abel was also proud of growing the USWA into a colossal 3,700 locals with 1.2 million paying members in the United States, Canada, and Puerto Rico. It was a part of the AFL-CIO and one of the most powerful unions, along with the United Auto Workers and Teamsters, in the United States. Abel was instrumental in diversifying the membership, so much so that actual steelworkers made up less than 50 percent of the rank and file. Since the 1959 strike, the USWA had drafted iron miners, copper smelters and refiners, aluminum workers, can-factory and metal-fabricating-plant employees, and even some police and Chock full o'Nuts coffee-shop waitresses. Having a broader base of dues-paying members buttressed the union when one or the other of its labor divisions had to go on strike. There were individual collective-bargaining agreements for each industry, so having several groups under one roof meant stability for the greater union. Even if every steelworker walked off the job, there would be 700,000 others paying dues monthly.

But this was a union, after all. The radical fringe was always alive. And as soon as a union leader begins to look comfortable, he becomes a target. That's what happened to Abel. In 1969, after just one term, he was challenged for reelection by a young union lawyer named Emil Narick.

A former star running back for the Pitt Panthers, Narick accused Abel of the same tuxedo unionism that Abel had said his predecessor suffered from. He said Abel was a dictator, a patsy for the Washington politicians, a guy who went to lavish parties hosted by the big steel manufacturers and sold the workers out for scraps. Narick charged that a real union leader would never break bread with management or hobnob with Washington elites. And there was no way the big steel manufacturers would give the workers a 16.3 percent increase unless it was a pittance compared to what they made in profit. According to Narick, the Abel administration was "old fashioned and unresponsive to the will of its members."

Abel's response: "You've got the younger element. They think we've always had good wages because employers believed in paying good wages. They think they get benefits like we have and holidays, vacations, medical insurance, and all that because employers want to give that."

But Narick, who Abel predicted wouldn't get more than 20 percent of the vote, was relentless. Fueled by his popularity as a local football hero, his candidacy gained momentum. He stood outside western Pennsylvania mill gates, asking for "a buck for Emil," and workers responded with grease-stained singles and five-dollar bills. In the closing weeks leading up to the February 1969 election, Narick compared his campaign to the fresh New York Jets up against Abel's tired Colts. Narick predicted an upset win.

After all the ballots were tallied, Abel was shocked. He'd won, but Narick got double the anticipated votes. While his win was never in real jeopardy (257,000 to 180,000), Abel could not deny that there was growing unrest on the shop floor.

Abel was still President of the USWA, but he didn't have anywhere near the power he thought he had.

17

THE STEELERS HAD A NEW QUARTERBACK. AND FOR THE first time in their history, a new stadium to play in, too. Three Rivers, built where the Allegheny and Monongahela Rivers meet to form the Ohio River, was a dull, concrete, multisport facility that the Steelers would share with the Pirates. But the players didn't care. Compared to South Park, it made them feel like real-live professional athletes. "It had these sumptuous locker rooms, carpeting on the floors," Noll once told NFL Films. "These guys are just sitting there glowing, they are thinking they are really something special."

Noll, however, made sure no one felt too special. While NFL teams around the league often gave—and still give—stars the biggest spaces in the locker room or grouped players according to positions, Noll arranged the Three Rivers dressing quarters as logically as the way he ran the team. The locker room was a big square, and locker assignments began with low numbers in the lower left-hand corner from the entrance and then wound around. It forced linebackers like Russell, who was number 34, to mingle with running backs and defensive tackles like Greene, who was number 75, to get dressed next to offensive linemen. It was hard to form cliques. Not that any of the players cared where they got dressed at first, as long as it was Three Rivers.

"It was," says Russell, "phenomenal."

So was the enthusiasm they felt for Bradshaw. Mansfield, the center who'd be snapping the rookie the ball, told *Time* magazine, "This guy is going to be Moses, he is going to lead us out of the desert." No pressure.

The weekend of Bradshaw's first rookie minicamp in Pittsburgh,

Russell arranged to have a barbecue at his house. But when he called the Steelers facility to find the rookie, he wasn't there. Bradshaw, Russell was told, had gone to pray at a local church.

The Steelers were a tight group, but they were not the most pious of teams. They drank as hard as they played. Nights were spent at a club called The Attic, listening to jazz. During training camp, nearly every night was spent breaking curfew at a motel bar the players called the 19th Hole. "As soon as the assistant coaches were pulling out of the parking lot, we were pulling in," remembers offensive lineman Gerry Mullins. Russell and Mansfield, holdovers from the early 1960s, believed that drinking away from the stadium brought the team together. It's how they were taught, and it's the lesson they were trying to pass down. The new realities of the big-money NFL, like rookies holding out for bigger contracts, were foreign to them. They always had jobs during the off-season and had never made enough for the game to be anything but fun. Just like for the fans, football was an escape from reality. And, really, they liked to party, and they liked the rookies to party with them.

That night, Russell went to the church to find Bradshaw. When he arrived he found his future quarterback on the pulpit, speaking passionately about his faith, to people he had never met. Russell was uncomfortable, wondering if he shouldn't be "more devout," he wrote in his book *A Steeler Odyssey*. He sat in a darkened area of the church and waited. Bradshaw, he thought, was so genuine and confident.

Bradshaw made his way out to Russell's house a couple days later for the barbecue. He was the only rookie invited, and the veterans were "as nice to a rookie as we had ever been," Russell wrote. But they also didn't spare Bradshaw any tales of woe. All the misery they had been feeling, all the ugly losses they had endured, were shared. They were desperate, and they wanted Bradshaw to know what he meant to the franchise, how they thought he could save them. This wasn't bonding, this was pleading. Bradshaw left the party early. "And some of the veterans wondered out loud if he would be the man our offense needed," Russell wrote.

His teammates were looking for a connection. As dominating as Joe Greene could be, and as much as he affected his teammates' attitude, a defensive tackle is not the quarterback. Only the quarterback controls tempo, makes play calls in the huddle, touches the ball on every offensive down. The pulse of the team runs through his hands. Receivers run better routes when they know a quarterback can get them the ball. Linemen explode out of their stances faster to protect if they believe in him. The quarterback can make every other player on offense look good. You never hear baseball players say "My pitcher" but you always hear receivers praising "My quarterback." Bradshaw had to create that relationship.

But Bradshaw wasn't Greene. He couldn't whip someone with one arm and command respect just by standing there, glowering. He didn't like to lose, but he didn't exude the same kind of hatred for it that Greene did. He'd grown up comfortable and loved by a big family. To him football was a game he was passionate to play, more than anything, sure, but he wasn't desperate to win. The game was just fun and because of that, the wins followed. It had always been that way. In high school he cocked his arm, threw the ball, his team won. In college he did the same. There was no pressure—from fans who identified with the team, from teammates who needed to keep their jobs. His transition from fun-loving gunslinger to professional quarterback, playing with grown men he was supposed to lead, was hard. "Nobody at Tech thought the world was going to end if we lost to Delta State," Bradshaw wrote in *It's Only a Game*. "I figured the Steelers had finished last without me; they'd won one game. How much worse could I make the situation?"

Much, much worse. It wasn't just that Bradshaw liked going to church while his teammates liked going to bars. It was the game. College football was Terry Bradshaw's domain; pro football was Chuck Noll's. It was the difference between checkers and chess. Bradshaw had never studied film before. In high school and college, if his first receiver wasn't open, he tucked the ball and ran. He didn't know how to read defensive coverages at the line of scrimmage. He underestimated the speed of the game, the intensity, how hard opponents were going to hit and how high a standard his coaches were going to hold him to. He was, in every way, overmatched. And no one had any sympathy.

In his very first game, against the Oilers, Bradshaw completed just four of sixteen passes with an interception and was pulled from the game to a chorus of 75,000 boos. This is where a new Chuck Noll emerged. The calm teacher who preached technique, the master manipulator who looked the other way when Joe Greene attacked opponents with scissors, handled Bradshaw like he was an abusive father. He grabbed his quarterback's face mask, his jersey and unloaded obscenities that would make the bluest of comics cringe. The anger shot from his knuckles through Bradshaw's pads. "I couldn't believe how cruel Chuck was," Bradshaw once said. "You would think someone as smart as Chuck was would be a better psychologist, but he beat me down. I totally lost my confidence. I was the kind of guy who needed a pat on the back—shouting at me only made things worse."

So did the fact that, on his first play from scrimmage in place of Bradshaw, local hero Terry Hanratty threw a touchdown. After the game, Bradshaw sat in his car in the Three Rivers parking lot and cried.

The Steelers lost their first three games that season, with Noll shuffling his quarterbacks practically every quarter. It got so bad for Bradshaw that his mom came to stay with him. One night he took her to a hockey game and fans in the stands started booing the both of them. Another time, before a game, he was standing outside the doorway of the locker room talking to Art Rooney Sr., within the eyesight of Noll. The owner was telling his young quarterback to keep his confidence, that everything would be all right, with Bradshaw's blond locks bobbing up and down in agreement. When the conversation ended and Bradshaw walked into the locker room five minutes late, Noll, who had seen the conversation between rookie and owner taking place, fined him.

It didn't help with fans that he was burly for a quarterback. His blond hair was thinning and unruly and his face lacked the kind of angles Madison Avenue likes in its football idols. He had a funny Louisiana accent that, to those in the North, made him sound simple. He preferred spending time on his farm with his parents to drinking at the Jamestown Inn in Pittsburgh's South Hills with his teammates. He wore buckskin coats with fringe hanging from the sleeves. "I was an outsider who didn't mingle well," Bradshaw once told *Sports Illustrated*. "No one liked to fish or do the things I liked to do. The other players looked upon me as a bible-toting Li'l Abner."

The criticism of Bradshaw, for his play and for his intelligence, was fierce as he threw four interceptions for every one touchdown that rookie season. But he wasn't the only one suffering. Noll's first season was about installing a program and teaching his players. Every frustration was met with encouraging signs of progress. Even at 1-13, players saw improvement. Not true that second season. The rookie quarterback was lost. The coach couldn't decide who should lead the team. While the team won four of five games in the middle of the year, it was 5-8 and on a two-game losing streak as it headed into the last game of the season in Philadelphia.

The Steelers opened the game strong, taking a 7–6 lead. But by halftime they were down 20–14. While they tied it at 20 in the second half, it was clear they were getting beaten up by the Eagles. It was so bad that even the Steelers punter got hurt. And Noll's solution was to have Bradshaw take over the punting duties. Late in the game, Bradshaw, who used to kick in his Louisiana backyard until the ball split in two, stood at the back of his end zone, waiting to punt. "The only thing Chuck told me," Bradshaw wrote in *It's Only a Game*, "was to keep my head down."

The Eagles were on him so fast it was as though the Steelers offensive line had lain down. The punt was blocked, Philadelphia recovered it for a touchdown and Bradshaw was injured when an Eagle player's spike opened a gash in his leg.

That would have been bad enough, an injury-to-insult moment fitting for the end of a horrible season. Luckily for Bradshaw, he had Joe Greene to steal the spotlight. The only defense against Greene was to hold him.

There was no other way for a single NFL offensive lineman to stop him. He was bigger than most, faster than most, and angrier than all of them. He did all the things on the field—hitting, stomping, helmet twisting—that other players were afraid to try for fear of retaliation on the field or punishment from coaches. But no player was crazy enough to stand up to Greene, and Noll had no interest in disciplining him. He saved his blisterings for Bradshaw.

That day in Philadelphia, Greene had four sacks despite being held all day long. Between this kind of personal affront and the humiliating loss to end a losing season, Greene had reached his breaking point. Late in the game, Russell remembers Greene saying to an Eagles offensive guard, in a voice that sounded like rumbling thunder, "If you hold me one more time, I'm going to have to hurt you."

The player held, and Greene hurt, with an uppercut to the guard's unprotected belly. His fist went into his stomach, and the air went out. So did the player, who was carted off to the sidelines. Greene made the same warning to the replacement, who, at the snap, held just like his predecessor—and suffered the same fate. Off to the sidelines he went. Finally, the Eagles brought in the third-stringer, who happened to have been a college teammate of Greene's. And he held Greene, too. But now Greene was stuck. He didn't want to hurt his old buddy, but he needed to make his point. As the official placed the ball at the line of scrimmage and the Eagles broke their huddle, Greene picked it up, walked toward his sideline, flicked it toward his bench, and said to the ref, "If you can't see these guys grabbing me, this game is over."

The officials put another ball down, and Greene glowered in their direction. Then he walked to middle of the field, picked up the new ball, and casually started walking toward his sideline again. Only this time he didn't toss it toward the bench. He threw a perfect, high, arcing spiral into the second deck of Franklin Field. Then he walked off the field. "It seemed like the ball took forever," Russell remembered in *About Three Bricks Shy of a Load*. "The crowd was dead silent. And the players—there we were, we didn't have a ball, we didn't have a tackle. It was like he was saying, 'Okay, if you won't play right, we won't play at all.' Nobody else would do such a thing."

"No one ever said anything to me about it after the game," Greene says. "The only day that moment ever came up again was the day I told Mr. Rooney I was going to retire. He said, 'You remember that day back in Philly when you threw ball in the stands?' I said, 'Yes, sir, I do.' He said, 'Well, I felt that same way.'"

18

CLINT MURCHISON KNEW WHAT THE COWBOYS NEEDED. JUST after the 1967 loss to the Packers at the Cotton Bowl, a number of disappointed fans fell victim to crime in the parking lot. A man was shot and his wife was seriously beaten during a robbery. Another was repeatedly stabbed and a dozen or so other fans mugged.

Murchison had been hoping to build a new downtown stadium in a better neighborhood for his Cowboys for years, but had always been blocked by Erik Jonsson, the city's mayor. Jonsson was a Brooklyn-born Yankee who cofounded the computer-chip manufacturer Texas Instruments. His creation of an entirely new economic engine for the city turned him into a favorite of Dallas society, a group that drafted him to run for mayor.

Jonsson's staid civic-minded use of his wealth clashed with the shoot-from-the-hip style and unapologetic attitude of Murchison's. And, given his popularity, Jonsson had Dallas's old guard by his side. To press the city into reconsidering his request, Murchison bought ninety acres of land fifteen miles away in Irving, Texas, and threatened to build his stadium there. Jonsson was unmoved. He agreed to renovate the Cotton Bowl at taxpayer expense, but he would not approve a downtown stadium complex.

After the '67 bloodshed, Murchison announced that he'd build Texas Stadium, what he called "the finest football stadium to date in the world," in Irving, if he could arrange for $13 million in financing. Because the majority of the Cowboy fan base was blue collar and located in South Dallas, near the Cotton Bowl, a new stadium in Irving would be no small move. But the consummate dealmaker Murchison deeded the land to the city in exchange for approval from the Irving City Council for a bond issue to fund the construction.

Murchison put the engineering and math skills he had learned at MIT and Duke to good use. With only minimal architectural consultation, he designed a remarkable amphitheater dedicated to football. "The problem with almost every modern stadium today is that they were designed to house both football and baseball," he said, decades ahead of his time. The innovations were remarkable. He knew the importance of television, and with that in mind, he limited the stadium seating to 58,000, almost 20,000 fewer than the Cotton Bowl. The seats would be secured on a steep grade overlooking the field, rather than set back away from the field. There would be a roof that would cover the fans, but a rectangular chunk removed to keep the field open to the elements. The field would be impeccable, made of the same artificial grass—Astroturf—that was used at Houston's Astrodome, and this would keep his Cowboys impeccable, too.

But the biggest innovation was the "Circle Suites," the first NFL luxury boxes. They were marketed to wealthy football fans and placed at the very top of the stadium, offering the most complete view of the game as well as separation from the regular ticket buyers below. The brochure said it all, "Your personalized penthouse at Texas Stadium . . . the ultimate in spectacular luxury and comfort . . . similar to a second residence, like a lake home or a ranch." A sixteen-by-sixteen-foot suite could be had with the purchase of two hundred Texas Stadium Corporation Bonds at $250 each ($50,000). But that was just for the concrete box. The owner would be required to decorate and outfit the suite at their own cost. The owner would also have to buy twelve $1,300 season tickets for thirty-two of the next thirty-five years. After thirty-five years, the bonds would mature at an anemic $300.

The bonds weren't required just for the swells at the top. In order to purchase a single season ticket, a regular fan was required to buy one

$250 bond (the first iteration of today's "personal seat licenses"), plus pay the cost of the individual game tickets. If you wanted seats between the coveted thirty-yard lines, the minimum purchase was four bonds per seat. And you also had to commit to buy the tickets for twenty-one of the next thirty-five years or lose your option on the seat. Those hit hardest were the blue-collar fans that filled the Cotton Bowl in the early years, the loyal ones who stuck with the team even when they lost the big games. "I'd say we lost a whole group of fans in the $12,000 to $20,000 a year salary range who could afford season tickets at the Cotton Bowl but couldn't afford to buy bonds," Murchison said. "If we discriminated against them, we discriminated against them, but no more than all America discriminates against people who don't have enough money to buy everything they want."

Where you sat, if you could get in at all, defined your position in Dallas's economy and, by proxy, your social value. Going to see a Cowboys game meant that you had money. Once you were there, you could look around and see who was above and below you in the race for more. Professional football was once a game for guys who didn't go to college. It gave them teams to identify with and root for as their own. The players on the field were much like they were, working hard for a decent wage to support their families. While the Cowboy players remained blue-collar, the Cowboy target market for the 1970s and beyond was decidedly white-collar.

They were also finicky, which made Murchison's football temple that much riskier. Because despite the Cowboys stellar regular-season record, attendance figures decreased 13 percent between 1966 and 1970. Dallas fans were losing interest in their team. Falling in the playoffs year after year to hardscrabble cities like Green Bay was humiliating. Dallas newspaper writer Steve Perkins summed up the city's frustrations with his book, which came out in 1969.

He called it *Next Year's Champions.*

19

BORN IN DALLAS IN 1947, DUANE THOMAS CAME OF AGE PRE-integration, when North Dallas meant white and South Dallas meant black. After being pushed from their home by an eminent-domain seizure for a government housing project, his mother, Lauretta, and father, John, moved the family to a yellow wood-framed house a few blocks from the Cotton Bowl. Their neighbors were field hands, laborers, and domestic service workers, the future fans for Dallas's expansion pro football teams. When his father's undertaking business failed, there was only enough food money for four children. The middle child and one of three boys, ten-year-old Duane was sent to Los Angeles to live with his Aunt Madie. Thomas "couldn't get over the freedom of it—you could actually go up to a white lady and talk to her without everybody looking at you funny."

Before he left for California, his father sent Duane and his older brother, Sonny, to their grandfather's farm in Marshall, Texas. Their grandmother woke them at four thirty in the morning. In pitch black, the boys slopped pigs, fed the cows, horses, and chickens, chopped wood, and drew water from the well. They'd come home to a huge breakfast made from the farm's fresh food, then head out to the fields for the rest of the day with a packed lunch. They'd pick cucumbers, cotton, corn, alfalfa—whatever was ready—and head home at dusk for dinner. Duane learned that if you worked hard enough, the world would provide.

When he turned fifteen, Duane returned home to Dallas and attended Lincoln High School, part of the all-black league of secondary schools. Textbooks were hand-me-downs from North Dallas's white schools, and there wasn't budget money for mimeographing football play-books or fancy mobile blackboards. Duane followed his older brother to football practice his first day at school in slacks and a Ban-Lon shirt. He scrimmaged without protection for two days before freshman coach Rabbit Thomas found him a uniform, who recalled, "The first thing I noticed about Duane was his speed . . . he always could run . . . but he had an explosion, too." Lincoln players were taught to memorize their assignments. Coach Thomas ran drill after drill and play after play until there was no longer a delay between a call and his players' performance. With football habits so deeply ingrained in each and every player, the team became larger than the sum of its parts. Players no longer worried about forgetting a play, they concentrated on their block or their tackle or how best to run the ball. Duane Thomas thrived in this environment. By his senior year in 1965, Duane Thomas grew into an intense, 6'1", 215-pound fullback who rushed for 1,443 yards and led Lincoln to the city championship.

Thomas was a weekly story in Dallas's sports pages, and Gil Brandt paid attention. He started a Duane Thomas file for the Dallas Cowboy computer. He even called his alma mater, Wisconsin, and urged them to offer Thomas a scholarship. Self-motivated, with piercing eyes, a perfectly maintained and trained body, and an "I'm getting out of here" vibe, it was obvious that Thomas had ambitions. But by necessity, Thomas stayed close to home and went to play for West Texas State, a little-known program that played against the major football powers (the NCAA did not institute Division I classifications until 1973). A choice that sent most young men directly into the workforce—his new teenage wife gave birth to his child during his senior year of high school—would not keep him from his destiny. Football would be a way for him to provide for his new family. Deep down he hoped that it would also eventually bring enough money to free his parents from the humiliating and debilitating work they continued to do to survive.

Thomas modeled his professional life on the Cleveland Browns' legendary running back Jim Brown, a black man who lived in the white world with dignity. To prepare himself, Thomas devised innovative training regimens to reach his physical peak and religiously took care of his body. "My day would start off at 5:30 A.M. I'd do thirty minutes of stretching, then eight hundred push-ups and sit-ups in flights, then fifteen miles of roadwork . . . in the evening I'd work on speed trials—twenty-six to thirty reps of eleven-yard striders at half to three-quarter speed, followed by four to six 220-yarders for speed-endurance. Then I'd do four to five miles of roadwork," Thomas recalled.

Pro scouts who had come to see West Texas's Mercury Morris—the lightning-quick tailback who would star for the Miami Dolphins and was a year ahead of Duane—took a hard look at Thomas, too. But at the end of his sophomore year at West Texas, all that Thomas was working for began to fall away. His father, John Thomas, was in excruciating pain from a long and eventual losing battle with pancreatic cancer. Ten months after his death, Duane's mother collapsed in front of her house with a massive heart attack. Her death pushed Thomas's youngest sister over the edge and she suffered a debilitating mental breakdown. In his grief, Thomas drew inward. He pressed himself even harder on the field. In his senior year, he averaged 5.4 yards a carry and rushed for 1,054 yards.

Throughout the season, pro scouts would come to check him out, so Thomas reached out to the only man left that he could trust, West Texas State head football coach Joe Kerbel, for professional advice. Kerbel recommended an agent from White Plains, New York, Norman Young, to represent him. Mercury Morris had used him for his contract with the Dolphins, and from what Kerbel understood, he was pleased with the result. Kerbel hoped that Vince Lombardi, who had just taken the head coaching job at Washington, would draft Duane. "He said he'd be my kind of coach," Thomas said. "He didn't like the Cowboys, though. He said they played sissy football."

But the Cowboys loved Thomas. In fact, the team's IBM 7090/7094 had him at number one for the 1970 draft. When he was still around for their pick in the first round of the draft, twenty-third overall, the choice was easy to make. Thomas hired Young, who took a 10 percent commission on Thomas's entire three-year deal ($87,000) up front out of Thomas's signing bonus and had Thomas sign over power of attorney to him so that he could handle his finances. Young's company would cash all of Thomas's paychecks, take care of the living expenses, bills, etc. for his wife and now two children, and then turn over the remaining portion at the end of each month. Duane would concentrate on learning the Dallas offense and making the team.

Thomas was handed jersey number 33 by the Cowboys. He liked it. It was one higher than Jim Brown's 32. In his rookie training camp, Thomas memorized the playbook (no small accomplishment considering the intricacies of head coach Tom Landry's alignments, sets, and motions), never missed a meeting, and buried himself in the Cowboy life. He did not get distracted when he discovered that his new agent had failed to pay any of his bills, his wife asked for a divorce, or he took multiple poundings on the field. In one particularly sensitive moment, Landry had to bring Thomas into his office to meet with an officer from the sheriff's department. The cop handed Thomas a bill from a clothing store that was never paid and demanded immediate attention. Thomas coolly thanked the man for his time and said he would take care of it.

When his rookie season started, Thomas played behind second-year sensation Calvin Hill. But he didn't complain. When he got into a game and was handed the ball, he delivered. As Hill began to struggle, Landry gave Thomas more and more touches. In two games alternating with Hill, Thomas rushed for 213 yards, at an average of 6.5 yards per carry. Hill then injured his shoulder in a game against the St. Louis Cardinals, and Landry made Thomas his starting tailback. At that point, the 1970 Cowboys were 5-4 and in danger of missing the playoffs for the first time since 1965. They needed a spark.

Thomas provided it. He led the Cowboys to victory in the last five games of the season. He averaged 5.5 yards per carry and went over a hundred yards three times, leading the team in rushing and kickoff returns. At the end of the regular season, he was the unanimous choice for NFL Rookie of the Year. And he did it exactly the way he was told. Roger Staubach remembered, "He was perfect at practice, and when he got in a game, he seemed to know what everyone else was supposed to do. The guy was amazing. A mind." During the 1970 playoffs, he was even better, with 135 yards against Detroit in the first round and 147 yards against San Francisco in the NFC Championship. Behind Thomas's dazzling running, the Dallas Cowboys made it to their first Super Bowl. They would face the Baltimore Colts in Super Bowl V.

For Landry, this was one more opportunity to test his mettle and his methods. He didn't buy into old-school coaching pep talks. The so-called intangibles—chemistry, heart, camaraderie—had no place in his system. Players' emotions were to be held in check, and then channeled to best effect on and off the field. Lean and professorial, Landry maintained an unflappable cool no matter the circumstance. He gave off an aura of all-knowingness. If his players did their job and executed the plans he laid out for them, the final outcome of the season—a championship—would be ensured. And the best way he felt he could get the players in line to do what he required was to manipulate them psychologically. He cut them off from the rest of the world, constantly testing them with physical and mental drills. He knew who responded best to criticism, challenge, flattery, or ambivalence, and he fed them what was necessary to keep them in check. To be a Cowboy was to be controlled.

Meetings were strict and intense and all practices were filmed to ensure that every mistake was documented. Levity was not allowed and tardiness could get you traded. Landry also had a strict rule about wearing baseball caps in meetings and he fined players for any and all infractions. On the road, the players were supervised from dawn until dusk, with security on every floor. No visitors were allowed in a player's room. If family came to visit, the player would have to go to the lobby to meet them. The message was abundantly clear to all players: Don't get comfortable, you are expendable. Landry spoke of the importance of the "system" and the "organization." His players found him emotionless and passionless. Asked if he had seen Landry smile, fullback Walt Garrison said, "Nope. But I've only been here nine years."

He was a coach who demanded everything a player had, and then gave little in return. Success was expected. Touchdowns and stellar defense were the result of planning, not of individual effort. Little praise with constant criticism kept the players unbalanced and hungry for recognition.

And, to Landry, Duane Thomas was the ultimate football player—a perfect machine that would take his elaborately choreographed directions and execute them without fail. He played with pain, under personal duress, and yet when the game was on, he never lost his composure, was as cold as ice.

The Cowboys would be playing another team with the "can't win the big one" moniker plastered on its back. The Colts had still not fully recovered from their loss to the New York Jets in Super Bowl III. Landry believed the game would come down to execution. And he was certain that Thomas was the missing piece to the Cowboys' championship puzzle.

The "can't win the big one" bowl was a dud. The Orange Bowl didn't even sell out, forcing the NFL to black out the televised coverage in Miami. There were ten turnovers in the game, and the biggest gain on one play was the result of a deflected pass. In the third quarter, the Cowboys led 13–6 on two field goals and a seven-yard Craig Morton pass to Thomas, and they were threatening to score again. Two yards from another touchdown, Thomas took the handoff and was hit just shy of the goal line. He tried to spin away from the tackle and in his second effort, the ball came loose. Cowboys center Dave Manders fell on it and, as Morton argued with the line judge to blow the play dead, the Colts piled on top of Manders and wrestled the ball away. The referee signaled Colts' ball on their own one-yard line. Months after the game, Colt defensive lineman Bubba Smith told a reporter that the referee had obviously blown the call. A stunned Thomas buried his head in his hands on the bench, but with almost a full half of play left in the game, he recovered his confidence and prepared for his next opportunity.

The Cowboy offense sputtered, and penalties (they had ten for more than a hundred yards) kept them in poor down and distance. Embittered by the fumble, Landry abandoned the weapon that had brought the Cowboys to the Super Bowl. Duane Thomas had just two carries the rest of the way. Landry put the fate of the game in the hands of Morton. Three fourth-quarter Cowboy drives resulted in Morton interceptions, the most crucial from a ball that bounced off halfback Dan Reeves' hands and into the waiting arms of Colts linebacker Mike Curtis, who returned the interception to the Cowboy 13. The Colts kicked a field goal in the final seconds and beat the Cowboys 16–13. Speaking to reporters after the game, Landry pinpointed the "big play" as Thomas's fumble on the one-yard line at the start of the second half. Ignoring the two later interceptions that had led to ten Colt points, he pinned the blame on Thomas's mistake, which had led to none. "If he had scored, they would have had a lot of catching up to do."

Thomas was stunned. Football had been his escape from his grim reality—two dead parents, being fleeced by his agent, and his wife abandoning him in the middle of his first professional season. In deference to his job, he neglected his problems, put his head down, and gave the organization everything he had. He gave Landry everything he had. The Cowboys were 7-1 with him as the starting tailback and had scored 175 points. Without him as a starter they were 5-4 and no sure thing to even make the playoffs. He rushed for 1,116 yards in those eight games and scored the only touchdown for the Cowboys in Super Bowl V. And now he was being blamed for the Super Bowl loss because of an aggravating but minor fumble? "After that game, I knew the only way I could survive was to make no errors," Thomas resolved.

20

TEXANS DIDN'T SPEND A LOT OF TIME DISCUSSING HOW COAL
and steel barons from western Pennsylvania—Men like James Guffey and
the Mellon family—financed the Lone Star State's turn-of-the-century oil
boom. In 1968, James J. "Jimmy" Ling, a Dallas businessman, came to
Pittsburgh and returned the favor when he bought five million shares of
Jones and Laughlin Steel.

Born and raised in Hugo, Oklahoma, James J. Ling never graduated
from high school. After a stint in the Navy and correspondence-school
training in electrical contracting, Ling settled in Dallas in 1946. With
$2,000 from the sale of his home, he opened up a small electrical supply
business. He'd read about the rise of the big Texas rich and closely followed the methods of men like Clint Murchison Sr. Murchison was famous for making his fortune in oil, but it was his business acumen that
impressed Ling. The young Oklahoman marveled at the way Murchison
had built an entirely new fortune by buying and selling stakes in companies. As Ling would later describe, Murchison knew when "two plus two
equaled five."

After eight years of collecting clients the old-fashioned way (service
and word of mouth), Ling grew restless. He needed capital to grow his
supply business, so he printed up prospectuses and sold shares of his
company at $2.25 per share to people he met at the Texas State Fair. In
ninety days, he had raised more than $700,000 from small investors,
practically one share at a time. Then he went shopping. He bought a California aerospace company, then Temco Electronics and Missiles, then
another defense contractor, Chance Vought Corporation. From 1955 to

1965, Ling-Temco-Vought (LTV Corp.) was the fastest-growing company in the United States, as Ling diversified into a multi-industry conglomerate. By the end of the 1960s, LTV Corp. had 29,000 employees and offered 15,000 different products—hamburgers, missiles, jets, and footballs among them. So many that Ling could no longer keep track. He created nothing himself, he simply owned.

Ling joined a growing list of modern leaders driving the new American economy—Harold Geneen of International Telegraph and Telephone, Charles Bluhdorn of Gulf and Western, Troy V. Post of Great America Corporation, and John and Clint Murchison Jr. of Murchison Brothers. They were rogue dealmakers controlling billions of dollars' worth of American manufacturing. They owned mansions and traveled by jet. Ling's spread in Dallas, a Louis XV–like monstrosity, included reproductions of the grounds at Versailles.

Almost every product LTV Corp. made required some form of steel. The car industry was booming in Detroit, and demand had remained steady year after year since the end of World War II. Ling's research indicated that technological improvements at mills would increase productivity and reduce labor costs. Plus, the eleven major steel manufacturers basically set their own prices based on their costs. If costs rose, they just unilaterally raised the price of steel. The federal government also imposed tariffs on foreign imports of steel, so that the big steel manufacturers wouldn't lose customers. What better prize to add to a dazzling array of companies than a large stake in the American steel industry?

Ling's method to get J&L Steel would later be termed a leveraged buyout. He used LTV Corp.'s roster of subsidiary companies as collateral to secure $425 million in cash on credit. The $425 million bought him a majority 63 percent share in the steel manufacturer. J&L's board of directors—who had more than a hundred years of institutional memory between them—accepted Ling's offer and gave LTV Corp. the option to buy the remaining shares at a future date.

After conferring with Ling, J&L's chairman, Charles M. Beeghly, informed the board that, "there will be no management or personnel changes at Jones and Laughlin."

That was the good news. The bad news was that, after the takeover, managers no longer owned shares and did not participate in the profits of the company. The tension inherent in their relationship with the workforce slackened, as their new cars and vacations were no longer dependent on J&L productivity and profits. Their lives became about punching a clock, in essence, as they hoped to get through the day with as little turmoil as possible.

With little pressure to perform, the J&L steelworkers slackened their pace. The monotony involved in much of the work—shovel this here, move it over there, pick this up, dump it over there, press this lever, pour it into the molds, tap the blast, etc.—is at best mind-numbing. What held the men up was the united effort for a common goal. When massive orders came in and demand exceeded supply, the men responded and quickened their pace. But that energy was short-lived and came with consequences. When demand slowed, workers were laid off. Almost always, in the "last hired, first fired" tradition of the unions, it was the younger guys. Their attitude became: Why bust my ass and work myself out of a job? "You wear two to three shirts a day, it's so hot. There's lots of gas, smoke, dirt. Some guys just tell the foreman 'No' and then rely on the union to protect their jobs," Ronald Koontz, a Johnstown, Pennsylvania, steelworker told *The New York Times.*

When James Ling diversified LTV Corp. with the purchase of J&L Steel, two and two seemed to add up to five. It would soon be more like zero.

21

THE 1971 OFF-SEASON UPENDED THE TWENTY-THREE-YEAR-old Duane Thomas in a way he'd not thought possible. The coach he respected and admired had singled him out as the bad cog in the machine. How had he gone from the key to Dallas's success to the rotten core of the Cowboy failure? He expected Landry to recognize his contributions, even if they disagreed about his role in the Super Bowl loss. It remained crystal clear in Thomas's mind: "Tom never once called me in and said, 'Duane, you had a great year.' That was all I ever asked," Thomas said. "Instead, what I got from him was this . . . and this . . . and this . . . the face, the chin, the compressed lips."

A season that he had spent trying to ignore his personal life so that he wouldn't be distracted from his professional life had come to a head. His divorce was proceeding. The IRS claimed he owed $10,000 in back taxes. His agent cashed his checks and paid none of his bills. Now he had to fix his financial mess himself. The first time he met Gil Brandt— before he'd been signed—Thomas asked him how a man can make a good living playing professional football. Brandt had told him, "By producing."

No one produced like Duane Thomas had in 1970. The evidence was incontrovertible. He'd asked other players in the league about their financial packages and discovered that just being Rookie of the Year on the Kansas City Chiefs was worth $50,000. He was Rookie of the Year for the entire NFL, and his bonus was just $10,000. Even the Oakland Raiders' owner Al Davis would tear up a contract if the player outperformed his salary. And Davis was known as the most business savvy owner in football. Thomas steadied himself and went to speak with Schramm and Brandt.

"The day that Duane went in to renegotiate, I was waiting in the outer office," Calvin Hill recalled. "I was getting ready to see them about redoing my own contract. I saw Duane walk out and storm to the elevator. I didn't know what Tex and Gil had said to him, but it scared me so much that I turned around and went home without even seeing them."

As a matter of policy, the Cowboy organization did not renegotiate signed contracts. Drafted rookies were expected to sign three-year deals with a signing bonus. Thomas had signed a deal that gave him $25,000 upon signing; salaries of $20,000 for 1970, $20,000 for 1971, and $22,000 for 1972; the $10,000 bonus for NFL Rookie of the Year; $5,000 for being named All-Pro; and $5,000 for rushing for more than six hundred yards. His 1969 predecessor, Yale's Calvin Hill, had signed a similar deal. "He came in with two Ivy League lawyers from Yale," Gil Brandt remembered. "It was like taking candy from a baby."

"From the first to the tenth rounds, I'll bet the pay wasn't more than $500 out of line on Cowboy contracts," said former Dallas lineman Blaine Nye. "We were in perfect lockstep. The difference came in the bonus money. But the base was always low. Maybe that's why we tried so hard to make the playoffs every year—for the money."

Brandt explained to Thomas that the best that they could do was to extend Thomas's deal another year and increase his annual salary. "I told him we'd rewrite his contract and tack on an extra year, and we'd pay him $40,000, $45,000 and $50,000 [he'd asked for $70,000 and $75,000 for his last two years]. We had a scale to follow. Hell, Bob Lilly [a Hall of Fame defensive lineman who was considered the finest in the game] was only making around $42,000 at the time," said Brandt. Thomas had two choices, the same ones that most Cowboy players faced eventually. Take the security of the new deal. Or "play out his option" and sign with another team three years later.

The NFL had twenty-six owners controlling the entire professional football market in 1971, and the option clauses in player contracts made sure wages stayed artificially low. Playing out an option for an NFL player required him to abide by the initial contract he signed (for Thomas a three-year deal) and then play an additional year at the "option" price set by the league's owners, a punishing 90 percent of their previous salary. If the player played out his option, he was allowed to sign as a free agent with any other team in the league.

But there was a catch. In 1963, Baltimore Colts owner Carroll Rosenbloom signed wideout free agent R. C. Owens from the San Francisco 49ers. Commissioner Pete Rozelle was concerned that Rosenbloom's move would encourage other NFL owners to begin poaching players from one another. Competition from the AFL was already escalating player salaries, and Rozelle didn't want infighting from his owners to do the same. So he came up with the NFL's compensation rule to discourage free agency. It effectively crushed the ability for a player post–AFL-NFL merger to attain his market value. Later called "the Rozelle Rule," it required one team to compensate another for signing one of its former players. If the two clubs could not come to a mutually agreeable exchange, the commissioner was given the power to assign players, draft picks, or money to the franchise that lost the player.

Thereafter, Rozelle took on the role of Solomon, tabulating what he believed was fair and then imposing his decision on the respective teams. A franchise never knew if Rozelle would award one of their star players to compensate another team for signing one of their free agents, so very few deals were done. In the four years before the merger, only eleven of the forty-two players who had played out their option were signed by a different team.

Thomas understood that playing out his option was a ludicrous choice. The average career for an NFL player is less than five years. The Dallas Cowboys would get the best years of his football career, and then he'd still be at the mercy of the owners and their commissioner.

Thomas reconsidered their offer to extend his contract and realized that the new deal would cover his debts and alimony, but would leave him with only subsistence wages. He'd be a star on the field, but a lackey off of it. Sharing his personal problems with the Cowboys gave them the opportunity to punch his situation into one of their computers. It spit out the best possible deal for the organization—keeping its star running back under their thumb at the lowest possible price. Schramm and Brandt had him just where they wanted him—insecure about his position with his head coach and saddled with debt. Some of the greatest players in the history of professional football—Lee Roy Jordan, Bob Lilly, Rayfield Wright—had faced the same circumstances before Thomas had. They had cowered and taken the Cowboy contract extensions.

Thomas spoke with the other players and learned the dark truth. "We had to keep winning to make any kind of money at all. Practice times had even been readjusted so we couldn't work a second job in the evening and try to make some extra money. It wasn't just the black players who were getting screwed, it was all of them, even great players like Jordan and Lilly."

Finally, Thomas reached out to Tom Landry for help. But Landry refused to intervene. He just repeated the oft-spoken Cowboy management mantra: "We don't renegotiate contracts."

Thomas spoke with Schramm again and offered to sign a contract that paid him purely for his performance, so many dollars for so many yards rushed, etc., for the upcoming 1971 season. Schramm refused, telling Thomas, "We can't structure a contract that way." At his wits' end, Thomas called Gil Brandt in March 1971 and told him he was retiring. Later that night he told the Dallas CBS affiliate, too. Schramm called his cronies in the media and set the record straight. The newspapers, radio shows, and TV stations attacked Thomas for being ungrateful and disloyal to the franchise, adding more fuel to the fire. Month after month, Thomas refused to live by the terms of his contract. Other Cowboys watched the drama. "A lot of players supported him but were afraid to come out publicly. It makes no difference what kind of ability you have.

If an organization wants to rid itself of you, it can do it. We knew there were plenty of players out there who could have been playing the game but were denied the chance. The whole system is based on insecurity," Rayfield Wright later commented.

Just before the start of the 1971 summer camp, Thomas reached out to his hero, the retired football great Jim Brown, to represent him. Brown agreed and arranged a meeting with the organization. Schramm, Landry, and Brandt met with Thomas and Brown at an Executive Inn across from Schramm's favorite meeting place, Love Field. Brown was unmoved by Schramm's rants, but when Tom Landry looked in Brown's eyes and said, "Look, we want him to play for us," the old player in Brown relented. Even Jim Brown crumbled across the table from a head coach. He told Thomas to play the 1971 season under his current contract, and that he'd go to bat for him again the following year.

Thomas went to camp and performed like he always had, flawlessly. The media kept on him all the while, calling him militant, unappreciative, and cocky. Thomas bottled it all inside himself and resolved to play that season in silent protest. On July 20, 1971, he called a press conference at the Thousand Oaks, California, training-camp facility to announce that he would not be speaking the rest of the season. Goaded by the beat writers to tell his side of the story, Thomas said that the Cowboys had never made it to a Super Bowl before him and would not go back again without him. He was rational and kept his cool until he was asked about the three men at the top of the Cowboy pyramid. He called Tex Schramm "dishonest, sick, and totally demented," and Brandt a flat-out "liar." But he saved the most vitriol for the man he had once respected the most. Tom Landry was nothing but "a plastic man, no man at all." Thomas had lost any semblance of composure—calling a press conference to announce that he wasn't going to speak and then attacking his employer made him look and sound almost as crazy as Schramm had characterized him to the press.

After the controversy, Thomas asked to be traded, but not before he freaked out the entire organization by parading around camp in a dashiki, "shadowed by a small, dark man with only one name," as one writer put it. "There was a rumor going around camp," Calvin Hill remembered, "that Duane and the Muslims were going to kidnap Tex. Next morning Tex had four or five guards around him. It was wild." Brandt was more than happy to get rid of him. They traded Thomas to an old scout of Brandt's who had become general manager of the former Boston, now New England Patriots, Bucko Kilroy. The Patriots got Thomas, backup lineman Halvor Hagen, and wide receiver Honor Jackson, while the Cowboys received halfback Carl Garrett and a first-round draft choice.

But just five days after the trade, Kilroy called Brandt and told him the deal was off. Thomas had refused to listen to head coach John Mazur and walked off the field after Mazur had him line up behind fullback Jim Nance in a three-point stance. "I told him I wanted to stay up because I was having trouble seeing. We were in an I-formation. The fullback in front of me was big Jim Nance, 245 pounds, wide, a broad ass. How was I going to see around that? It became a clash of wills. 'You'll do it because I say so!' I never liked that phrase," remembered Thomas. The Cowboys said a deal's a deal, but NFL commissioner Pete Rozelle stepped in and ruled in favor of New England after Thomas refused a physical and blood test. Rumors began in earnest that Thomas was addicted to drugs.

Thomas went to California and took the blood test and physical, which he passed without incident. He hired yet another agent to speak with Schramm, who again refused to budge. At last, Thomas reported back to the Cowboys in September. He was put on their inactive list. Despite all of Thomas's distractions, Landry wanted him back. He decided that he'd put up with his militancy and let him run rogue in the locker room. The truth was that Thomas had alienated many of his teammates. He didn't appear to have any followers.

Thomas shut down completely, refusing to speak to the media, his teammates and even Landry himself. But on the field, Thomas was spectacular. After losing to the Washington Redskins in the third game of the 1971 season with only eighty-two yards to show on the ground, Landry activated Thomas. His first game was against Landry's former employer, the New York Giants, on the evening of Monday, November 11, 1971. It was the very first game played in Clint Murchison's brand-new, $25 million Texas Stadium. In front of Dallas's finest citizens on *Monday Night Football,* it was a game Tom Landry could not afford to lose.

Landry put Thomas on special teams—the blue-collar units that covered kickoffs and blocked for kick returns. Even more dangerous than line-of-scrimmage play, kickoff coverage is a place to test a man's resolve. They gave Thomas the wing, the position closest to the sideline on kickoffs. And they put him in the wedge, the brutal impact zone for opposing tacklers on kickoff returns. Thomas sped down the field on the opening kickoff and made a textbook tackle that caused a Giant fumble. He made two more tackles on kickoffs and made a pivotal block—upending his man—to pave the way for Cliff Harris's twenty-seven-yard touchdown return. When Calvin Hill sprained his knee in the second half, Thomas took over at tailback. He ran for sixty yards on nine carries. The Cowboys won, 20–13.

Thomas was back and better than ever on the field. But he still refused to speak. Beat writers started calling him "The Sphinx." As his resistance to the organization grew, so did his influence on his fellow Cowboys. Calvin Hill recalled, "I suppose that in the deepest part of me was admiration. He was like the silent slave. He said nothing, but maybe he took the gear out of the machinery. Once Dr. Marvin Knight, our team doctor, came into the trainer's room, looking for Duane. 'Where's Duane?' he said. Oh, there's the son of a bitch. How ya doing?' Duane said, 'When you learn how to address me, I'll tell you how I'm doing,' and he got in the whirlpool and turned his back. I felt like pounding on the table. 'Yeah! Yeah!'"

With Thomas, the Cowboys cruised through the season and compiled an 11-3 record. His play was so outstanding that even Landry reached out to shake his hand after one remarkable touchdown run. Thomas stared Landry down, refused to shake, and then bypassed the outstretched hands of teammates Rayfield Wright and Jethro Pugh. When player-coach Dan Reeves was tasked to take roll call at every meeting, Thomas refused to answer. Reeves was so incensed that he went to Landry for justice. But Landry ignored him. "I still have nightmares about that roll call. Duane made Landry bend to him and do something I thought was unfair, and I've never forgotten it," Reeves recalled.

The Cowboys beat the Vikings in the first round and the 49ers again in the NFC Championship to reach their second Super Bowl in a row. Thomas scored touchdowns in each of those games. Media day for Super Bowl VI spooked every journalist who walked past a corner of Tulane Stadium in New Orleans. There Duane Thomas sat, as he was ordered to do by his boss, for picture and interview day. He remained silent for his allotted twenty minutes, refusing to add more verbiage and hype to an already overblown American ritual. Pete Rozelle didn't dine out on this performance.

The Cowboys dominated the Miami Dolphins in Super Bowl VI. Thomas ran for a seemingly effortless ninety-five yards and one touchdown on nineteen carries. As the writers cast their ballots in the press box for the Most Valuable Player of the game, some Thomas backers thought the outcome would be unanimous. But when *Sport* magazine's editor Larry Klein announced that Roger Staubach (12 of 19 for 119 yards passing) was the MVP, they realized what had happened: The winner was expected to fly to New York and give a speech at a banquet. That was something that Duane Thomas would not do.

"Duane represented what was in the hearts of most players, but we didn't have the courage to stand up like he did. Duane did what he did for a reason, but we didn't give him the support. We just went along with the system," Rayfield Wright said.

Thomas faded from the game as quickly as he arrived. The Cowboys traded him to San Diego in 1972 and the Chargers traded him to the Washington Redskins in 1973. By the end of the 1974–75 season, Thomas was out of football for good.

The Cowboys, meanwhile, would not win another Super Bowl until they found someone as talented and uncontrollable as he was.

22

AS HE HAD IN HIS FIRST TWO SEASONS, NOLL MADE WISE draft choices in 1971, picking up Jack Ham—the All-American Penn State linebacker—in the second round, Dwight White—the East Texas State defensive end—in the fourth round, and defensive tackle Ernie Holmes from Texas Southern in the eighth round. But he made another move, much less noticed, that helped transform his defensive line from Joe Greene and the Greenettes into something cohesive and brilliant. He hired Dan Radakovich as the defensive-line coach.

Noll had a theory about assistant coaches, one that wasn't all that different from his feelings about veteran players from other teams: If they've been somewhere else in the pros, he didn't want them. They'd have too many bad habits to break, and Noll wanted guys who were clean slates. It would be too easy for them to say, "Well, this is how we did it in . . ."

But Noll wasn't a dictator. He encouraged and appreciated discourse on day-to-day ideas and game plans. In a sport that relied on regiment and experience, he wanted fertile football minds. That's what made Radakovich the ideal candidate for his staff. Radakovich had been a center and linebacker at Penn State in the mid-1950s. He earned the nickname "Bad Rad" for the way he constantly attacked and cajoled not just the opposition, but also his teammates and even his coaches. He was Pennsylvania-steel tough with an in-your-face disposition, although he never planned on being a football coach. "I was going to go to law school," he says. But after getting into an argument with his Penn State coaches late in his senior year about how to play linebacker, they told him, "If you're so good, you coach it." And that spring he did, getting $100 to teach his former teammates. After an NFL tryout ended with an injury, he was back in State College, working as a grad assistant.

By the spring of 1971, he had worked his way through the college ranks—a dozen years at Penn State, a stint as the defensive coordinator at the University of Cincinnati—while trying to fit in law school classes at night, along with helping his wife raise their four kids. "I was going broke, and the Steelers had had a coach die a few weeks earlier, so I said to my wife, 'I wonder if they've hired anyone to replace that guy,'" says Radakovich. "So I called, and lo and behold they hadn't hired anyone or interviewed anyone because Mr. Rooney had put a freeze on interviewing until six weeks after the coach had died, out of respect. That's right when I happened to call. Noll didn't know me, but he said if I could get there the next day he'd talk to me."

Radakovich showed up at 8:15 the next morning, driving from Cincy. No one was there. Noll and his staff rarely showed up before nine. At nine on the dot, a secretary unlocked the door, and "within 15 minutes, the whole organization showed up," Radakovich remembers. "By 9:30, Noll sat me down in front of a blackboard and asked me about the defensive line. I had never coached it before. So I talked for two minutes and that was it. He said, 'That was it?' I said, 'Yeah, but if you want to know about coverage, I can do that.' He said, 'Show me.' So I was at the board for 20 minutes. Finally he told me that was enough. Then he turned to Charlie Summers, the secondary coach and said, 'Gee, wouldn't it be great to have a D-line coach that knows coverage?' Charlie looked goofy because that didn't make sense."

At least not to Summers, but to Noll it was revolutionary. He was a contrarian. The trend in the NFL at the time was to build lines—on both offense and defense—that were as big and bulky as possible. But Noll wanted speed. The faster his defensive line was, the easier it would be to get around those lumbering blockers. The more disruptive it would be to the timing of the offense. And the less time his linebackers and defensive backs would have to spend in coverage. Finding Radakovich, who could emphasize the importance of coverage to his linemen and teach them how to move like linebackers, was a happy accident.

It helped that he had drafted the right talent. Greenwood had played sparingly his first two seasons, but Noll saw him consistently improving— the young lineman was learning to combine power off the edge and superior hand-to-hand combat skills with his 4.7 speed. When Joe Gordon, the Steelers PR man, was tinkering with the team's media guide after the season, Noll told him to give a little extra room to Greenwood because he thought he'd be ready to make bigger contributions.

White, meanwhile, impressed from his first day in camp. Rookies always reported before veterans and were timed in the 40. White, running a 4.9, was just a step slower than Greenwood. And he played angrily and recklessly. Not desperate, like Green, but aggrieved, as though he'd been slighted. He'd grown up around junkies and drunks in Dallas. He was bright, but his teachers in school ignored him. "Some tried," he once said. "But most just wanted to get away at four o'clock." At home, as the oldest of three boys, his parents handed down the brunt of punishment and responsibility to him. He had gone to East Texas State and was, admittedly, bitter while he was there, constantly thinking how he could have ended up somewhere better if anyone had pushed him as a student. He was so frenetic when he played that coaches nicknamed him "Mad Dog." Years later, Joe Greene would say that the hardest hits he ever took during games were from White.

Through those first few days of camp, Radakovich couldn't stop thinking about how dominant White was. But he was a rookie coach, evaluating a rookie player who was competing against other rookies. He didn't trust his assessment. Until the veterans came in, that is. When he first studied his new team on film, Radakovich kept telling Noll how slow he thought the Steelers defensive ends were. "My teams at Penn State were faster," he says. Once he saw them live, and saw White blowing past them, he became convinced his original assessment was right: The kid had to get on the field right away.

This was the kind of proactive coaching that Noll wanted. Radakovich wasn't beholden to the veterans, didn't care about the status quo. More important, he wasn't afraid of talent, no matter how young or the potential for mistakes. "Some of the assistants thought I was messing with the best part of the team," says Radakovich. "But Noll was for it right away. Moving Dwight and L.C. to first string was a no-brainer. It improved the defensive pursuit by ten steps every play by having them both start. They were skinny, but they could fly."

Radakovich expanded their minds while expanding their games. He explained the nuances of coverage for the back seven defenders, which helped his young D-line understand the importance of getting to the passer quickly. Greenwood weighed in at 245 pounds. And Dwight White, the other defensive end, was 255. Noll wanted that speed to overwhelm the edges of the offensive line, while Greene collapsed the middle of it. So Radakovich trained them like he would a linebacker, teaching them how to move laterally and how to change direction. Stopping them in the close spaces of the offensive line was like trying to stop a drop of mercury. Slow-footed linemen looked bewildered trying to keep up with them.

The results on the field were immediate, with the Steelers starting 2-1 and allowing a little more than two touchdowns per game. Through the first 10 games in the season, the Steelers were 5-5. And while they'd finish 6-8, it was their best record in nine seasons and good enough for second place in their division.

More importantly, the Steelers defensive line forged an identity. Greenwood was as calm and cool as he was fast. Greene was the reluctant, brooding star. And White was a man whose mouth worked as hard as his body. He had so much to get off his chest, so much to prove. Mostly, they bonded over the fact they were young black men from the South who had been transplanted to the industrial North. They supported each other, pushed each other, protected each other, and taught each other. Greene and White would eventually share an apartment. "We all came from basically the same background," White once said. "Living in the ghetto, where you had to work, had to get up and get it for yourself. We all happened to meet in the utopia of pro football, but a lot of the ways we think now are influenced by the way we were then. That's why we all seem to think the same way."

That year, a Pittsburgh radio station looking to capitalize on the Steelers exciting young defense held a contest to give it a nickname. Playing off the dreaded Iron Curtain, seventeen fans submitted "The Steel Curtain." It stuck.

23

SLOWLY, METHODICALLY, NOLL WAS BUILDING THE TEAM—from players to staff—that he had envisioned when he was first hired in 1969. He had the defensive tackle, the defensive ends, the quarterback. But his strategy during his first three seasons had been as much about not losing as it had been about winning. He wanted mistake-free football and, as talented as Bradshaw was, he was still prone to the hubris-induced, confusion-caused interception. Noll needed a dynamic running back, someone who matched the speed and power of his defensive line.

As the 1972 draft neared, Noll eyed a running back from Houston named Robert Newhouse. An All-American, Newhouse finished his senior season with the second-most rushing yards in a season in NCAA history. He wasn't big, but he was squat and ran low to the ground. He used his forty-four-inch thighs to churn through tacklers, earning him the nickname "The Human Bowling Ball." One arm wasn't enough to bring him down, and neither were two. It took an entire team. Noll looked at Newhouse and thought he was the antidote to the Steelers' offensive ills.

But Art Rooney Jr. and Radakovich loved a Penn State running back. It had become a habit for the Steelers to think of Penn State as their own farm team. That was true for players like Jack Ham, who displayed such smarts and instincts that he earned a starting linebacker job as a rookie, and coaches like Bad Rad. Part of it was the respect the Rooneys had for Joe Paterno. And the other was that because the school was so close, and the players always so good, it was easy to scout them.

Of course, everyone in the country was high on a Penn State running back in 1972. Lydell Mitchell was a powerful, 5'11", 200-pound runner who scored twenty-nine touchdowns his senior season—twenty-six of them on the ground—and gained more than 1,500 yards. He was an All-American who finished fifth in the Heisman voting. But that wasn't the guy Rooney and Radakovich wanted. They wanted Mitchell's blocker, Franco Harris.

All Penn State players were required to spend a week or two practicing on the opposite side of the ball every year during spring drills. During Harris's sophomore year, Radakovich tutored Harris as a linebacker and marveled at his speed, at how fluid someone that size—Harris was 6'2", 220—could be when he moved. That sophomore season he went on to earn honorable mention All-American status. That put him on NFL radars. But he was injured the following year, and his senior year, while Harris was a threat, Mitchell was Paterno's primary weapon.

Harris had an open, inviting smile under a mustache he'd had since puberty, and the manner of a student who thought everything was trippy. Off the field he moved a beat slower. Surveying, appreciating, thinking. Words didn't roll off his tongue, they gathered in his mouth and formed full sentences before passing his lips. He wondered why things were and contemplated the answers until he was satisfied, either with the answer or the fact there may not be one. He had the gait of a man who lived lightly and without judgment. During their senior years Penn State promoted Harris and Mitchell as Mr. Inside and Mr. Outside, with the hook being that the bigger, brawnier Harris, who preferred running on the edges, was Mr. Outside.

It was the perfect campaign angle for a man so full of contradictions. He was half-black, half-Italian, the son of an Army vet who had married an Italian woman he met during World War II. Franco was so lax that he was considered lazy by his college coaches, but he was so determined that he spent much of his childhood working odd jobs around Fort Dix, New Jersey, where his father was stationed after the war. He rarely spoke, yet had bushels of friends who testified to his human decency. He grew up in a strict household where he feared punishments from his father. Yet had so much dignity that he refused to be belittled. During Harris's senior year, Joe Paterno was screeching at players before a practice, trying to get them energized. Harris walked onto the field a few minutes late and Paterno lit into him in front of the entire team, telling him that the next time he jogged onto the field after practice started he'd be benched. The next day, as all his teammates emptied the locker room for practice, Harris just sat by his locker, in full uniform, and waited. And waited. Until he was sure practice had started. Then he casually walked out onto the field. Paterno benched him.

Because of that, NFL scouts didn't know what to make of Harris. He was big, but didn't play physical. He was fast, but spent a lot of time blocking for Mitchell. Around campus he had a reputation for being relaxed and welcoming, but to scouts, at least, he had a rep as a disciplinary problem because of his clashes with Paterno. As for Harris, he was only partially aware that he was even a prospect, let alone of his reputation. "No one worked me out and no one called me," says Harris. "I never entered college thinking I was going to play pro football. It was not part of my plans. I wanted to get my education in hotel and food management and go to work and see the world."

But Rooney and Radakovich were constantly in Noll's ear. It was an interesting time for Radakovich. After just one season with Noll, he had been offered the defensive coordinator job at the University of Colorado. He had decided to take it, but Noll insisted he stay at least through the draft, partly because he was one of the people pushing hardest for the Steelers to take Harris. Up until the minute it was time to make the choice, Noll was waffling. "He had so much pressure on him to take him, all the scouts and Art Rooney liked him so much," says Radakovich. "When he finally did [take him], he picked up the phone and called Franco for the first time. They had a quick chat. Then he hung up the phone, looked at me and said, 'Man, he sounds like a Dead Head.' I answered back, 'Yeah, he's a nice shy kid, you'll like him.' Then I left town."

Harris meanwhile, had singled out Pittsburgh as the one place in the

NFL he was afraid to play. When he heard it was possible he might be drafted, by anyone, he considered writing the Steelers a letter asking them not to pick him because he didn't want to play where fans threw snowballs at the players. His agent stopped him, afraid it would make his client with the rep for discipline problems seem like more of a head case. "I was probably the most surprised person there was when I went in the first round," says Harris. "The first time I heard from any pro team was when I got that phone call from the Steelers."

Maybe the only person more shocked was the man who picked him. Noll had no idea what he had.

24

WITH EMIL NARICK'S 1969 CHALLENGE BEHIND HIM, UNITED Steelworkers of America President I. W. Abel took on a new decade with a familiar stance, shoulder to shoulder with the big steel companies. Despite the substantial backing that Narick had received from Pittsburgh's local union houses, and despite the continued grievances at individual mills—whether or not there was ample air circulation on the shop floor, getting better protective gear, making sure that a worker wasn't passed over for a higher-paying job because of discrimination, or a grievance about overtime pay—Abel did not reach out to the rank and file. Their concerns were beneath him. He had his eye on the big picture. And there were serious problems ahead.

Abel's biggest concerns were layoffs, foreign imports, and a decline in U.S. productivity. He was convinced that all three of these were occurring for one reason only—the threat of a USWA strike. Every three years, Abel had witnessed the big steel buyers (automakers and heavy machinery) ordering massive amounts of steel prior to a contract negotiation between the union and the steel manufacturers. Worried that talks between the two would break off and lead to a strike, GM, Ford, Chrysler, and the others would make sure they had enough steel on hand. The result would be a wild period of "hedge buying" that created massive demand six months before contract talks began. Then, once a deal was complete, the demand for steel would plunge. It put Abel in the awkward position of cheerfully announcing a wage increase just days before the big eleven manufacturers, with no future orders in hand, announced layoffs, which would often approach a quarter of the entire workforce.

Another effect of the possibility of a strike was increased imports of foreign steel. While the USWA and the big steel manufacturers were successful getting a 10 percent tariff on steel coming into the U.S., the demand during the hedge-buying period was often too high for U.S. mills to meet. Even when the U.S. mills ran at their highest possible capacity twenty-four hours a day, they could not meet demand. So orders would go to foreign markets, and once a manufacturer established a relationship with a foreign producer—many of whom were notorious for demanding long-term supply contracts—they felt all the more comfortable buying abroad. With imports flooding U.S. markets during a negotiation, stockpiles of surplus steel built up. The surplus would often last a full six to eight months after the USWA contract was settled, and it often took a full year before all 500,000 steelworkers were back at work. Since each contract was three years long, the process would soon begin all over again. Imported steel in 1965 accounted for 10.4 million tons. By 1971, it had reached 18.3 million tons.

With regular layoffs and increased competition from foreign steelmakers, the youngest generation suffered the most. The "last one hired, first one fired" refrain became a popular one. The newest workers had no seniority and so, in the unique vernacular of Pittsburgh, they loafed around and waited to be recalled. On his drive into the city every morning, Abel would see the crowds of young men hanging around the Carson Street bars, drinking at the crack of dawn. When the young men got back on the job, it took time for them to get back in the swing of things. Once they did, the supply of steel would rise, demand would remain constant or even dip, and the cycle would repeat itself. Many of the men came to expect their "mini-vacations" and often questioned the very nature of their work. USWA statistics in 1970 showed a turnover of 187,000 jobs a year.

Abel had to consider the needs of steel manufacturers. If there were no mills, there would be no workers. But as the 1971 contract negotiations began, he had to deliver for his men. And what the old guard wanted was more money and more benefits. When he tried to get a deal together before the massive hedge buying began, the steel companies would not listen. Abel was forced to threaten a strike to get them to the table. Once he did, the hedging was unprecedented. Steel buyers bought an astronomical 17 million tons of hedge before the 1971 contract was ratified. A more radical USWA president would have pushed a national strike and refused to fill orders. But Abel thought a strike would be disastrous. Japan and Germany would happily supply the hedge, further weakening U.S. Steel production. While Abel delivered a massive 30 percent increase in wages over the next three years, as well as a cost-of-living increase, the glut in the market put a stop to orders. More than 105,000 seething young steelworkers, most of them from western Pennsylvania, lost their jobs.

They filled the local bars and drank ten-cent drafts, wondering why the old guard had sold them out.

25

IT WAS DICK HOAK'S JOB TO FIGURE OUT WHAT FRANCO HARris could do. The Pittsburgh native and Penn State alum, whose brothers and father worked in the mills, had retired as the Steelers all-time leading rusher after the 1970 season. He had taken a job as a high school football coach at a catholic school in West Virginia, where his team went 1-9. "But I liked it," says Hoak. "I could have stayed there forever."

Instead, shortly after drafting Harris, Noll called Hoak and asked him if he wanted to come back home and coach the Steelers running backs. "It just so happened I had an offer from the Pitt coach to come work for him, too," says Hoak. "When I told him about the Steelers he said I'd be crazy to turn them down. So I took it. Good thing, too. Pitt went 1-9 that year and everyone got fired."

Hoak wasn't hired until after the Steelers had drafted Harris. The first time he ever saw him on the field in person was at training camp. It didn't go well. Harris played in a college all-star game and arrived at camp a week late. During those first few practices, he was constantly caught by tacklers behind the line of scrimmage. Instead of hitting the hole he was biding his time, looking for a place to cut back against the grain that was never there. "He wasn't setting camp on fire," says Hoak. "Some of the guys were looking at each other like what the heck?"

"When I first saw him I didn't think he was going to make it," says Russell. "He would stop before he hit the hole. He would backtrack, go left, go right. He wouldn't hit the hole. I thought, what's he doing?"

Harris never bought into the kill-or-be-killed mentality of football. He liked running, he liked eluding. When he watched films of opponents' defenses he always found himself focusing on the running back instead of the linebackers, trying to imagine himself making the same moves he was watching on screen. While most guys compartmentalized their lives, becoming someone new and scary on the field, Harris was the same on and off the field. A thinker in pads. With his curly hair and dark beard and chiseled nose and olive skin, he took on the look of a Grecian philosopher. Just because it was a contact sport didn't mean you had to crave contact. "The art of running is being able to change and do things because what you thought would be there is not there," Harris once told NFL Films.

It took one exhibition game for his coaches to realize that Harris wasn't the problem in practice, it was his teammates. "We went down to Atlanta for an exhibition," says Hoak. "We put him in the game and we run this play where he is supposed to go around the left end. He starts over there and there is nothing there. Then all of a sudden he puts his foot in the ground, cuts back to the other side, and runs seventy-five yards for a touchdown. These little defensive backs are chasing him and they can't catch him. When he took off down that sideline you said, 'holy cow.'

"After that, the coaches sat around and thought about why he looked so bad in practice. Well, in practice sometimes guys don't go full speed. So if he started cutting back there was nothing there because these guys weren't going all out and they'd be sitting in the lanes, so there was no place to run. You get in a game and these guys are pursuing, it's a different story. After that exhibition game Chuck just came up to me and said, 'Dick, don't over-coach him.'"

Still, Noll didn't start Harris right away. He'd usually bring him in off the bench sometime in the second quarter. But by the seventh game of the year—after Harris had rushed for 138 yards and two touchdowns on just fifteen carries against the Bills—he was Pittsburgh's primary offensive weapon. "Every time Franco ran for a hundred yards my wife would make him a lasagna," says Pittsburgh's then trainer Ralph Berlin. "For a while it seemed like she was making him one every week."

During his first few years as coach, Noll's constant tinkering with his roster had dramatically changed the makeup of his offensive line. While the trend in the league was to put big beefy men up front, Noll wanted his guys to be smaller and faster. His preferred method of running the ball wasn't to overpower a defensive line, it was to use a defender's aggressive nature against himself by executing trap blocks. In a trap the offensive lineman doesn't initially block the defensive lineman across from him. He just lets him go, while another offensive lineman pulls from his position and blindsides the onrushing defender.

But the most important key to a trapping running game is to have a runner who's patient enough to wait for those blocks to develop. The Steelers hadn't had that until Harris arrived. "It's not a forty-yard dash coming out of your stance," says Hoak. "You had to run under control and see what was happening. If you were out of control you would run right up your guard's back. That is what made us so good. Franco had great vision—he could see the whole field and feel people around him. He was a great trap runner."

"We didn't have big, bull-you-over linemen like Kansas City or Oakland," says Harris. "Our guys were small, and all the traps worked perfectly for me. It was tailored to my running style—I was lucky with that. At the point of contact, once the ball is hiked, there is nothing but chaos, and where the hole is supposed to be, half the time or more it's not there, and there's so much chaos that you have to be able to have your keys and read and respond. I was fortunate enough that I was good at that."

Harris not only made the offense more explosive, he made it more respected. No longer did the defense have to keep opponents out of the end zone and then pray the offense didn't screw up. There was competitive balance on the team. Practices were more intense. And that elevated everyone. Through the first month of the season, the Steelers were 2-2, with wins over the Raiders and Cardinals and losses to the Cowboys and Bengals. But in the fifth game of the year, they introduced themselves to the league as grown-ups in a 24–7 home win against Houston. The offense, led by Harris's 115 yards rushing, gained 295 total yards, 249 of those on the ground. And the defense gave up only 108 yards total, with no passing yards. None. The next week they beat New England by thirty. Then it was Buffalo by seventeen. The week after that they played the Bengals again. They had won three in a row, but Cincy was the defending division champ. It was no contest. The Steelers went up 26–0 by halftime. When Harris scored the last touchdown of the game, late in the fourth quarter, he iced a 40–17 win.

That Bengals game was the fourth of seven straight in which the Steelers would gain more than 200 yards on the ground. Their dominance was so obvious to everyone watching the NFL that, after the game, Steelers guard Bruce Van Dyke was named the AFC's Offensive Player of the Week. On one play against the Bengals he pulled to trap block a linebacker, fell, got back up and, from his hands and knees, lunged at a defensive back to make another block. Even for an offensive lineman, it's hard to stay anonymous after an effort like that.

The next weekend Pittsburgh beat the Chiefs, just three years removed from their Super Bowl win, and who, along with the Dolphins, were considered the class of the AFC. It was the kind of win no one in Pittsburgh had ever dreamed could happen, perennial losers beating up one of the best teams in football. Even more remarkable, it was the fifth straight Steelers win.

Two weekends later the Steelers were closing in on an accomplishment that had once seemed impossible for a franchise that couldn't win a Pee Wee title: clinching a division championship. Really, it should have been easy. They were in Houston, facing an Oilers team that was 1-11. But L. C. Greenwood was out with an injury. Two of the five starters on the offensive line—Jon Kolb and Gerry Mullins—had the flu. Later in the game, Van Dyke would injure his leg and be pulled. A fourth starting offensive lineman, Jim Clack, injured his ankle. To top it all off, Bradshaw left the game with a dislocated finger. Running backs, even ones as talented as Harris, are only as good as their offensive line. And this line—this team—was in trouble.

At halftime, the score was tied 3–3. But when the Steelers came out for the second half, "Joe Greene just took it over," says Hoak. "He was sacking the quarterback, getting the running back, forcing fumbles. I don't know if I can say I ever saw a defensive lineman control a game. I've never seen anything like that."

Greene had five sacks that day and two forced fumbles, both of which led to Steelers field goals. He also blocked an Oilers field goal attempt. "I decided this was our chance, we were so close," says Greene. "And I just didn't want to lose."

He didn't. And neither did the Steelers. They toppled the Oilers that day, 9–3. And the next weekend, after beating the Chargers in San Diego 24–2, they were 11–3 and crowned AFC Central Division champs.

AS BIG AS ANYTHING HARRIS OR GREENE DID ON THE FIELD, there was another phenomenon at Three Rivers in 1972. In support of it, people marched on the stadium, in groups eighty-strong. They wore green army helmets with the Italian flag painted on the side. They carried hollowed-out loaves of Italian bread, stuffed with bottles of red wine. There were plastic wineglasses with stems in their bags, along with enough meat and cheese to feed, well, an army. Which is what this group of fans called themselves.

Al Vento, a pizza man, and Tony Stagno, a baker, and their families had been going to Steelers games for as long as there'd been a team. From Forbes field, to Pitt Stadium, from bad to worse to "Can it be worth it?" But when the team moved to Three Rivers, they bought tickets anyway. And hatched an idea. "We looked around the stadium and there were no banners, there was no enthusiasm," Stagno told NFL Films. "Someone we were sitting with said, 'It'll take an army to get fans going.' We said, 'Okay, we'll be the Italian Army.'"

Every game they sat in their section, with two seats reserved just to hold the food, wearing their Italian Army helmets and waving Italian flags. Other signs sprouted up around Three Rivers: GERELA'S GORILLAS, for kicker Roy Gerela, or DOBRE SHUNKA, which meant "Good Ham" in Polish, to honor Jack Ham. But no one could compete with the roar of the Italian Army. Especially after Stagno and Vento anointed the Steelers half-Italian running back as their leader.

As a rookie, even while ripping through defenses, Harris was as un-assuming as he had been on Penn State's campus. "We loved his style because we were old-school guys who were taught you didn't talk to the crowd and ask them to applaud," says Russell. "Franco would run, pick up his yards, and never play to the crowd. He was old school, and we loved that."

Harris didn't even bother buying a new car that first year, and the one he had was often in the shop. Many times he hitchhiked or took the bus home from practices and games. So when Vento and Stagno wanted to talk to him and ask if they could rename their uprising "Franco's Italian Army," he wasn't too hard to find. "They just approached me about it after a game one day early in the season," says Harris. "I said, 'Sounds good to me.' Never in my wildest dreams did I think that it would get as big as it did."

It wouldn't have, had Harris not blown up the way he did. Once he became a starter, he began a streak of eight straight hundred-yard-or-more rushing games, breaking the record that had been held by Jim Brown. He finished the year with 1,055 yards and was voted into the Pro Bowl by his peers. But mostly, in the same way he brought the offense and defense together by putting them on equal ground, his talent turned Three Rivers into a melting pot. Signs all over read RUN, PAISANO, RUN. There was an Israeli Brigade of the Italian Army and an African-American Brigade and Irish one, too, that christened the running back "Franc O'Harris."

By season's end, when Harris was introduced before games, the scoreboard flashed the words "Franco's Italian Army," and 50,000 people roared until their throats were raw, waving red, green, and white Italian flags that had been passed out before the game. Even the players couldn't ignore it. "What's this red, green, and white, man? What's that? Red, green, and white?" Joe Greene asked on he sidelines before a game once.

"That's the Italian flag, maaaaan," Harris responded, as chill as the Pittsburgh air that winter afternoon.

"My season kept getting bigger and bigger and the fans really started to connect with us," says Harris. "At that time the army kept telling its story, and it grew of such significance that people from around the country joined it, and people are calling out to me."

The Monday before the Steelers division-clinching game against the Chargers, Noll flew the team out to Palm Springs, to get it acclimated to warm weather and the time change. Vento and Stagno decided that, since the team was out there, the unofficial mayor of Palm Springs and the number-one Italian in the world, Francis Albert Sinatra, should be drafted into Franco's Army as a one-star general. They begged Steelers announcer Myron Cope to make it happen.

After a couple days, Cope had grown frustrated trying to track down a contact for Sinatra. Six different people had said they could help him, that they were Sinatra's top lieutenant, and none had come through. He was having drinks with a buddy one night and said, "I've had it, I'm not wasting any more time on this project."

"Waste a little more," his buddy said, pointing to the door as Frank Sinatra walked through it. Sinatra was escorted to a back room as Cope scribbled a note as fast as he could. It read:

Dear Frank:

We are press and front-office bums traveling with the Steelers. We do not wish to disturb your dinner except to say this: Franco Harris, who as you probably know is a cinch for Rookie of the Year, has a fan club called Franco's Italian Army. Franco is half-black, half-Italian. So a baker named Tony Stagno started Franco's Italian Army and is its four-star general. The Army hopes you will come out to practice tomorrow to be commissioned a one-star general. There will, of course, be an appropriate ceremony in which you will be given a general's battle helmet, and there will be ritual dago red and provolone cheese and prosciutto, and there will be much Italian hugging and kissing.

P.S. Franco's from Hoboken.

Of course, Harris wasn't from Hoboken. But Sinatra hustled up front to Cope's table, and being the bettor he was, asked how Bradshaw's dislocated finger was doing. Then he agreed to show up at practice the next day, share some wine with Franco, and accept induction into the Italian Army.

Cope called Stagno and Vento, who booked first-class flights to Palm Springs. It was the first time Stagno had ever been on a plane. They had an Italian Army helmet made that read "Sinatra" on the back. On the sidelines at practice they had a table set up with wine and cheese and Italian flags waving in the soft California breeze. Film crews were ready to shoot. The only thing missing was Sinatra. Ten minutes went by. Thirty minutes went by. Finally, after an hour, Cope said out loud, "I guess he's not gonna show."

Then, everything got quiet. Cope turned around and found himself face-to-face with Frank. "When Sinatra says he'll show," Sinatra said, "he shows."

Stagno and Vento handed him the helmet. They shook his hand and kissed him on both cheeks. They all shared wine and cheese and called each other "compad." Then Cope realized that Harris was missing out, since it was all happening in the middle of practice. So he ran onto the field and yelled, "Franco, the man is here." Practice stopped. All eyes turned to Noll. And then to Cope, who was frozen, realizing what he had just done. And then they turned back to Noll who said simply, "Franco, get over there." On the sideline, in the middle of practice, Harris and Sinatra each raised a glass of red wine and toasted to Franco's Italian Army.

On his way back to the airport Stagno called his wife. When she asked him how it all went with Sinatra he told her, "It was like kissing God."

The next week, back at Three Rivers, the Steelers prepared to host the Raiders in the opening round of the playoffs, Pittsburgh's first-ever post-season game. The Italian Army joked they were going to kidnap John Madden, the Raiders animated coach. And, in fact, a pep rally a few blocks away at the Hilton became so frenzied that fans marched down to the

Raiders hotel, where they saw Madden relaxing in the lobby. Several hundred fans started pounding on the hotel's plate-glass window, someone threw a bottle that crashed into a second-floor window and then a Pittsburgh police officer, called in for crowd control, fell and was stepped on. Before the night was over, paddy wagons had been called in and people were being hauled off to jail, including two Raiders reserves who had been caught in the melee on their way back to the hotel from the movies.

Watching it all through the lobby window was Madden, thirty-five, and still built like the burly offensive tackle he had been in college. He had been hired three years earlier by Raiders owner Al Davis, and he'd led Oakland to a 12-1-1 record that first year and had been named the AFL's best coach.

Earlier that season, in the first game of the year, the Steelers and Raiders played at Three Rivers. It was a game the Raiders, who had finished 8–4 the year before, expected to win handily, but instead they were beaten 34–28. It was an especially bitter loss for Davis, who had coached with Noll on Sid Gillman's Chargers' staff. No one in the league had a reputation for being as angry and competitive and belligerent as Davis. He took traffic personally. And he especially hated old-guard NFL families like the Rooneys.

Davis was an original AFL guy. After working for Gillman, he became the head coach and GM of the Raiders. And he was at the heart of the upstart league's attempts to break the NFL by pushing his colleagues to bid up salaries for the biggest college stars. Of course, Davis had always been full of ideas. Once, as an assistant coach at the Citadel, he was recruiting a linebacker from Brooklyn. Davis took the kid to one of the nicest restaurants in the borough, where the tables were set with fine silverware and real tablecloths. In the middle of dinner he got so excited describing a defensive scheme that he started drawing on the tablecloth. Then he jumped out of his seat and got into a three-point stance, right in the middle of the restaurant.

He was just as committed to the AFL's success as to the NFL's failure.

In 1966 the league's owners, who were negotiating with the NFL to merge, knew how passionate Davis was, how he didn't compromise, how he didn't just want to win, but to humiliate opponents. So, in a Machiavellian move, his fellow AFL owners named him league commissioner, which forced him to give up his job with the Raiders. He was at the pinnacle of football, leading a league that had stolen Joe Namath from the NFL, had high-flying offenses, and money to burn. "He wanted nothing to do with the NFL," Dan Rooney wrote in his autobiography.

But the rest of the AFL owners felt differently. While letting Davis take a hard-line stance publicly as the league commissioner, Hunt and Schramm were having their back-room talks to finalize a merger deal. Davis had been a patsy, someone to help them look strong. Three months after Davis took over, in June 1966, the two leagues announced the merger. "No doubt Davis felt betrayed," wrote Rooney in his autobiography. "Not only by the merger itself but by the way he had been deliberately cut out of the negotiations."

When the Raiders landed in Pittsburgh for that opening-round play-off game, not only was Davis, who returned to the Raiders as part owner in 1966, still fuming from that season-opening loss, he carried the baggage of the merger with him as well. "Davis still played by the old rules," Rooney wrote. "Treating NFL teams like the enemy."

This game played out like a front-line battle—a few yards on either side of the line constituted victory. At the end of the first half, the score was tied at zero. In the third quarter, the only points scored had come from a Roy Gerela field goal. Gerela added another in the fourth, giving Pittsburgh a 6–0 lead late in the game. Desperate, Madden pulled his starting QB, Daryle Lamonica, replacing him with a rookie southpaw, Kenny Stabler.

In the stands, the raucous crowd tried to rattle Stabler. Vento and Stagno and the rest of Franco's Italian Army waved hollowed-out red peppers at the Raiders and put the *malocchio* curse—the evil eye—on Oakland. It didn't work. Three times on the drive, Stabler and the Raiders faced third down. All three times they converted. Finally, with less than two minutes left, Stabler, nicknamed "The Snake," slithered his way for a thirty-yard touchdown run. After trailing the entire game, the Raiders had gone ahead with 1:13 remaining. "Yeah," Noll said after the game. "It wasn't a fun time."

He wasn't the only one thinking it was over. Art Rooney had already left his seats in the owner's box to make his way down to the locker room, where he'd be waiting to shake every Steelers hand and thank them. At this point in the game, Bradshaw had completed just 10 of 24 passes for 115 yards. "I wouldn't have wagered my momma's tooth on our chances," Bradshaw wrote in *It's Only a Game*. Noll sent in a play, 66 Circle Option, which was a pass over the middle to a rookie receiver named Barry Pearson. "Oh no," Harris muttered in the huddle. "Not that play." It was a rare moment of exasperation from the rookie, whose assignment was to stay in and block. The plan was to get enough yardage for a Gerela field goal attempt. "I was next to our safety, Glen Edwards, and I was thinking it was over," Russell says. "Right before the play Glen was giving our offense a hard time. We had played pretty well that game and we were about to lose and I said to him, 'Hey, be positive, something good can happen.' It was just standard thinking. I didn't believe it."

Vento and Stagno did. Just as they waved peppers at the Raiders, they pointed a tiny man carved from ivory, a good luck charm, at the Steelers goal line. "The crazy thing," Stagno once told NFL Films, "is that it really worked."

The Raiders read the play and jammed Pearson at the line. With his primary receiver nowhere to be found, Bradshaw scrambled in the pocket. He ducked a Raider and sprinted right. As Bradshaw broke from the line, Harris's blocking assignments roamed away from him, so he released from the backfield and put himself in position to be a safety valve for his quarterback. But Bradshaw, pursued by five Raiders who were diving for his ankles, never saw him.

Meanwhile, Stagno dropped his good luck charm. As Vento scrambled on the cement between the steps to find it, Bradshaw rifled a pass downfield to the Raiders 35 in the direction of running back John "Frenchy" Fuqua, who, for an instant, had come free on the broken play. At that moment, the ball, Fuqua, and Raiders defensive back Jack Tatum all collided.

Just then, Vento jumped up, holding his tiny ivory man to the sky.

Bradshaw's pass ricocheted off Tatum and Fuqua and hurtled toward midfield. "I saw it deflected and I dropped my head," says Russell. "I thought we lost."

But Harris, with no one to block, had been trailing on the play. As the ball sailed toward the ground at the forty-two-yard line, he scooped it up by the nose as it passed his shins. He seemed to be the only one moving. The Steelers watching on the sidelines believed the game had been lost. The Raiders on the field saw the deflection and were sure they had won. Only Harris kept the play alive, galloping down the sidelines, as if he were running out a play in practice.

There were five seconds left in the game. The Steelers were ahead 13–7, and about to win their first postseason game in thirty-nine years of existence. And the man who started it all, Art Rooney, was alone in the locker room. He'd missed what would one day be voted by NFL Films as the greatest play in league history.

Forty-five minutes after the game, as the team celebrated in the locker room, Harris got a note from one of the locker-room attendants. It was a telegram that read: "THE FOLLOWING IS AN ORDER: ATTACK, ATTACK, ATTACK, ATTACK. COLONEL FRANCIS SINATRA (OF FRANCO HARRIS' ITALIAN ARMY)."

Later that night, a local reporter called Harris's mom, who had been watching the game. She wasn't a football fan, and barely understood the game. But she knew how important this day was to her son. "She told me and everyone who would listen that something special was going to happen," Harris says. Before the game, she lit candles with pictures of the Virgin Mary on the holders and placed them around her living room.

When the reporter called, she told him divine intervention saved that ball from touching the ground.

She wasn't the only one who believed.

That night on TV, while doing the local sports broadcast, Cope said he got a call from a fan who told him a friend had named the play. Then Cope said the words on the air. "It was," he said, "the Immaculate Reception."

THIRD QUARTER

1973–1974

TWO DAYS BEFORE ST. PATRICK'S DAY IN MARCH 1973, DAN Rooney was sitting in his office. It was after five. Most of the people on the Steelers' staff had gone home. For the past few months the entire franchise had been reveling in the glory of the Immaculate Reception. The fact that the Steelers lost to the Dolphins in the AFC title game the next week—everyone lost to the Dolphins in their undefeated 1972 season— hadn't taken away the hope that everyone had for the future.

Then Rooney's phone rang. It was his private line. When he picked it up he heard his wife. She sounded anxious, concerned. "Ernie Holmes just called me," she told him. "He's in trouble. You better call him right away."

Holmes, a defensive tackle, was the final piece in the Steel Curtain defensive line. While he had been drafted out of Texas Southern in 1971, the same year as White, he wasn't as polished a player. His playing weight in college was close to three hundred pounds. He worked furiously to get down to 265 before his first training camp, as the Steelers had asked, but when he did, he lacked the strength that had made him so dominant. The Steelers cut him and offered him a job on the taxi squad for $1,000 a month, where he could wait and hope someone got hurt. Holmes refused. "I could make more back home on the docks," he said, insulted.

Holmes was country strong—his nickname had been "Fats" from the time he was a boy—and built like a powder keg. He had the same temperament. When he first arrived at a reception for Steelers rookies in 1971, he kept eyeing White from across the room, staring at him but never talking to him. When they eventually came face-to-face, White stuck out his hand, but the stockier, broader Holmes just looked at him and said, "Yeah, fat boy, you know you're going to have to leave here. There's not room for more than one of us here."

Holmes *needed* to make the Steelers. He had grown up on his family's forty-five-acre farm in Jamestown, Texas, halfway between Dallas and the Louisiana border. But while at Texas Southern, in Houston, he had married his girlfriend. And they had two kids before he graduated. While he struggled in Pittsburgh, his family was waiting in Houston for his checks. The distance, and the stress he felt financially, was straining his relationship with his wife.

When Holmes refused the taxi-squad assignment and moved back home to Texas, Holmes's father sat his son down and asked him, "What the hell are you doing?" But Holmes couldn't be moved. He was despondent and disappointed, convinced that conspiracies had kept him off the team, and frustrated that he wasn't being recognized right away. Finally his dad called Art Rooney Jr. and asked him to talk to his son. "He was kind of a poor soul," remembers Art. "He and Bradshaw were the same way. They could be cheerful, but there was always something sad about them. You felt sorry for them."

The Steelers brought Holmes back and hid him on their practice squad, which was already full, asking him not to dress for the team picture so they didn't get fined for carrying too many players. And that off-season he rededicated himself to training. He knew he'd never be svelte, but he wanted to at least have the stamina to match his strength. He ate one meal a day, drank water, took vitamins, and ran for his life, sometimes as many as ten miles a day in three separate sessions around Pittsburgh's Squirrel Hill section. By the time he reported to camp in the summer of 1972, he weighed 260 pounds but was as strong as ever. Holmes had decided that the only time he'd leave Pittsburgh again was if "they dragged me off the field."

He went all out on every play, in practice and in games, blindly attacking—every snap he didn't win was a threat to his livelihood. But the ferocity with which he played came from a deeper well than where most players find personal motivation. Something seethed inside him. "I don't know what my life is," he once told *Time* magazine, "except there's something pounding in the back of my head." Occasionally he'd stop by Dan Rooney's office to talk, worried that people were out to get him. During practices veteran Steelers offensive linemen had to ask him to slow down so they didn't get hurt. Holmes played low, and used his helmet like a ram's horns, butting opponents under the chin to knock them off balance and, literally, make their head spin. "He had a look that was really scary," says former Steelers safety Mike Wagner. "I think he wanted to beat people to death—within the rules of the game."

But this is how he lived, all the time, at the extreme edges. "He and I were pretty tight," says Terry Hanratty. "We used to play poker on the road, and it was up to the guy hosting the party to look up in the yellow pages the barbecue rib joint and bring it in. You would have thought you had walked into a shoe store because there were so many boxes of ribs: 20 rows, six boxes high, cards covered in sauce. Ernie would eat ten boxes, go to the bathroom, throw up, and then repeat that three or four times."

Once, at a party in a restaurant hosted by defensive line coach George Perles, the Steelers entered a back room to find a gluttonous spread: A full roasted pig, piles of pasta, roast beef. They attacked the food at first, pouring it down their throats, before they finally slowed down, everyone settling into chairs with full bellies and heavy breaths. Hanratty walked in at that moment. "And there is Ernie Holmes almost contented," Hanratty says. "Then he looks at the pig's head, throws it down, cracks it, and starts eating the brains."

Holmes had split time at defensive tackle in 1972 with Ben McGee. But McGee retired after that season, and Holmes got the job. He had the stability and recognition he craved, which he fought for on every play. Players and coaches hoped it would help mellow him off the field.

But in March 1973 Holmes was in Texas when he and his wife separated. He worried he'd never see his kids again. He was overextended financially—"I was the successful one in my family and helped people out," he told a reporter back then—and knew he was facing an expensive divorce. He needed money, and he'd asked Rooney to help him. Without promising anything, Rooney told him to come see him in Pittsburgh, that he'd help him work it out.

That night, Holmes jumped into his car and raced through the night and the next day to Pittsburgh, without sleeping. He arrived after the Steelers offices had closed, so he kept driving, onto the Pennsylvania Turnpike until it became the Ohio Turnpike. He was distraught and tired and battling demons in his head, real and imagined. At the scene of an accident he stopped and told a police officer that trucks were trying to cut him off. But the cop ignored him. Back in his car, Holmes grew more paranoid as traffic built up around him, blocking his car. He pressed on the brake, he pressed on the gas, lurching forward ever so slightly.

The trucks were after him. He pulled a shotgun from the floor, blew out his window, and started shooting at the tires of passing trucks. The state police were on his tail now, chasing him at ninety miles an hour. He veered off the main road, blew out a tire, and jumped out of his car, running into a nearby forest. He carried his shotgun with him.

A police helicopter swirled overhead and Holmes, surrounded by state police, began shooting at it, hitting an officer in the ankle. Moments later, surrounded and exhausted, he was finally in cuffs. Said one officer afterward: "We could have killed him a dozen times."

That night in jail, Holmes called Dan Rooney. "We'll do everything we can for you," Rooney told him. "Try not to worry." It was a Saturday. Holmes would be in jail for the weekend, until a judge could hear his case and consider bail.

That Monday, represented by a lawyer paid for by the Rooneys, Holmes was released on $45,000 bail, also paid by the Rooneys, and admitted to a psych hospital in western Pennsylvania, again paid for by the Rooneys. He was supposed to be there for a month. He stayed for two. Art Rooney visited nearly every day. L. C. Greenwood took him on supervised trips around town. This was a kid who had quit on the team once, had to be coaxed to come back, and was a part-timer who showed only flashes of the kind of mental strength necessary to be a consistent starter. Yet he was treated as if he were Joe Greene. "We all thought," says Art Rooney Jr., "he needed mercy."

That summer, after his stay in the hospital, Holmes went back to Ohio and pled guilty to assault with a deadly weapon. At sentencing, a psychiatrist testified that he suffered from acute paranoid psychosis. Holmes was given five years' probation. That July he was back in training camp. And that September he was the Steelers starting defensive tackle.

The success of 1972 turned Three Rivers into Pittsburgh's biggest block party every Sunday. The first home game of 1973—against the Lions—was sold out, a streak that continues to this day. And with Holmes firmly entrenched alongside Greene, the Steelers played as well as they ever had. In the second game of the year, against the Browns, they won 33–6 in what Noll described after the season as his team's most perfect game of the year. Holmes had three sacks, and after one of them, he just sat on Browns QB Mike Phipps, as if he had found the most perfect spot to lounge all afternoon.

Even before the game, they showed the confidence and swagger of a team that knew how good it could be. That year, NFL commissioner Pete Rozelle had issued rules forcing all NFL players to wear the same uniforms as their teammates, from the tape on their shoes to the stripes on their helmets. A lot of the players had come of age on college campuses in the late 1960s. They had been raised on rebellion and freedom of expression. Rozelle's rules, while harmless, were stifling. At least L. C. Greenwood thought so. For that Browns game he protested by debuting a pair of gold cleats. "We all live to be different or our own selves," he said. The

Steelers were fined by the league, but Noll's response when asked about the shoes by reporters after the game was typical of his it-doesn't-bother-me-if-it-doesn't-bother-the-team approach:

"What shoes?" he asked.

"The gold shoes," he was told.

"I don't watch shoes," he answered. "That's Peter's province. I'd feel bad if L.C. went out there barefoot."

They started that season 4-0, giving up just eleven points per game. After a loss in the fifth game of the season to the Bengals, the Steelers won four straight again, including a win at Oakland. They were 8-1 and had a three-game lead over Cincinnati in the AFC Central, with only five games to play.

And it wasn't just the front line that was dominating games. Noll had hired another longtime college coach, Bud Carson, to be his defensive coordinator in 1972. He installed a complicated zone defense called the Cover Two, which essentially forced the quarterback to solve a moving puzzle whenever he stepped to the line.

The Steelers were the first NFL team to use the Cover Two, and it was a radical shift from the coverage schemes that most pro teams were using. Around the league, the preference was for man coverage, with corner-backs tracking receivers down the sidelines or across the field. But the Cover Two was a zone, with corners funneling receivers toward the safeties, then protecting the short to middle portion of the field. That was their zone, while safeties covered the deeper area of the field. The system not only confused quarterbacks who could never be sure who would be covering receivers, it also created very small seams in which to throw passes between the two levels of defensive backs. "We first installed this with Bud in 1972, but by 1973, it was our base defense," says safety Mike Wagner. "As a safety, you have to read as the QB drops back. The first thing you look for is a pass read, and if it's a pass you look to the outside receiver and see which way he is releasing. Our corners would push for an inside release, but if it's an outside release he would follow for a few steps and I would have to widen my base and get outside and sprint to a spot. But it worked because of our corners. They had to be able to jam the receiver, read the play, and then funnel the receivers all within seconds. And if it was a run, they had to support, because they were bigger than the safeties."

In much the same way Noll counteracted league trends by preferring smaller, quicker offensive linemen, he went after bigger physical corners, like Mel Blount, whom he drafted in the third round out of Southern University in 1970. He was just playing the rules in the book. And they allowed for cornerbacks to manhandle receivers, hitting and chucking them from the moment the ball was snapped, all the way across the field. Noll's theory was, if a receiver can't get loose from a corner, he can't catch a ball. And the 6'3", 205-pound Blount was the perfect corner for such a theory. He eliminated half the field for every offense.

But no matter how great his defense was, no matter how many games in a row the team won, this season felt different than the previous one. The euphoria that came with winning that first division title had ceded to expectations—from fans and from players. And despite the wins, Noll saw constant mistakes, especially at quarterback. In a way he never did with Greene or the defense, Noll refused to cut his quarterback any slack. Every mistake by Bradshaw, every missed read or wrong call, resulted in an eruption. "Noll was more focused on what the offense was doing during games," says Russell. "He wanted Terry to make the checks the way they had talked about during the week. If Terry didn't audible what he told him to audible to, which was almost always a running play, he was angry. You got to follow the boss's instructions."

"Joe Gordon had the best line: One of them wanted love; the other couldn't love," says Vito Stellino, who covered the Steelers for the *Pittsburgh Post-Gazette* in the 1970s. "Noll's idea is that the game was the final exam—he spent all week teaching them, and the game is their job."

That 1973 season, despite all the wins, Noll played yo-yo with his quarterbacks. No one was good enough. Bradshaw had the skill but not the confidence or the discipline, and he was often injured. Hanratty had the confidence and the understanding of defenses, but not the skill. They were the same way off the field. Bradshaw was self-conscious and rarely hung out with his teammates. The more he was ridiculed and manipulated by Noll, the more he kept to himself. It got to the point where, if he told a joke in front of his teammates, he'd look Greene's way to see if it had gone over. "After a game, Bradshaw would say exactly what you wanted him to say," says Stellino. "And then another wave of reporters would come up and he'd tell them something entirely different if that's what they wanted to hear. He had tremendous insecurity."

Hanratty, meanwhile, was the guy sitting at his locker every morning when his teammates came in, smoking a cigarette, drinking coffee, reading the paper, and making wisecracks. Mansfield used to call him Yosemite Sam because of his hook nose and mustache. He'd walk into the huddle during a game and be ready to wing it. He had nothing to lose. He was the local kid backing up the mercurial superstar. "I'd say, 'I have no clue what to call. Check with me on two,'" Hanratty says. "I had thirty seconds to check out the defense and then I would see what was happening and I would call it."

Hanratty took over from Bradshaw in the middle of the Steelers' second four-game win streak, a 20–13 win over the Bengals. He won his next two starts, but then he struggled—the Steelers lost to the Broncos in the tenth game of the season, and Hanratty was replaced for a game by Joe Gilliam, the third-string, second-year quarterback. When Gilliam lost his first start, the Steelers second straight loss, Noll had no choice but to go back to Bradshaw, who lost as well. The Steelers, who had been 8-1 with a three-game lead in the division and five games to play, were now 8-4 and tied with the Bengals.

The next week, during a win over Houston, Joe Greene became so disgusted with his team's lack of effort and intensity that he pulled himself from the game. While the Steelers made the playoffs that season as a

Wild Card, finishing second in the division to the Bengals, they ended the year pitifully, with a 33–14 loss to the Raiders in the opening round. When asked to summarize his team, Greene told a *Pittsburgh Post-Gazette* reporter, "We are a team in danger. We are in danger of living on potential, and no one can do that. You are powerless with potential."

28

THE FIRST TIME THE UNITED STEEL WORKERS OF AMERICA'S new District 31 director, Edward Sadlowski, walked into the union's glittering new headquarters, he found himself surrounded by suits. He later told a group of followers, "You go in there, and after a while you start relating to the mahogany more than you do to the guy out in the mill."

The union bought the brand-new, thirteen-story high rise on Pittsburgh's Boulevard of the Allies in 1973, while thousands of western Pennsylvania steelworkers remained laid off. Five Gateway Center had diamond-shaped windows formed by crisscrossed beams, reminiscent of the U.S. Steel logo—the hypocycloid. With manicured walkways and a neat plaza funneling into a viaduct that took pedestrians into Pittsburgh's Signature Point Park, the message that USWA President I. W. Abel wanted to send was clear: Steelworkers had arrived.

The truth was as dusty and black as a Pittsburgh sunrise. The USWA was steeped in problems piled as high as its new tower.

There were four major unions in the 1970s—the USWA, the Teamsters, the United Mine Workers, and the United Auto Workers. The latter three gave their members—the rank and file—the right to vote on national contracts. When the president of those unions banged out a deal with the trucking, mine, and auto-manufacturing companies, the deal wasn't done until the members agreed to the terms of the contract. In exchange for the right to approve new agreements, the rank and file gave up the right to vote for their local reps. Those men—always men—were appointed by the union's national leaders, who were elected by all the union members. Basically, the rank and file were citizens who had the right to vote for president of the United States, but who also allowed the president to appoint their congressmen. The leadership of the Teamsters, UMW, and UAW held on to their power by putting strong-arms in charge of the locals. Their primary role was to get the membership to rubber-stamp contracts and to make sure that the president was reelected for national office at massive convention gatherings. With that kind of power, these union bosses could walk into a negotiation with a sledgehammer in hand—a strike threat that would completely shut down an industry.

That wasn't the case for the United Steelworkers of America. The steelworkers did not have rank-and-file ratification power. Contracts were approved in an executive committee, made up of district leaders—who repped hundreds of locals in specific areas of the country—and a select number of USWA presidential appointments called staff reps. It was actually easier to consolidate power in this system. The USWA president only had to find allies in a handful of district presidents to push his agenda.

With his weathered leather coat, blue khakis, and work shirt, thirty-five-year-old Ed Sadlowski came from Chicago to Pittsburgh in the spring of 1974 to turn over the desks and start a revolution. He was attending his first meeting as District 31 president, a position he earned the hard way. Only a year earlier, Sadlowski lost his district election to I. W. Abel's man in Chicago, Sam Evett. But after Evett was exposed for giving kickbacks and payoffs to union members counting the ballots, the U.S. Justice Department forced the USWA to hold another election. In November 1973, with government agents at each union hall observing the counts, Sadlowski won by a 2–1 margin.

Sadlowski thought I. W. Abel and his bureaucrats dressed in their Saks Fifth Avenue best were shafting the rank and file. To Sadlowski and his followers, Abel had gotten into bed with big steel and was complicit in men losing their jobs. The insurgents' case got stronger after Abel worked with the steel companies on a film in 1973 called *Where's Joe?* It was shown at every major steelworks. George Bogdanovich in *The Nation* magazine described the film best:

"Where's Joe? tries to frighten the American steelworker into thinking that 'Joe' lost his job because of competition from 'Hans' or 'Oda,' who, by outworking Joe, enabled German and Japanese companies to undersell their American competitors. 'They got to be kidding,' is the typical reaction of steelworkers, especially younger ones . . . It is hardly surprising that many young workers view the union bureaucrats as an extension of [steel company] management."

Like his Polish immigrant grandfather and father before him, Ed Sadlowski went straight into the mill when he came of age. An autodidact troubled by the working conditions at his South Chicago mill and with a family history of activism, Sadlowski became a force in his local union. He read up on the history of the American labor movement between shifts, and by twenty-one, he was elected shop steward. In 1964, at twenty-five, he was elected president of Local 65's 10,000 membership. He ran for the job on a tried-and-true platform—the differences between the guys in the blast furnace and the guys with their feet up on the desk at the union hall. Put a guy from the shop floor in power and watch things change. Physically, he was imposing. At a linebacker-solid 240-plus pounds, with wavy black hair and a granite chin, he had a faraway look in his eyes that seemed to see a better landscape than the one in front of him. He wore the same clothes and drank in the same bars as the men he represented. Sadlowski looked like the kind of guy who could take a punch and keep on coming. He was Dick Butkus in work boots.

In *Which Side Are You On?*, his memoir of organized labor, Thomas Geoghegan described Sadlowski's appeal: "[He] could say the word 'Boss' with fifty-five different nuances of contempt, and use just the right one for each occasion. . . . Sadlowski was the younger son who reminded them [the older workers] of their own fathers. . . . Yet he wasn't from the Stone Age. He was in *Rolling Stone.* He was sixties, and hip."

When Abel renegotiated the union's last contract with the steel companies in 1971, he committed to pursuing a no-strike policy. He believed that hedge buying would end if steel consumers were confident that steelworkers wouldn't strike. It would keep his men employed and, knowing there would be no strikes, would keep the companies that purchased steel from hedge buying in advance of a stoppage. No hedge buying meant more consistent production and, in theory, fewer layoffs.

Having read everything about legendary union leaders, Sadlowski railed against the no-strike clause. If his heroes hadn't had the power of the strike, there wouldn't be a union. Now he had the backing of his more than 100,000-member-strong District 31. He thought that mattered.

In Pittsburgh, though, Sadlowski's Chicago connections meant nothing. His battle cry "Steelworkers Fight Back!" made no sense to the staff reps at Five Gateway Center, and he had no way to reach out to the men working along the Monongahela. "I went on the executive board in December of 1974. There'd be votes of 28 to 1. We'd break for lunch and there'd be seven or eight tables in the lunchroom. I'd sit alone. I was ostracized," Sadlowski remembered.

He needed an ally who could get his message to the men on the shop floor. Like La Cosa Nostra, steelworkers were insular and suspicious of outsiders. They wouldn't give a guy the time of day without an introduction.

Pittsburgh-based USWA staff rep Pat Coyne found a kindred spirit in Eddie Sadlowski. Disillusioned by the Abel administration's deaf ear to the rank and file, he'd read the same labor history books as Sadlowski and thought the USWA was moving dramatically away from its roots. Born in 1929 and raised in Pittsburgh's Brookline neighborhood—on the south side of the Monongahela—Coyne had the connections Sadlowski needed.

At 6'3" and a hair under 300 pounds, Coyne could fill out a suit, but he wasn't very good at keeping his hands in his pockets. He had side stepped the mill himself as a football star at Pittsburgh's Central Catholic

High School and went to N.Y.U. on a scholarship. But when the university cancelled the football program, he was back in Pittsburgh for good.

The first thing he did was knock on a door twenty-eight steps above Oakland Avenue. The AOH (Ancient Order of Hibernians) clubhouse was where Pittsburgh's Irishmen went to make names for themselves. It was where favors and side deals were done. The only problem was getting through the door. The man who guarded it was Joey Diven, whom *Sports Illustrated* called "the greatest street fighter who ever lived." To get into the AOH, you needed a card. If you didn't have one, Diven wouldn't let you in. Seas of Irishman walked the three flights to take Joey on. One night, the legend goes, a guy walked up and asked Joey to let him in because he's Irish. Diven threw him down the stairs. The guy climbed back up again and said, "Really, I'm Irish." Diven threw him down again. The third time the guy walked up, Diven looked at him again and said, "You're right, you must be Irish." He let him in.

Pat Coyne and Joey Diven—who would one day bodyguard Art Rooney at Super Bowl IX in New Orleans—were cut from the same cloth. The Hibernians found work for Coyne at the Allegheny County Commissioners Office. He joined the Young Democrats of Pennsylvania and spent a lot of time with steelworkers at Joe Chiodo's pub in Homestead and the hole in the wall bars along Carson Street. He knew a lot of them from the high school gridiron—Pittsburgh's proving ground for future mill hunks. In 1962, when he was thirty-three, Coyne had never worked in a mill, but he still had the credibility and connections to walk into USWA President David McDonald's office and say, "Hire me."

McDonald did. He made Coyne a staff rep, someone from the national office who worked with the rank and file at their local union halls. Coyne was just the kind of muscle McDonald used to keep the membership in line. But Coyne, the son of a cop and nephew of a Pittsburgh ward boss, was an empathetic brute. From his father and his uncle, he'd seen all sides of power, the kind that comes from strength, the kind that comes from influence, and he had ideas about how it should be used. Once inside the USWA's "official family," he knew enough not to like the way McDonald wielded his.

Coyne supported Abel in his bid to oust McDonald in 1966. With Abel's hard-fought victory—Coyne was jumped by three McDonald men in a convention hallway and took a hard shot to the back of the head—Coyne expected a new militancy. Abel would go toe-to-toe with Big Steel. Instead, he felt like Abel took up where McDonald left off—private dinners to "lay the groundwork" for upcoming negotiations, U.S. Steel/USWA think-tank junkets to resorts, sharing planes and cars to lobby together in Washington.

Coyne stewed. But he'd had four kids by 1966. He called in the favor Abel owed him for his support in '66 and was transferred to USWA charity initiatives. Coyne proved a convincing fund-raiser and worked with an institution dedicated to children with brain injuries. But by 1974, Coyne was forty-five years old and itching for another fight.

When Ed Sadlowski took District 31 and was shunned at the USWA headquarters, Coyne reached out to the young troublemaker from Chicago. He pulled him out of the Gateway Center's lunchroom and took him into the union halls, ethnic lodges, bars, football games, and picnics where steelworkers congregated. Coyne put his own kids at the mill gates to hand out Sadlowski's FIGHT BACK! literature, daring the management to kick them out. With Coyne in Pittsburgh hitting the streets, the Sadlowski message began to grow roots. Patrick Stanton, a welder at J&L, complained to *The New York Times*, "All the union bosses talk about is productivity and partnership. The company gets the profits and we get the layoffs and the injuries, so where is the partnership?"

By January 1976 Pittsburgh was in a deep recession. While Sadlowski railed against the union bosses, Coyne was getting calls in the middle of the night from desperate workers threatening to take their lives. There were 270,000 steelworkers out of work, close to 100,000 from western Pennsylvania, more than half of the entire steel industry workforce. Laid-off workers from Clairton, Braddock, Homestead, the South Side, and

Aliquippa would show up at Coyne's house on Sundays to drink his booze, watch the Steelers game, and plot strategy.

At the end of the year, I. W. Abel provided them with an option they hadn't considered. The longtime union leader had decided to retire. The USWA would need a new president. Coyne had a good idea of who should run.

29

ART ROONEY JR. WAS IN HIS ROOSEVELT HOTEL OFFICE ONE morning in 1968. "I liked to call it the boiler room," Rooney says. He was always playing the part of the put-upon brother. And this day was no different. Dan and his father were making him meet with a sportswriter named Bill Nunn, who worked for the *Pittsburgh Courier*, the largest African-American newspaper in the country.

Every year, Nunn traveled across the United States covering black college football games for the paper. At the end of the season he put together a black college All-American team. It was a tradition that had been started by his father, Bill Sr., who was the paper's managing editor and good friends with the Chief. One afternoon Dan and Nunn ran into each other, two sons whose fathers were friends, and began a conversation. A writer from the *Courier* often hung around the Steelers offices at the Roosevelt, and Rooney asked Nunn why he never saw him there. "I told him about certain things I felt and things he wasn't aware of," says Nunn. "I told him how I put out this All-American team every year and got calls from some NFL teams about the players, but no one on the Steelers ever called."

After that, Dan told Art Jr. to pick Nunn's brain. Maybe there was talent the Steelers should be paying attention to. "At first, all we did was look at each other," Rooney says. "I was thinking, this black guy is getting a free job and he was thinking I'm just a rich white kid who couldn't get a job anywhere else."

But they were stuck in a room together. So they started talking. Nunn told Rooney about what he looked for in players he named to his

All-American team and how he put it together. He went to the biggest black college football game every week, anywhere in the country. On top of that he had an extensive network of coaches feeding him the names of players who were, for the most part, playing in places that weren't on an NFL scout's itinerary. "After twenty minutes of talking I was blown away," says Rooney. "I told my dad, 'We've got to hire this guy.'"

Nunn paid immediate dividends after joining the team full-time in 1969. He helped the Steelers find Blount, who was playing at Southern University, in 1970, and Ernie Holmes the next year and Joe Gilliam from Tennessee State in 1972. "I wasn't just a black college players scout," says Nunn. But the credibility he had with black college football coaches was now the Steelers' credibility.

In 1974, Nunn was with scouts from several teams making a swing through the Deep South. Scouts often traveled in packs, partly to share notes, partly to reassure each other that they weren't missing anything, and partly to figure out who their opponents liked. One rainy afternoon the group was at Alabama A&M scouting an all-conference receiver named John Stallworth. They had him run some pass-catching drills and then, on a slick field, timed him in the 40. His times were slow, too slow to keep anyone's interest. But Nunn believed that Stallworth had just had a bad day.

The next day, as the scout patrol left town, Nunn told the group he was feeling sick and was going to stay behind to rest. Then he snuck over to A&M, picked Stallworth up, and drove him to a high school field far from campus. Unlike the other scouts, he had seen Stallworth play several times and watched him run away from defensive backs with ease. He was convinced the receiver was special and he wanted to time Stallworth again, on a dry field, without anyone else around. He was much faster than the day before. "I found when I first started that nobody lied to any-body," Nunn says. "All these scouts shared information, and a lot of that is because everyone was afraid of making mistakes. Well, a part of doing the job is not sharing info with the Giants or Browns."

Nunn became so enamored with Stallworth that, when he received the player's game film from the A&M coaches, he ignored their request to pass it along to other teams when he was done watching. He kept it hidden in his office. As the draft neared, he had Noll convinced that Stallworth was a game-changer. But he was so sure of his subterfuge that he told Noll not to draft Stallworth in the second round, when the coach preferred, because he knew he'd be around in the fourth. Nunn was right. And his strategy helped shape the draft that compelled the Steelers to do the one thing Joe Greene worried his team never would: fulfill its potential.

The Steelers' first-round pick in that 1974 draft was Lynn Swann, the acrobatic receiver from USC who was the most prolific pass catcher in school history. Swann's mom had wanted a girl, thus the name, and she enrolled her son in ballet lessons, thus the twisting mid-air pirouettes he executed while catching a ball. Like Stallworth, scouts had clocked Swann in the 40 and been disappointed with his times. But Noll didn't care about stopwatches. He cared about what he saw on film—when judging football players, that was the only thing you could trust, and he simply couldn't believe that Swann wasn't faster and more graceful than anyone else playing.

In the second round, where Noll had been desperate to take Stallworth, he instead took a beanpole linebacker from Kent State named Jack Lambert. This was an Art Rooney Jr. special. Lambert was 6'5", 210 pounds, but he was as mean as a snake—and he looked just as nasty. Where his two front teeth had once been was a gap as big as a mouse hole. From inside his helmet he looked like a jack-o'-lantern.

The Steelers liked what they saw of Lambert on film. It wasn't his physicality that impressed them—at his size he actually looked lacking compared to other players—but it was his speed and instincts. He was as technically sound as any pro—his feet moved laterally, his hips stayed square to the line of scrimmage, and his shoulders were low when he tackled. These minor things, the steps more talented players let slide, helped him get where he was going a half step faster than anyone else.

When he exploded on a ball carrier or a receiver, the force didn't come from his lithe frame. It came from his being in perfect position on nearly every play.

What clinched the Steelers' decision to take him was what one of the scouts saw the day it rained—a drenching downpour—at a Kent State practice. The field was too muddy, so Kent State practiced on a nearby blacktop in light pads and at half speed. Well, almost half speed. On one play Lambert dove across the line to make a tackle, skidded on the pavement, and stood up with gravel embedded in his forearm from his wrist to his elbow. He looked at it, picked out the rocks, and went back to the huddle.

After choosing Stallworth in the fourth round, the Steelers picked up Wisconsin center Mike Webster in the fifth. Webster was no bigger than a linebacker—225 pounds, tops—but during the Senior Bowl that year he consistently knocked the defensive tackle lined up across from him—a highly rated prospect—in the opposite direction of the quarterback. Coaches like that. "He was just crushing it," Noll once said. "I thought to myself, if the guy he's playing is a first-rounder, what's Webster?"

Noll felt lucky to get him when he did.

30

ABOUT TWENTY-SIX MILES NORTH OF PITTSBURGH'S THREE-river triangle, Aliquippa, Pennsylvania, sits on the western edge of the Ohio River.

For more than a century, Aliquippa and the hundreds of acres of surrounding Woodlawn farms remained much as they always were—dense hillocks descending into lush valleys abutting the Ohio. But as the nineteenth century ticked into the twentieth, it became ground zero for a grand social experiment.

The late 1800s in the steel industry were marked by two massive changes: First, the richest industrialist in the world, Andrew Carnegie, sold his two thousand Carnegie Steel mills to the richest banker in the world, J. P. Morgan. Morgan then combined his new company with two other major steel producers he owned, Gary's Federal Steel and National Steel. Together, they were known as United States Steel, which became the largest corporation in the world and controlled 67 percent of the nation's steel-mill capacity. With so much work controlled by one company, steel workers from all over Pittsburgh—mostly immigrants, all long-suffering, doing dangerous work for menial pay, and finding few options for more gainful employment—began to rise up in defiance.

By 1900, Christian reform movements—inspired by Rev. George Hodges at Pittsburgh's Calvary Episcopal Church—that wanted to better the living and working conditions of laborers were gaining momentum, too. One Iron City steel magnate—and dedicated churchgoer—named B. F. Jones Jr., who ran the Jones and Laughlin mills, had difficulty facing fellow worshipers at Sunday service. J&L's South Side works hugged the Monongahela, and the shanties that climbed up nearby Mount Washington were deplorable. With such a small plot of land convenient to the mill, landowners gouged their tenants, making grown men and families share tiny rooms in unsanitary conditions. To make ends meet, a typical man and wife with at least one child would share a two-room apartment with up to twelve other "boarders." Each bed—stacked one above the other in bunks—was shared by two men. One man slept while the other man worked.

Jones reasoned that if he could somehow raise the standard of living for his workers—a cause that was becoming a prime focus of progressive politicians—while still keeping the laborer dependent on the company, he could keep J&L vital. He mapped out a "vision of the family," a self-contained city fully owned and run by J&L management. And soft-selling the takeover of an entire community as a "family" project proved remarkably effective.

What attracted Jones Jr. to the notion of a J&L town was not only the ability to manage the workers at the mill, but to oversee their private lives. Vices would be forbidden, and with the ties the company had to the county's Republican political machine, law and order would be sponsored and controlled by J&L. He had great faith that steel corporations would not only build the country's railroads and high-rises, they would build the next generation of hearty, healthy, law-abiding American laborers. Capitalism would make the new American man.

In 1905, as the radical Industrial Workers of the World union formed to unite all workers as a single concern, Jones and Laughlin acquired the land around Aliquippa Park and bought up other massive swaths of acreage around the town. He set aside seven miles of waterfront for the Aliquippa Steel Works. Its first tin mill began production in December 1910, and by 1916 rod, wire, nail, and blooming mills were on line.

The workforce would enter the Aliquippa Works through a gated viaduct under an Aliquippa & Southern Railroad embankment off of Franklin Avenue—the town's main street—which merged with Station

Street at the entrance to form a "Y." The funnel was both an efficient way to control shift changes and to monitor outside agitators. It was also a perfect metaphor for a steelworker's transition from home to hearth and back again. One side of the tunnel was work, the other the rewards of work—"the best possible place for a steelworker to raise a family," B. F. Jones Jr. called it.

The town was laid out under the auspices of the Woodlawn Land Company (a wholly owned subsidiary of Jones and Laughlin) which averaged building one house a day for several years on a series of twelve "plans." The houses were offered for sale only to J&L employees (at cost plus 6 percent interest), which removed any possibility of land speculation. By 1914, the majority of the community and much of the works were in place, and the draw of affordable housing with indoor plumbing, electricity, and in most cases central heating brought wave after wave of inner-city escapees, Southern black migrants, and immigrant settlers. With the blast furnaces, hearths, and finishing mills churning out thousands of tons of finished steel a day, the Aliquippa mills proved to be a crucial national resource.

Thirteen different ethnicities made up Aliquippa, with Slavs, Serbs, Italians, and Greeks making up the largest segments. Each of the twelve plans were defined by hills, one per plan. To get from one plan to the next required going down the neighborhood hill to Franklin Avenue, walking to the next plan's central street and then back up that plan's hill. Plan One and Plan Two were closest to the mill and housed mostly unskilled laborers from Serbia and Croatia. Plans Three, Four, and Five housed more senior workers made up of German, Irish, and Polish immigrants. Plan Six was the highest hill and the perfect distance away from the soot and ash. It housed the senior management of the plant and J&L's in-the-pocket politicians. Plans Seven, Eight, and Nine extended farther away from the plant and housed skilled workers from Northern Europe, usually former puddlers or sons of puddlers given skilled jobs. Plan Ten housed the company's midlevel foremen and supervisors. Plan Eleven was originally made up of

Italian immigrants from the Southern province of Patrica and later transitioned into a predominantly Southern black neighborhood. Plan Twelve was made up mostly of older generations of Irish. J&L's management kept a keen eye on the makeup of each plan so that there were clearly defined pockets for each ethnicity. Keeping the workers divided down cultural and ethnic lines maintained important prejudices between the workers. If they fought among each other—and they did—it was that much more difficult to organize. By 1920, Aliquippa's population increased from 3,140 to 15,426 and 40 percent of the arrivals were foreign-born, few with any formal education.

With upward of $20 million invested in Aliquippa, J&L hired a version of the "Coal and Iron Police," privately paid but recognized as law and order forces by the State of Pennsylvania.

Part of keeping Aliquippa clean meant keeping out the union. The only public access to the rank-and-file workers was at "the tunnel," and local police huddled at the entrance shift after shift. With their headquarters directly adjacent to the J&L's offices, and with its own shooting range directly behind, the message could not have been clearer to organizers who might enter town: You are not welcome here.

For the Aliquippa workers, though, economic dependency was much more effective than physical threats. Forty percent of the workers had mortgages with the Woodlawn Company. Their payments were taken directly out of their paychecks. And at any time the company could kick them out of their houses and repay them what they put in minus a 3 percent financing charge and cost for depreciation. The threat of eviction was enough for most workers to refuse any home visits from union officials. The company owned the stores, the houses, the electricity, the busses, the trolleys, the railroad, the water company, and for all intents and purposes the *Aliquippa Gazette*, which supplied ample pro-company, anti-union editorials every day. All company-owned services were deducted from worker's wages, making payday a practical farce, since credit purchases at the company store, mortgages, police fines, etc. would be deducted. Families would be left with just a few dollars a week. And those dollars were spent in the beer halls, bars, and gambling joints on the one patch of land J&L inadvertently neglected to purchase, a crooked lane known as McDonald Hollow, forcing the family to live off company credit again until the next payday.

By the 1930s, Jones and Laughlin Steel was the fourth-largest steel maker in the country, with just under 5 percent of the total market and a capitalization of $181 million. The Aliquippa Works alone, if cut out from J&L, ranked as the nation's sixth-largest steel producer, employing 10,000 of the town's 30,000 residents.

But to those who didn't live there, the area became known as "Little Siberia."

In February 1944, Wesley and Myrtle Dorsett boarded a train in North Carolina with their two young children—Juanita and Melvin— plus Myrtle's parents and their most valuable possessions in tow. Myrtle was pregnant with her third child and knew that tobacco farming would not put enough food on her growing family's table. The jobs were in the north. And like more than 1.5 million Southern blacks, the Dorsetts went to better their lot, where a black man could work for an honest wage and vote without harassment.

World War II left a large hole in the Aliquippa Works labor pool. Wesley joined the mill march and eventually moved the family into a shared two-story on the black side of the Plan Eleven hill. Each morning, afternoon, or evening (depending upon his shift assignment) Wesley would go through the tunnel and turn left, making his way to one of J&L's open-hearth furnaces that converted the nearby blast-furnace pig iron. Myrtle kept the house, and by 1959 had filled it with five more kids: Ernie, Tyrone, Keith, Anthony, and Sheree.

The first four Dorsett sons—Melvin, Ernie, Tyrone, and Keith— became street legends. Wild, fast, and fearless, the Dorsett boys held their own in Aliquippa's pool halls and back alleys. One neighborhood kid from Plan Eleven's Linmar Terrace had gone from a skinny, chicken-legged crybaby to a terror on Aliquippa's high school field. With his brush cut, cuffed jeans, and white T-shirt, Mike Ditka Jr., the son of a union leader for the A&S Railroad, was carving a fresh path out of town. As a senior starting end for the Fighting Quips in 1957, Ditka had offers from twenty colleges to come play football for them. Recruited by an assistant coach, Joe Paterno, Ditka agreed to go to Penn State, until the University of Pittsburgh relentlessly lobbied him to switch. Agreeing to automatically admit Ditka to dental school after he graduated sealed the deal. He ended up in the Pro Football Hall of Fame instead.

The Dorsetts played football, too, but not at Ditka's level. They masked their frustration with trash talk and left a legacy for their youngest brother that demanded a brio the young boy just didn't have. Wes Dorsett spent his rare off-hours chasing his first sons with a switch, meting out traditional mill-town punishment. But like most Aliquippa sons, they took their licks and wrote them off as a fair price to pay for their ganging, drinking, and hustling ways.

Anthony cowered in fear of his father's belt. He was a mama's boy comfortable in the kitchen at the hem of his mother's skirt and by her side at the Ebenezer African Methodist Episcopal Church. His big eyes continually scanning his environment for dangers, his father coined him "Hawk."

The Dorsetts weren't easy to catch. They could flat-out run faster than any other boy or man in Aliquippa, Pittsburgh, or western Pennsylvania. Hopewell High School football coach Richard "Butch" Ross, an Aliquippa-born son of a steelworker who parlayed football into a college education and a teacher's certificate, noticed. "The name Dorsett was synonymous with speed, with being a good athlete. There was a line of progression from Melvin, who was a track star, to Ernie, to Tyrone, to Keith. We kept our eyes on the line because we knew when we had a Dorsett, we had someone who could really run." A small number of Plan Eleven kids were bused into coach Ross's Hopewell School District (fifteen out of fifteen hundred students). Every Dorsett child made the short list.

Vince Lombardi once said, "Football is blocking and tackling. Everything else is mythology." While it's true that without the proper technique for blocking and tackling a team has little chance to succeed, the part of the game that decides an outcome can't be taught. The difference between two teams is often speed. It is the most important attribute an athlete can have, and it's as rare a quality as charisma. At every level of the game, the boys and men who carry the football have to be able to outrun the opposition.

For a while, the Dorsetts outran everyone and everything—their mother, their father, the street, school, the mill, and themselves. Ernie, ten years older than Anthony, used to pull him away from his mother's hearth and get in his face before he hit elementary school. "Hey, man, you ain't gonna be anything. Your brothers have got speed, why don't you be like us?" Then Melvin would join in and push the boy around the living room, forcing him to fight back. The kids on the block had no use for Anthony, either—they'd call out for his younger sister Sheree to play pickup football, ignoring him.

While he grew ever more fearful on the street and at home, Anthony understood the necessity of playing football. He went out for the Midget Football League Termites and made the team based on his last name alone. But he played little, and to compensate, he would drag his pants in the mud to make it look like he'd played four quarters. His brothers drilled him for the play-by-play of the game as soon as he got home. During street touch football games he struggled. "You can't even play the game. You're going to be the sorriest Dorsett of them all," his brother Ernie would say. Anthony steeled himself and committed to proving his worth in the only arena that mattered in Aliquippa, high school football. "I remember the first time I touched the football," Dorsett recalled. "It was on a kickoff return. I was so afraid of getting hit that I just took off like a rabbit. I ended up running seventy-five yards for a touchdown. After that, it was a snowball effect. Things began falling into place for me."

Anthony channeled his fear and found that his hawk eyes were invaluable as a running back. Later on he'd rely on this ability to see "flashes of color—sometimes it's just this feeling for everything that's happening around you, almost like an outside force."

The terror of the steel mill did not escape the boy either. Wes Dorsett, like many uneducated fathers who went back and forth through the tunnel, warned his youngest son about life in the mill. "Do something better, son. At the mill you go in, but you never know if you'll come out." Anthony got a look at the place firsthand. "Once I was sent down to the mill to get the keys to Dad's car. I was waiting at the gate when I saw this guy come walking toward me. He was filthy, covered with dust and a mask of grime, and it wasn't until he was right before me that I recognized him—it was my own father." Anthony would never step foot in the mill, refusing summer jobs throughout high school.

In January 1965, ten-year-old Anthony Dorsett, like every other kid in western Pennsylvania, heard about someone like him hitting the jackpot. The pride of Beaver Falls (one of Aliquippa's rival towns across the Ohio River) signed the biggest contract in the history of professional sports. Joe Namath, son of Babcock and Wilcox steelworker John Namath, agreed to a $400,000 deal with the American Football League's New York Jets. In just five years, a kid who quarterbacked the WPIAL (Western Pennsylvania Interscholastic Athletic League) Champion Beaver Falls Tigers and played on a national championship team at the University of Alabama had made it big. The game could not only keep you out of the mill, it could make you rich.

31

THE FRUSTRATION DUANE THOMAS FELT ABOUT HIS CON-
tract wasn't an isolated incident. Throughout the league, as the NFL's
influence increased, as TV revenue grew and owners got richer, players
vented. They wanted better pensions. They wanted to get paid a decent
wage for a preseason game. "When I was a rookie in 1969 I made $54 after
taxes for a preseason game," says Hanratty. "I remember when Joe Greene
got his check for a game he tore it up and threw it in the business manager's face."

But, mostly, they wanted unfettered free agency. And in the summer
of 1974, they decided to strike. On the picket lines, they yelled, "No freedom, no football!"

But striking, in Pittsburgh, while playing football for the Steelers,
was complicated. It was a union town, but one whose steelworkers were
losing jobs every day. And those people, largely fans of the Steelers, didn't
empathize with the striking players. "They wanted to know why we
weren't being loyal and going to play a game," says Rocky Bleier. "It wasn't
like we were working eight hours a day and spending forty years in the
mill. That's how fans felt—they didn't equate sports with work."

Bleier was a particularly favorite target of venting fans. After star-
ring as a captain at Notre Dame, he was drafted by the Steelers in 1968.
But compared to pro talent he was a slow, small running back who, from
all appearances, had no reason to be in the NFL. Some people thought he
had only made the team because he was charming and eloquent, or because the Chief had a soft spot for Catholic kids. But those feelings

changed when Bleier was drafted to fight in Vietnam after the 1968 season and it was assumed his career was over. No one knew when, or if, he'd come back. "I liked pro football," says Bleier. "I liked the status it gave me. I didn't want to give that up."

While on patrol with his unit in Vietnam he was caught in an ambush and shot in his left thigh. As he struggled to crawl away from the gunfight a grenade in his path went off. Shrapnel ripped through his right leg and foot. With both legs badly wounded and losing blood, and his unit pinned down, Bleier waited seven hours for the firefight to end and support to arrive. He says that his first thought while lying in his hospital bed was, "I want to play pro football."

Over the next several months Bleier struggled through several surgeries to repair his foot. But he was encouraged by constant postcards from the Chief, who would write, "We need you, Rock." But when he rejoined the team for training camp in 1970, he was slower than he had ever been. Hanratty, his buddy from Notre Dame, encouraged him to try law school. Instead, Bleier went through every two-a-day, limping off the field at the end of every practice, keeping the pain to himself. His comeback try was valiant, but he had no business playing professional football, and Noll cut him at the end of training camp.

The next day, Dan Rooney called Bleier and gave him a gift: They were going to put him on injured reserve, pay him a salary and let him continue rehabbing so he could try again next year. "I had an internal drive mechanism," says Bleier. "Everyone likes to be a hero and have someone look up to you. And I just didn't want to be like everyone else who was working a regular job."

Bleier had another operation to remove scar tissue from his foot and regain some flexibility. "Still, I tried to talk him into retiring," says former Steelers trainer Ralph Berlin. "If you saw the back of his leg, it looked like someone had been working on it with an axe. He just wouldn't take no for an answer. I used to go in at night and take his foot and massage and manipulate it to try to get more movement to it, and he wouldn't quit. Some nights we would be doing it and it would bring tears to his eyes."

Bleier tried everything to get back on the field. After visiting his family in Appleton, Wisconsin, he saw his father, who owned a bar, sitting in the lotus position in the living room. The yoga helped him relieve the pain in his hamstrings, which ached from the years he had spent standing on his feet and pouring pitchers. So Bleier started doing yoga. He progressed enough that, in 1971, Noll put him on the taxi squad. And in 1972 he made the roster, becoming a special-teams standout. "We had a stretching coach; they hired him in 1972," Bleier says. "They had never had that before. I went to him and asked how to get faster. And we had a weight-lifting coach in the early seventies. I worked with him. I really worked out—in 1973 I came back and weighed 218 pounds and had eighteen-inch biceps."

Occasionally, he used steroids. "I used it to get bigger, to make my muscles stronger so I could come back and play football," Bleier says. "It helped me get my weight back and overcome my injury. From a professional standpoint it made sense. I was asked to perform at a high level and it helped me do it longer. Why wouldn't I? If I can recuperate faster, that's what you're paying me to do."

He wasn't the only player on the team—or in pro football—who was using the performance-enhancing drugs. They had become popular in the early 1960s with the AFL's Chargers, after Sid Gillman hired a strength coach named Alvin Roy. Roy had worked with the U.S. Olympic team and first learned about the steroid Dianabol from the Russians. He introduced them to the Chargers—"it showed up on our training table in cereal bowls," one former player once told espn.com—and from there, word of the little pink pills spread throughout the game.

Jim Clack, a Steeler lineman during the early 1970s, admitted in *About Three Bricks Shy of a Load* that he used steroids to gain thirty pounds. "You knew guys were doing it. You heard them joking about it in the locker room," says Hanratty. "But it was so new, no one knew what the hell they were doing or putting in their bodies. I wish we did. I've seen too many guys die from steroids. Jim Clack died of a heart condition. But the obit doesn't say it was caused by steroids."

Even if the players knew what kind of damage steroids caused, they were athletes, in their prime, trying to be the best in the world. The future wasn't a consideration. "No one on our team ever asked me if I wanted any," says Russell. "And I'm glad. Because I can't say I wouldn't have tried if they did."

By 1973, Bleier, recovered and a full-fledged member of the team, had become a national hero, someone whose life story Hollywood producers wanted to—and eventually did—make movies out of.

But in the summer of 1974, as far as the fans were concerned, he was just an ingrate. As one of the Steelers player reps, he was the face of the strike. And Steelers backers took their frustration out on him. As much as any other player, it was his name they muttered when they vented about how disloyal the players were being. It left him conflicted, and concerned for his job. "I remember I came back from the picket line one night and there was a message that Mr. Rooney called," says Bleier. "It said he was going to call me back. I'm nervous, convinced I'm going to get cut. So he calls back, at eleven that night, and he said, 'Rocky, I called earlier because I was driving around and listening to a radio show and people were complaining about players and their loyalty and especially that Bleier kid and it bothered me. I called to let you know that what I did for you I would have done for any of my boys. If you believe in the strike, you be back in that picket line and we'll get this thing cleared up. I didn't want you to worry about what people are saying.'

"How can you not like that guy? It just made me want to play for him even more."

The Rooneys did their best to straddle the line between being the owners of an increasingly valuable NFL franchise and the proprietors of a family-run business. Dan negotiated with Bleier and the other player rep, Preston Pearson, to let Ernie Holmes cross the picket line so he could keep his routine and avoid any trouble. One afternoon, while Jack Ham and Gerry Mullins were picketing on a dusty road near training camp, across from a local cemetery, the Chief rode up to say hello. "Don't you boys worry about this," he told them. "We'll get it settled." Then he left them a six-pack of beer. Remembers Mullins, "The next day's story in the paper read 'The players striked until the beer was gone, then they got into their Porsches and drove home'."

Against the advice of his fellow owners, Dan Rooney stood before the picketers that August, with Bleier by his side, and told them there would be no hard feelings once all this had been worked out. Their approach compelled players to confide in the Rooneys. After Dan addressed the team, Joe Gilliam, the third-year quarterback, pulled the owner aside and told him, "Mr. Rooney, I have to cross. It's my only shot to make this team."

In another time, in another era—when black quarterbacks like Gilliam didn't have to purposely run slow 40s so they weren't switched to defensive back—Gilliam might have been leading the strike, not trying to break it. He had a slingshot arm and a release so fast that, when Steelers scouts examined it in slow motion on film compared to Bradshaw's and Hanratty's, his hand was the only one that remained blurry. He was 6'2" but barely weighed 190 pounds. Unlike Bradshaw, who seemed to crave contact, the lanky Gilliam used his build to glide through tacklers. While winning two black college national championships at Tennessee State, he picked up the nickname "Jefferson Street" Joe. Jefferson Street was the main drag running through State's campus in the black part of Nashville. And to Tennessee State fans, Gilliam was every bit as talented and charismatic as the "Broadway" Joe who guaranteed titles.

But it was hard to prove that with the Steelers as the third quarterback on the depth chart, unless there was no one else to throw the ball in practice. So Gilliam crossed the picket line, and immediately supplanted the striking Bradshaw as the Steelers starter.

32

BY THE TIME ANTHONY DORSETT REACHED HIGH SCHOOL IN 1969, Namath was the coolest guy in the world leading a rebel football league's team to play another homegrown hero—Johnny Unitas—in Super Bowl III. The future and past of professional football, forged in western Pennsylvania, was on national display.

And then a congenital defect agitated by the wild life brought down Anthony's oldest brother, Melvin. The little brother who had dedicated himself to living up to his older brother's taunts watched him collapse and die of a heart attack in the family home. "When Melvin died, I almost lost it," Dorsett once said. "I couldn't stay in the house, and I had to move in with my sister for a time. I was always a scared kind of kid, afraid of the dark, afraid of dead people. I always slept with a light on. And Melvin's death was something else. I remember that time to this day, how I'd sit on the swings out in the playground, swinging, swinging, thinking for long periods at a stretch."

Dorsett grew more insular, failing to find solace at home, at church, or in the community. Aliquippa is not a place for sensitive and fragile young men. Dorsett learned to channel his vulnerability, fear, and isolation into the only acceptable emotional currency available to men around Franklin Avenue—anger.

His speed took on an entirely new dimension. Five foot eleven and 130 pounds, he was incapable of physically hurting anyone on the field. So Dorsett developed a remarkable ability to humiliate the opposition with cuts, jukes, and misdirection, all turned on a dime with dazzling quickness and grace. When he hit the open field, no one could catch him.

He'd shake the ball behind him, taunting those trailing. While the beauty of his performances on the field masked his inner turmoil, his anger could not be suppressed off the field. He got into numerous fights at school and on the street. By the end of his junior year at Hopewell High School, his reputation as a Dorsett had come full circle. "I overheard some teachers talking about me: 'That kid will turn out to be just like his brothers. The wildness is there now, and the wine will be there later. He's got lots of athletic talent like his brothers, and he'll wind up just like them—nowhere,'" Dorsett remembered.

While he was a great draw and was heavily recruited by colleges around the country, Dorsett was not the prince of the city. He led Hopewell to wins over Aliquippa in both his junior and senior years and talked as much trash as he got at the Franklin Avenue pool hall. Dorsett was gifted, better than everyone else on a football field, and his contemporaries hated him for it. He had a shot to make it like Namath had, while they were destined to walk the tunnel. The criticism and undermining that sidetracked his four older brothers came down with even more force on Anthony.

After his senior year, in which he rushed for more than 1,200 yards in ten games with twenty-three touchdowns, Dorsett was courted by a number of major college football programs. But what stuck with him most were the recruiters and schools that criticized him. The Pittsburgh Steelers' starting halfback in 1972 was Preston Pearson. He came to Hopewell one Saturday to scout Dorsett for his alma mater, the University of Illinois. He reported that Dorsett was too small to make it as a major college running back. Notre Dame's report was even less flattering. "That Dorsett's just a skinny little kid from Aliquippa. He'll never make it as a major collegiate running back."

He packed it away with all of the things his brothers and neighbors had said to him. It forged his internal fear and insecurity into a potent cocktail. The more people he proved wrong and shut up, the better he would feel about himself. The very drive that made Dorsett a terror on the field alienated him from the rest of his teammates. Blocking was not for him. That was for the other guys. He just had to be himself—scan the field and dart—and the touchdowns and applause followed. His team could lose with him, but they couldn't win without him. Dorsett stood out and took on all comers and with each win he went further and further inside himself. He looked for critics and fought anyone he could find because he needed to. It kept him from thinking about getting hurt.

Dorsett expected to play for Joe Paterno at Penn State. The Nittany Lions were on their way to a 10-1 season and an invitation to the Sugar Bowl. Since Paterno had taken the reins at Penn State in 1966, the school had won 63 games and lost only 12. But when Dorsett visited State College, Paterno explained to him that he'd have to sit a year or play defense before being handed the ball. He was committed to his junior running back John Cappelletti, and there would be no room for him in the backfield until his sophomore year. Good-bye, Penn State.

Between recruiting trips, the eighteen-year-old Dorsett learned that his senior year dalliance, a girl from West Virginia who frequently visited an Aliquippa Plan Eleven neighbor, was pregnant. With a baby due the following September and a dependence on his mother, Myrtle, the only person he felt had his best interests in mind, Dorsett knew he couldn't move far away from Aliquippa. That left him one option. It turned out to be the perfect fit.

By 1973, the University of Pittsburgh football program was one of the worst in the NCAA. After finishing 1-10 in 1972, there were rumors that the university's president, Wesley Posvar, would recommend that the school drop out of the NCAA's Division I and deemphasize football. They weren't true. Instead, he recruited a head coach who had led a perennial doormat, Iowa State University, to back-to-back bowl games. The day after the 1972 Liberty Bowl, Johnny Majors flew to Pittsburgh and announced that he would accept the job as the Pitt Panthers' head football coach.

Majors brought with him a young assistant, Jackie Sherrill, who

Female fans flocked to Joe Namath no matter where he appeared. (AP Photo)

"Chuck came in and said, 'Some of you aren't good enough to play,'" remembers Dick Hoak "It was nothing personal, he was going to be honest, you either produced or you weren't going to be there." (AP Photo/Harry Cabluck)

The blast furnaces and rolling mills of the Homestead Steel Works, Pittsburgh (Photo by Hulton Archive/Getty Images)

The tapped blast furnace molten iron is tested for purity before moving to a Bessemer, open hearth, or basic oxygen furnace. (AP Photo/Ivan Sekretarev)

Molten iron from the blast furnace is poured from a massive transport ladle into an open hearth that burns away the impurities to form steel. (AP Photo)

Molten Steel from the open hearth is poured into ingot molds, cooled, and then sent to the rolling mills to be processed into steel product. (AP Photo/Elizabeth Dalziel, File)

Steelworkers storm the Carnegie Steel company during the Homestead Strike of 1892 that killed ten men (AP Photo)

NFL owners and coaches meet with NFL commissioner Bert Bell (center) in Pittsburgh in 1947. (Left to right, seated) Art Rooney, Pittsburgh Steelers; Tim Mara, New York Giants; Bert Bell; Curly Lambeau, Green Bay Packers; Fred Mandel Jr., Detroit Lions. (Left to right, standing) Dan Reeves, Los Angeles Rams; George Halas, Chicago Bears; Jack Mara, New York Giants; Roy Benningsen, Chicago Cardinals; George Preston Marshall, Washington Redskins; Al Ennis, Philadelphia Eagles; Ralph Brizzolara, Chicago Bears (AP Photo/Daniel P. Jacino)

The original American Football League owners: (left to right, front row) Robert Howsman, Denver; Max Winter, Minneapolis-St. Paul; Lamar Hunt, Dallas, the League's founder; and K. S. "Bud" Adams Jr., Houston; (left to right, back row) Barron Hilton, Los Angeles; Ralph C. Wilson Jr., Buffalo; and Harry Wismer, New York (AP Photo)

Pete Rozelle answering questions in New York on June 9, 1966, about the merger agreement between the National and American Football Leagues. At left is Tex Schramm, and at right, Lamar Hunt (AP Photo/John Duricka)

Joe Greene
(Focus On Sport)

Art Rooney (left) and his oldest son, Dan, in front of the Steelers draft board after they made Terry Bradshaw the number-one pick in the pro football draft on January 27, 1970 (AP Photo/Harry Cabluck)

Terry Bradshaw and Chuck Noll at a Pittsburgh news conference on February 13, 1970. Their relationship was destined to be strained. (AP Photo/Harry Cabluck)

Running back Franco Harris (number 32) warms up prior to the AFC Divisional Playoff Game on December 23, 1972, against the Oakland Raiders (Photo by Tony Tomsic/Getty Images)

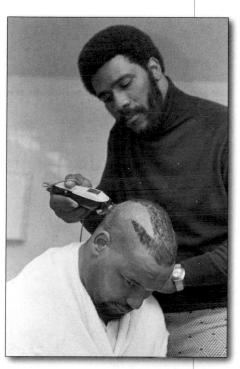

Joe Greene shaves the head of teammate Ernie Holmes (AP Photo)

Franco's Italian Army encouraging Harris in a 13-7 win over the Raiders in the 1972 AFC Divisional Playoff Game at Three Rivers Stadium (Photo by Ross Lewis/NFL Photos/Getty Images)

Cowboy coach Tom Landry (center) celebrates the new eleven-year contract he signed on February 5, 1964, in Dallas with team owner Clint Murchison Jr. (left) and general manager Tex Schramm (AP Photo/DMN)

Clint Murchison's game-changing Texas Stadium (Photo by Glenn James/NFL)

Dallas Cowboy running back Duane Thomas sits alone on the bleachers. He refused to pose for any pictures or be interviewed by sports writers. (AP Photo)

Bill Nunn and Chuck Noll share a joke during training camp at St. Vincent's College in Latrobe, Pennsylvania (Photo by George Gojkovich/Getty Images)

Andy Russell, Jack Lambert, and Jack Ham before Super Bowl IX (AP Photo/Jim Kerlin)

In 1969, Rocky Bleier returned from Vietnam. While in his hospital bed, Bleier received a note from Art Rooney that read, "Rock, the team's not doing well. We need you." (AP Photo)

By 1975, Bleier and Franco Harris were the NFL's premier running back tandem. (AP Photo/NFL Photos)

Jones and Laughlin Steel in Aliquippa (AP Photo/LTV Steel)

Tony Dorsett at Pitt (AP Photo/Harry Cabluck)

Ed Sadlowski on Chicago's 106th Street Bridge
(Courtesy of Southeast Chicago Historical Society)

Sadlowski supporters (Courtesy of Southeast Chicago Historical Society)

Sadlowski's USWA campaign poster
(Courtesy of Mary Jo Coyne)

Pat Coyne at Central Catholic in 1946
(Courtesy of Mary Jo Coyne)

Coyne and family, Christmas 1966 (Courtesy of Mary Jo Coyne)

Sadlowski's photo in *Penthouse* (Courtesy of Mary Jo Coyne)

Chiodo's Tavern on Homestead's Eighth Avenue. The building
was demolished in 2005. (Gerard Thurman)

Dan Rooney, Art Rooney, Chuck Noll, and Art Rooney Jr. pose with the
Steelers four Lombardi trophies in 1980 (AP Photo/NFL Photos)

would help sign his first recruiting class. They desperately needed Anthony Dorsett. Sherrill spent so much time at Hopewell High School schmoozing anyone and everyone who might be able to influence his prize recruit that the principal asked him to fill in one day as a substitute teacher. The night before NCAA letters of intent could be signed, Sherrill was rumored to have slept in his car outside the Dorsett house. The next day, Dorsett signed.

The freshman superstar arrived at preseason camp in August 1973 weighing 157 pounds. And he found immediate inspiration. "If this is the guy who's going to lead us to the promised land, then we're in trouble," Dorsett overhead an upperclassman in a pack of offensive linemen mutter. He took the first ball from scrimmage eighty yards for a touchdown. Majors ran alongside him slapping his hat on his thigh and screaming, "We've got an offense!" He made him the starting tailback after two practices.

At the beginning of his freshman season, Pitt's sports information director, Dean Billik, sat Dorsett on a bench and told him that they were going to change his name. He'd be Tony instead of Anthony. They wanted to distinguish him from Anthony Davis, star running back for the University of Southern California. They'd build a campaign around him as T.D.—"Touchdown" Tony Dorsett. Not wanting to rock the boat, he agreed. But he was as quick to take insult as ever. He'd been told his entire life that he would not amount to anything. Anthony Dorsett finally meant something, and now he was told his name wasn't good enough.

Dorsett was overwhelmed by campus life. He made little effort to make friends because he didn't really know how, even with guys on the team. On September 14, 1973, Anthony Dorsett Jr. was born to unwed mother Karen Casterlow in Weirton, West Virginia, while his namesake played his first college game. Tony Dorsett ran for 103 yards against the Georgia Bulldogs and Pitt tied the SEC power 10–10, shocking the city and the entire college football world. The media bore down on him.

When word spread of Dorsett's child and his decision not to marry his son's mother, he alienated every steelworker who had ever knocked someone up but did the right thing and married his girl and then walked into the J&L hiring office. Western PA and working-class tradition always held that a man stepped up when he got a girl pregnant. You were no longer free to do as you pleased. But Dorsett didn't see it that way. His best opportunity to support the mother and child was to achieve his professional goals—not marry a girl he wasn't committed to and abandon his God-given gifts to take a job at the steel mill. He wasn't going to ruin his life to please other people.

The pressure mounted. "Even with my success on the football field, there were more than a few times during my freshman year when I was so down that I felt like dropping out of college. The limelight, the demands on me, being a part of everything and at the same time apart from everything—all of those things weighed heavily on me . . . I [have] to be around people that I know and trust." He went back to Aliquippa, again and again, until his mother told him enough. "If you quit, son, you'll break my heart."

Johnny Majors gained Dorsett's trust and Jackie Sherrill made sure he would want for nothing, often arranging private parties on Mount Washington for Dorsett's small cadre of friends. Tony lit up Notre Dame for 209 yards on 29 carries on his way to a 1,686-yard season, an NCAA freshman rushing record, and made consensus All-America. Pitt went to its first bowl game in eighteen years and finished the season 6-5-1. Majors was named NCAA Coach of the Year, but there was little doubt about who had turned the team around.

The 1974 season would test Dorsett's resolve. He was speared, eye-gouged, cheap-shotted, and harassed all year long, but he pushed through, played hurt, and racked up another thousand-yard season. His ego grew. Playing Army during his junior season, he caught a fifty-one-yard touchdown pass from Pitt quarterback Matt Cavanaugh, stopped at the goal line and held out the ball toward the Army defenders. He shook it at them as they approached, stepped over the line for the score and then tossed the ball at them. His showboating did not endear him to his hometown crowd. Pittsburghers loved to watch him play, but they had no use for his taunting. He'd become bigger than the team, and many resented the way he put himself in the spotlight.

At the end of his junior year, he expected to win the Heisman Trophy. Instead, when Ohio State's Archie Griffin was selected for a record second year in a row, Dorsett had no reservations about voicing his opinion. "I had outrushed him in total yards. And with all the other things I had accomplished, I was more deserving of the award than he was." Dorsett had the audacity to break western PA football-player code and speak about his own accomplishments above the team. Even Joe Namath spoke as part of a "we," not an "I." Dorsett gave no credence to the oft-repeated mantra of head coaches from peewee to pro: "There's no 'I' in team." If it were all team, why was he the lightning rod for media attention?

Pitt had steadily improved from 6-5-1 to 7-4 and 8-4 in his first three years, and Johnny Majors let his star speak and do as he pleased.

When asked about Archie Griffin's career rushing record of 5,177 yards, Dorsett calmly predicted that he'd finish his college career with at least 6,000, an unheard-of milestone. He became the go-to guy for headlines. Dorsett also started taking every gratuity and freebie offered, even taking a page from Namath when he accepted a raccoon coat from a Pittsburgh furrier. "The media made a big deal out of it," Dorsett said. "They thought it was too much for a college senior to be going around dressed in an expensive raccoon coat while the other guys on the team were wearing cloth or something. Hell, fur coat or not, I couldn't hide anywhere. Besides, the coat kept me nice and warm."

Dorsett's senior year was everything he had promised, and more. He'd adopted the habit of wearing tear-away jerseys—which were so effective that they were banned in 1979—so that opposing defenses couldn't grab him in desperation and pull him down as he ran past them. He'd go through box after box, game after game, leaving the indelible image of a man who could not be taken down.

The first game that season was against Notre Dame, which ABC had moved from the middle of the season. "As far as people tuning in to see Pitt versus Notre Dame, it was probably people tuning in to see Notre Dame play Tony," said Matt Cavanaugh, who knew that Dorsett had a bull's-eye on his back. He had ripped apart Notre Dame every one of his years at Pitt, rushing for an astronomical 303 yards the year before.

But Dorsett delivered another masterpiece, 181 yards in a 31–10 rout at South Bend. The Pitt Panthers finished the regular season with a domination of Joe Paterno's Nittany Lions, 24–7. Dorsett's guarantee of 6,000-plus yards in his college career was icing on the cake. He finished with 6,082 and picked up the Heisman Trophy. On January 1, 1977, Pitt blew out Georgia in the Sugar Bowl 27–3 to win the national championship with a perfect 12–0 record.

Tony Dorsett had backed up every claim he'd made.

33

THE STEELERS SPENT EVERY PRESEASON PRACTICING AT ST. Vincent's College in Latrobe, an hour east of Pittsburgh. But it might as well have been a century away. Nestled in the rolling Laurel Highlands, the school's steeple-topped buildings and campus full of Benedictine monks was far from the steel and dust the players were used to. It was the perfect place to bring a team together. Especially one being ripped apart. With the veterans picketing, rookies took every snap. They got one-on-one coaching and learned to play in the NFL at their own speed—first a walk and then a run. "We got an opportunity to show what we could do," says former tight end Randy Grossman, who signed with the team as an undrafted rookie that year. "My reality check came before the veterans came in, against a defensive back from BU who was a rookie. We were running a drill and I ran a really good pattern and he is all over me and the lightbulb went off: What I did to be good was not good enough anymore."

Of course, some rooks were more ready than others. After he was drafted, Jack Lambert spent every Saturday until training camp driving from his home in Ohio to Pittsburgh—two and a half hours each way—for film sessions with his new coaches. And on the first day of camp, for Noll's beloved Oklahoma drill, he put his tenacious but spindly middle linebacker against his undersized, pissed-off center, Mike Webster. "First set of plays, Bam! Lambert gets knocked on his ass," Art Rooney once said. "They lined up again and Wham! Lambert goes down again." Seconds later the two ended up in a fight. In fact, nearly every time Lambert lined up in the Oklahoma drill it ended with him winning or him fighting. "His attitude and his style, it was real," says Russell. "He was legitimately a tough guy and the way he exploded was genuine."

Russell already knew about Lambert's social skills. They had met at a Steelers off-season banquet, held after one of the days Lambert spent watching film. Russell, who worked as a banker during the off-season, arrived in a pinstriped suit. Lambert had blond hair hanging to his shoulders. After Russell introduced himself he remembered, "Lambert staring at me hard, without smiling, shaking my hand with a powerful grip, as though I was the rookie and he was the veteran." It didn't take long for the old-timers to learn this about Lambert once they abandoned the strike and reported to camp in mid-August. They were feeling frisky, having ended their strike after nearly six weeks without a resolution. Free agency would continue to be a battle they'd fight for years. But they still wanted penance from the rookies for the pickets they'd carried on their behalf and, in the grand tradition of training camp, one of them tried to make Lambert sing the Kent State fight song. His response was simply: "Kiss my ass—I'm not singing anything."

No one asked again.

It helped that on this team, there was very little divide. It was as Noll had intended when he set up the locker room: The offense and the defense came together as one. They played poker together every Tuesday night, usually at Harris's house. Frenchy Fuqua, the flamboyant running back who once wore platform shoes with goldfish in the heels, showed up. So did Greene, who started the game his rookie year. Gerry "Moon" Mullins, the offensive tackle, was usually there. Even Bradshaw, who kept to himself more and more, played a hand or two every once in a while. "It was a nice place for camaraderie," says Greene. "We were all bad. Frenchy and Franco never folded. Frenchy bet into the blind without even seeing his cards. Moon Mullins was the most consistent player. Lynn Swann lost every week. He wanted to win, sure, but that wasn't going to keep him from coming."

"Stallworth came every week, too, but he never played," says Mullins. "He just showed up with a bucket of Kentucky Fried Chicken and drank the beer."

Drinking helped lubricate the bonding process. After games, Three Rivers locker-room attendants left a garbage can filled with beer and ice in the sauna next to the showers. Still dressed in their pants and socks, players popped open a beer, set the steam on high, and rehashed everything that had just happened. "That period of time was just our time, no coaches," says Bleier. "And that helped pull the team together because you could bitch at one another."

But the beer bonding started during training camp, when veterans took the rookies out for chugging contests. The rooks had relay races, head-to-head, winner advances, loser sits. One year Bradshaw was cheering on Gilliam and Gilliam puked in Bradshaw's face. Inevitably, the rookie winners, one from offense and one from defense, had to face the veteran champs, who were always Holmes and Ray Mansfield. That's when the contest ended.

Mansfield and Russell, the two holdovers from the pre–Chuck Noll era, set the social tone for those teams. They were a decade older than a lot of the young stars who were starting to dominate. But their m.o. wasn't to haze, it was to adopt and teach. Mansfield earned the players' respect because he was so tough, so old school. "He regarded training camp as a place to get in shape, not to come to already in shape," says Wagner. "He had this willpower and big heart—you could see he was hurting, but he wasn't going to let his body succumb to fatigue and stress."

Russell, meanwhile, was still making Pro Bowls after a decade in the league. Talent follows talent. And from the beginning, when players saw he had bought into Noll's plans without complaint, they followed his lead. "He was the first guy I can recall during Chuck's time that provided leadership," says Greene. "He interpreted what Chuck said in meetings and would always come in after meetings and explain what he meant. He was also so good with the press—sometimes we would read his quotes in the paper to figure out what Chuck was saying."

In Noll, the players had a constant focal point of amusement, in the way employees rally around the ticks and mannerisms of the man who controls their fate. His axioms became their axioms, what they repeated at the bars when they were blowing off steam. If a guy was constantly screwing up in games, they'd sit around and tell him, "It may be time for your life's work," a Noll favorite when he was cutting a player. A lack of physical play earned this rip, in a stoic voice, "You are not winning the battle of the hitting." Poor performance in practice was followed later that night by, "You know what the problem is? The problem is execution—you are not executing."

But mostly, they laughed about his flailing attempts at motivation. Because while he could be so eloquent when explaining the details of the trap and parried so well with the press, he was utterly lost when trying to lift the team with his words. He always claimed he didn't want players he had to inspire, but professionals who inspired themselves. That may have been a ruse. "He would start out telling a story about two squirrels," says Bleier. "And he'd say, 'Okay, there were two squirrels, one lived high in the tree in the branches, and one lived near the ground. And so you guys have to know to work together and play hard and do what we planned. Good practice.' We'd look around and be like, what happened to the squirrels? But he never missed a beat, he didn't stutter or stop or apologize. He just said, 'You know what needs to be done.' That was it."

Says Grossman: "He was the kid who would tell a joke and at the end have to say, 'You get it, you get it?'"

No one ever did. But they picked up on almost everything else Noll said.

34

THE CONTROVERSY BY THE END OF STEELERS CAMP IN 1974 wasn't Lambert's defiance toward the veterans. Or residue from the failed strike. What had everyone so surprised was that, even though the veterans had returned to camp a month before the season began, Joe Gilliam remained the Steelers' starting quarterback. He had been perfect that preseason, literally, leading the Steelers to a 6-0 exhibition record. His passes were crisp and confident, his reads accurate. "Jefferson Street" Joe walked through camp as though he were taking a Sunday stroll, straight past Terry Bradshaw on the depth chart.

And that first game he played like he belonged, completing 17 of 31 passes for 257 yards, including a sweet, rainbow of a bomb to Lynn Swann that went for a fifty-four-yard touchdown, in a 30–0 win over the Colts. Noll, who let his quarterbacks call their own plays, tried to ignore the thirty-one passes. Instead, he focused on the Steelers' first shutout since 1972.

But in the next game, a 35–35 tie with the Broncos, Gilliam threw the ball fifty times. That was twelve more than the any Steelers quarterback had thrown in the first two games combined the season before. While Gilliam was being hailed as the league's greatest new gunslinger—he was *Sports Illustrated*'s cover man after the Colts game—Noll was quietly stewing. Gilliam was most comfortable in chaos, when the game played out like pinball, with the ball careening around at laser speed and him reacting. He had a zest for throwing the ball, and his was as pretty a ball as there was in the NFL. But he also played with the same desperation that forced him to cross the line. Being a third-stringer, being a black quarterback, and being Joe Gilliam and not Joe Namath all conspired against his better nature. And his freelancing—throwing from his shoulder, throwing with both feet in the air—defied the carefully calibrated plans that Noll had established. He had tailored his game plan, and his team, not just to his philosophies, but to the rules established by the NFL. The way to win was to run, not to gun.

But Gilliam consistently brushed him off when Noll asked for running plays. The third game of the season was against Oakland. And this time the Steelers were shut out, 17–0, their first goose-egg loss in ten seasons. By now, the word was out on Gilliam. There'd be no running game when he was calling the plays. Against the Raiders he completed just 8 of 31 passes. Several times on third and short he ignored Harris in the backfield and tried to throw into the teeth of the Raiders D. At one point Noll told Bradshaw to start warming up and, when he did, fans started cheering and chanting, "We want Bradshaw!" No one in Pittsburgh had said that since 1970.

But Noll didn't pull the trigger. Instead, he gave Gilliam more time to develop the talent that was obviously there. In return there was only frustration. Two more picks in a nail-biter win against the Oilers. The next week he threw twenty-three incompletions in a win against the Chiefs, and the week after that he went just 5 for 18 for sixty-six yards in a 20–16 squeaker over the Browns.

The Steelers were now 4-1-1 to start the year. But the quarterback situation had turned ugly. Bradshaw asked to be traded and practically went into hiding. He didn't go to restaurants or read the newspaper, for fear of what he'd read. "He was going home, being alone, staying in his apartment," remembers Greene.

Meanwhile, Gilliam received death threats. It wasn't just about who was the better player, Gilliam or Bradshaw. The underlying issue was always the color of Gilliam's skin. When he appeared on the cover of *Sports Illustrated* after that season-opening win against the Colts, Gilliam wasn't just tagged as the Steelers quarterback. He was "Pittsburgh's Black Quarterback." The death threats he received weren't because he was playing badly; they were because he was black and playing badly. While Noll didn't set out to be a groundbreaking coach, he had inadvertently become one. Gilliam was the first black quarterback to win an opening-day start. And Noll had to consider the consequences of benching a black quarterback who had won four of his first six games for a white one most people knew he didn't trust.

Everyone seemed to have an opinion. Dwight White openly backed Gilliam. John Henry Johnson, a Hall of Fame Steeler running back, lobbied in the *Courier* for Hanratty. Joe Greene, who had become close with Bradshaw during the players' strike, wanted his fellow number-one pick. "Bradshaw was really struggling with all this," says Joe Gordon, the Steelers' PR man at the time. "It was Joe who took him under his wing, took him to dinner, said everything would be okay."

"I didn't think about it as anything other than Terry gave us the best chance to win," says Greene. "The controversy was in the air, it was on the airwaves, there was madness. But there wasn't any in the locker room."

"White guys loved black guys, black guys loved white guys," says Hanratty. "Swann and I would bet on USC and Notre Dame. We all truly liked each other. If someone had a party, everyone showed. Back then everyone was poor, so color meant nothing on our team. Joe Gilliam was talking about how poor he was and his dad was a coach. My dad had W2s that had $2,500 for the year."

Before that seventh game of the season, against the Falcons, Noll named Bradshaw his starting quarterback.

His reign lasted three games, at which point Noll, who could tolerate Joe Greene throwing a ball into the stands during a game, could no longer tolerate Bradshaw. Despite winning two of those three starts, Bradshaw was replaced by Hanratty, who promptly went 5 for 15 with three interceptions in his one start. Afterward, even Noll recognized the folly of his ways and told reporters, "I just wish one of them would take the bull by the horns and win the job."

It wasn't until the eleventh game of the year, a 28–7 win over the Saints in New Orleans, the site of that year's Super Bowl, that the team's lineup was set. Bradshaw didn't win the job, but he would be the quarterback. And the next game, he promptly led the Steelers to a disappointing home loss to Houston. That week, Greene was so upset he held a players-only meeting and told his teammates that if they didn't win the Super Bowl, he was quitting. Then, for emphasis, he grabbed all the stuff from his locker, packed it in a bag and walked to the parking lot. "But, really, what I was thinking was, Man, I hope someone comes to get me," Greene says.

You'd think, with all the turmoil and handwringing, that this was a team in a death spiral. But in fact, the Oilers loss was only their third of the season. The Steelers were actually on their way to clinching the AFC Central.

The Steelers had a drill they ran during every practice. The first-string quarterback, running backs, and offensive line lined up against the defensive line, linebackers, and secondary. The Steelers defense would run the opponent's scheme against their starting offense. And then the offense would run the opponent's plays against the defense. But in the last five minutes of every practice, Perles, the defensive line coach, had Greene, White, Holmes, and Greenwood line up in what he called a Stunt 4-3. "George would put it out there and say, 'Dick, try and beat it,'" says Hoak. "He'd say, 'I don't care what you call or what you do, try and beat it.' So we tried to beat it and see what would work against it. There wasn't a whole lot, but every once in a while we would come up with something that would gash some yards on it. So George would go back in and later that night he would tinker around with it."

The Steelers defense had been dominant that year, at times carrying the offense while it worked through its identity issues. But no one thought that would be enough during the playoffs. Heading into the postseason's first-round matchup, in Three Rivers against the league's best running back, O. J. Simpson, and the Buffalo Bills, *Sports Illustrated* wrote that the Steelers were the only playoff team without a quarterback and predicted they'd lose.

This is when Perles unveiled his new defense. In most defensive alignments the linemen either set up in the space between offensive blockers or go head-to-head. Either way, the center was almost always left open. The theory for this kind of strategy was simple: It forced the offensive blockers to commit to a defensive player, making it more difficult for guards to pull or tackles to trap, unless those players were exceptionally fast. It also meant that linebackers had an easier path to the ball carrier, since the offensive linemen were occupied by their defensive counterparts. It was bland, but historically effective.

Perles flipped it on its head.

Holmes and Greene, the Steeler tackles, were not only exceptionally big but also remarkably fast. Their reaction time off the ball usually beat the blockers they faced. So he had them both line up in the gaps between the center and the guards on either side. Instead of waiting for the offensive line to attack them, they attacked the offensive line, and forced the guards to double team one of them with the center. To make matters worse, Greene lined up at an angle, making it more difficult for blockers to find something to grab on to, and Holmes added a stunt, meaning sometimes he'd slide over and dip behind Greene as he was occupied. Originally this was designed to be a pass-rushing scheme. Either Greene and Holmes would use their speed to split the blockers and have a shortened path to the quarterback, or they'd be double-teamed, leaving the defensive ends White and Greenwood in one-on-one situations.

But instead, it became the definition of a Steel Curtain against the run. The alignment plugged the middle on every down. One of them was always there, blowing up the point of attack. It also made it nearly impossible for guards to pull, since it left either Holmes or Green unblocked at the snap, giving them an unabated route to the running back. It was a simple yet ingenious adjustment by Perles, like slicing bread. The only option available to the offense was a wide sweep. Against the Steelers, whom Noll had built for speed, that was not viable. "Joe set the tone for us in that stunt 4-3," says Jack Ham. "He wouldn't get sacks but he bought into it and that was a domino effect. He took a beating in that stunt turned toward the center because he had to be double-teamed, but it was our main defense."

That afternoon, O. J. Simpson rushed for just forty-nine yards, and the Steelers won 32–14. Leaving the stadium that day, Joe Greene's wife said to him, "If you can hold O. J. Simpson under fifty yards, nothing can stop you now."

35

THE HEDGE BUYING THAT I. W. ABEL FEARED AND TRIED TO stop would eventually wipe out western Pennsylvania's workforce.

Steelworkers slaved night and day, working overtime and double shifts to grind out as much finished product as possible, meeting the heightened demand from steel-dependent manufacturers prior to new union contract negotiations. But there was a funeral pall in every mill, on every shift. The workers knew that as soon as Abel announced a deal with Big Steel, at least a quarter of them would be laid off. The cycle was always the same: Demand for steel plummeted, the older generation got a big pay raise and the young guys were sent packing until demand came back. They wouldn't be recalled for months, sometimes even a year.

Like squirrels storing nuts in the fall, the workers stashed as much cash in their bank accounts as they could during the hedge season and prepared for the inevitable.

At least the timing wasn't bad. Contracts were always up in August, which meant layoffs came in the fall. And that meant tens of thousands of rabid Steelers fans had nothing to do from September to January but loaf in union halls and old-time Pittsburgh joints like Joe Chiodo's tavern in Homestead. Chiodo's was on Main Street, not far from the gates of the Homestead works. The specialty of the house was the "mystery meat sandwich," which changed daily according to what Chiodo could get cheap in the strip district, Pittsburgh's wholesale clearinghouse for meat and produce. Hung from the tavern's rafters was an ancient collection of brassieres, along with a hodgepodge of unique Pittsburgh artifacts.

A rite of passage for a Pittsburgh son was to walk into Chiodo's with his father. The old man would order two and two (two drafts and two sandwiches) and the bartender would wink at the dad and tell the boy what each piece of garbage on the rafters meant. The stories were mostly about football players—Steelers like Johnny "Blood" McNally, Bobby Layne, and Ernie Stautner, some Pitt Panthers like Mike Ditka and coach Jock Southerland and a handful of high school stars—Johnny Unitas of St. Justin's, Dan Rooney at North Catholic, and big Pat Coyne at Central Catholic. Around 1973, there were rumblings from regulars to take down Stautner's and Ditka's pictures. Stautner was the defensive coordinator for Tom Landry's Doomsday Defense in Dallas, and Ditka was the Cowboys' receiver coach. But Joe Chiodo would have none of it. Once on the wall, you were there for good.

Joe Chiodo loved Art Rooney and his Steelers as much as he loved steelworkers. He used to explain to anyone who would listen, "When my father died, Mr. Rooney came to the wake. Can you imagine a guy like Art Rooney paying his respects to a poor immigrant who could barely speak English?" Chiodo loved Rooney's team so much that he revived a tradition started by another tavern owner in the forties: Owney McManus's "Ham and Cabbage" runs. McManus was a close friend of Art Rooney's from their boxing days. He'd load a carful of his patrons onto the same train as Rooney's Steelers when they played on the road. The boondoggles caught on and were named after the specialty of McManus's tavern, "Ham and Cabbage."

Chiodo began his own runs to Steeler games in the sixties, filling cars and buses with steelworkers looking for an excuse to go on a weekend bender. One Sunday, the gang made the short trip to Pitt Stadium together. It was a typical Pittsburgh day, the sky pouring down a mixture of rain, ash, and soot onto every miserable soul who chose to step outside. By the beginning of the second half, only the well-oiled ticket holders remained. The Steelers were getting creamed. Chiodo's gang took cover under the press-box overhang, sighing with each blown play. When one of them said "Fuck the Steelers" it wasn't long before most of them joined in.

Chiodo asked them to stop. He knew Art Rooney and his family sat in the press box. The steelworkers ignored him and added another line to the chant: "Fuck the Steelers . . . Fuck the Rooneys!"

Chiodo lunged for the biggest loudmouth, but the giant had a much longer reach. He grabbed Chiodo by the throat and wouldn't let go. The rest of the group came to their senses and pulled the leviathan off of Chiodo. But Chiodo's tenacity had helped him make his point: The Rooney family never heard "Fuck the Rooneys" from a steelworker again.

In the early seventies, Chiodo's buses were joined by tens and sometimes hundreds of others on the road. And when a home game was blacked out on TV because Three Rivers wasn't sold out, out-of-work steelworkers too poor to buy tickets would split cheap motel rooms in East Liverpool, Ohio, and Meadville, Pennsylvania. Any town outside the seventy-five-mile blackout radius. Those who couldn't afford even that trip wound up in American Legion or VFW halls, appliance stores, or anyplace that had a television. Some entrepreneurial families in the boonies even rented out places in their living rooms to Steeler Nation.

From road game to road game, laid-off hard hats chanting "Pittsburgh's going to the Super Bowl . . . we've got a feeling," became evangelists. Their faith sustained them.

36

THE DAY BEFORE THE STEELERS BEAT THE BILLS, THE RAIDERS had upset the Dolphins in Miami's bid to repeat as Super Bowl champs. The game changed leads several times, including three times with between five and two minutes remaining. Then with two minutes left and trailing by five, Ken Stabler drove the Raiders down the field. With thirty-five seconds left from the Dolphins eight-yard line, the Snake dropped back and looked right. No one was open, so he scrambled left. As a Dolphin tackler grabbed both of Stabler's shoetops from behind and he fell to the ground, the quarterback lofted the ball into the end zone. Between three Dolphins, the Raiders came down with the ball—and the last-second win. Afterward, in the heat of the moment, John Madden said, "When the best plays the best, anything can happen."

Madden wasn't the only one who acted as if the Super Bowl had just been played. Nearly every newspaper in the country wrote about that second-round playoff game as though the rest of the season were a foregone conclusion.

Chuck Noll disagreed. And that Tuesday, addressing his team for the first time since their win over the Bills, he let them know. "He didn't raise his voice, but his voice changed," Greene told NFL Films. "And he said, 'The best team in the NFL didn't play the other day, and the Super Bowl wasn't played the other day. It's being played in two weeks. And the best team in the NFL is sitting here in this room.'"

"Joe Greene was sitting next to me," Russell said to NFL Films. "He stood out of his desk chair, and it was almost stuck to his legs—the whole thing was turned sideways, because it's a small school desk—and he looked like he was ready to play right there."

The animus between the Raiders and Steelers was fierce. They had knocked each other out of the playoffs the previous two seasons, and split two regular-season games. The Raiders were still bitter about the Immaculate Reception. One game, the Steelers players complained that the Raiders were greased up. L. C. Greenwood talked about how they were constantly trying to clip him. After Pittsburgh was shut out in Oakland in the second game of 1974, the Raiders cornerbacks taunted the Steelers and pointed to the scoreboard. "It was a blood feud," Lynn Swann once said. "We disliked the Raiders. We had no respect for them."

It showed, even before the game began. While lounging in the hallway outside his locker room waiting to get taped, L. C. Greenwood watched the Vikings and the Rams in the NFC Championship, which was played before the Raiders-Steelers game. A Raider walked by and said, "Hey L.C., what are you watching?"

Greenwood responded: "Just waiting to see who we're going to play in the Super Bowl."

That week in practice, Greenwood, Greene, and White goaded Ernie Holmes every day, telling him how Gene Upshaw, the Raiders All-Pro guard, was going to make him look foolish. By the time the game started, Holmes—surrounded by black flag–waving Raider fans—couldn't wait to butt his head into a Raiders helmet. As the Steelers lined up on defense for the first time, Holmes started yelling to Upshaw, who was still in the Raiders huddle and had his back to him. "Gene, Gene . . . Hey, Eugene!" Holmes screamed. When Upshaw finally turned around, Holmes said, just loud enough to be heard, "I'm going to kick your ass."

For most of the game, that wasn't the case. It was 3–0 Oakland after one, 3–3 at the half and 10–3 Oakland after three quarters. But the Stunt 4-3 was wearing down the Raiders offense, keeping the score close until the Steelers could make a game of it. In the fourth, they finally did. Down a touchdown, Franco Harris ended a nine-play, sixty-one-yard drive with a nine-yard touchdown. On the next series, with the Raiders running game going nowhere, Stabler dropped back to pass and was picked off by Ham, who returned it to the Raiders nine. A Bradshaw to Swann TD pass gave the Steelers the lead for good.

But it still wasn't over. The Raiders had magically beaten the Dolphins in the final seconds the week before, and with a little more than a minute left and down 17–13, Stabler had the ball again. Before the first play of the drive he stood in the huddle and surveyed the field for a moment. He made eye contact with Russell, who was manning his linebacker position, and for a moment, they held each other's gaze. Then Stabler winked. He expected to break Russell's heart.

But it didn't happen. Three plays later Stabler was intercepted again. Harris scored a game-clinching touchdown as the Steelers won, 24–13, picking off Stabler three times and holding the Raiders to just twenty-nine yards on the ground. For the first time, the Steelers were headed to the Super Bowl, to face the Minnesota Vikings. "Our Super Bowl dynasty was born that day against Oakland," says Harris, who had 111 yards that day.

"You hear people brag about being in the zone," Greene told NFL Films. "They don't know what the hell the zone is all about. 'Cause you visit the zone probably once in your life. I don't want to trivialize it. Because I played thirteen years and I was in the zone one time. That day our team was in the zone."

Here's what Chuck Noll remembered from his experience with the Colts in Super Bowl III: His team lost to Joe Namath's Jets because the players were tight. The Colts were huge favorites, the biggest of the three Super Bowls up to that point, and when the game began he could see agony on their faces. Namath had been lounging by the pool, sipping drinks and guaranteeing wins, while his guys were too worried about losing to win the game.

He wouldn't make that mistake with the Steelers. So with Bourbon Street beckoning his rowdy group, he told them to go have fun. There'd be no curfew, no bed check. He made the Super Bowl week no different than a week of practice in Pittsburgh. The players had Monday and Tuesday off and wives were allowed to stay in their hotel rooms. "I think he learned that you can't make the game bigger than life," Ham says.

For vets like Mansfield and Russell, being let loose on New Orleans to play in the Super Bowl, after so many years of struggle, was like being freed from prison. Bourbon Street was the ultimate playground, and they tried every slide on the lot, bringing anyone who would come along. Mike Wagner learned to eat oysters and shoot them down with beers. At one point Russell wound up on top of Mansfield's rental car as though he were King Kong. That was the last they saw of the car that night. "We just drank way too much and had no idea where it was," Russell says. "We had to go back the next morning and look all over downtown New Orleans to find it. I'll tell you, by the time we started practicing on Wednesday, we were begging for a bed check."

That week, Russell and Mansfield had become media darlings. In the light of day they were the most eloquent, personable, happy representatives of the Steelers; the go-to quotes for every scribe covering the game. "Andy and Ray had such great personalities and [a great] understanding of [how to deal] with the press," says Greene. "That week they kind of showed the young team how to handle all this, and then I think I picked up on that, and so did Bradshaw, and Franco, and Lynn."

Others found different ways to distinguish themselves. Ernie Holmes carved his Afro into the shape of an arrow, pointed toward his forehead. "I'm an individual who has a dream," he said at the time. "A dream to go forward."

Noll just let his team be. Even with 11:00 P.M. curfews, players were roaming the hallways of the hotel with a couple of drinks in their hand. The night before the game, Greene and Holmes and friends were sipping bourbon and cokes and drinking beer and dancing.

The only player who seemed to suffer in New Orleans was Dwight White. Soon after landing in New Orleans he collapsed in pain in the lobby of the team hotel. Greene carried him into a cab and took him to a hospital, where White was diagnosed with viral pneumonia. For three days he lay in a hospital bed, shedding pounds. He tried attending a Thursday practice, lasted fifteen minutes and had to be readmitted. Come Saturday night, he had lost twenty pounds and could barely stand.

The doctors told Noll there was no way he would be ready to play.

When the players woke up on the morning of the game, it was pouring. The normally balmy New Orleans weather had turned chilly, with the temperature in the mid-40s. And in the Steelers locker room, it looked like a ticket-broker's convention.

Every player was allotted four Super Bowl tickets, plus the option to buy twenty more at $25 a ticket. Before they left for New Orleans, the players had been approached by Pittsburgh travel agents who were willing to buy tickets for $150 so they could use them in Super Bowl packages for customers. Some of the players took the easy deal right away. Others had bigger plans. And when they got to their hotel and the brokers came up to them with briefcases filled with cash, they got even greedier. For most of them, the bonus for winning the Super Bowl would be equal to or more than their salaries. A chance to earn a little extra dough couldn't be passed up.

"I concocted a plan with Bradshaw to get another twenty-five tickets," says Moon Mullins. "But when we got them, they weren't fifty-yard-line seats. So we couldn't unload them. Before the game I got to the locker room at like 10:00 A.M. and our equipment man had young kids working with him. So I sent a kid out to get face value for them. That was like $30 or $40. But because the weather was so bad he couldn't even get that, so I ended up eating eight or ten tickets."

"Swann thought he could get $300 if he waited until the game," says

Hanratty. "But by then it was 45 degrees and they were selling tickets outside the stadium for five bucks. I go into the locker room and ask him if he has his tickets and he pulls out twenty of them that he's got to eat. I asked him if he needed salt."

All the players dealt with the circumstances surrounding the day differently. Some of them were so relaxed they fell asleep at the foot of their lockers. Bradshaw was so nervous he hyperventilated, had sweaty palms, and a bout of diarrhea. At one point he was so anxious that he lit up a cigar to calm himself down. But Noll never wavered.

"He made a speech before each game," says the former trainer Ralph Berlin. "And basically it was the same speech about doing your job and letting your teammates do their jobs. When we went to the Super Bowl the first time I thought, boy, I can't wait to hear this talk. And he gave the same speech he made for the first exhibition game of the season."

Besides, inspiration came in another form. The night before the game, Dwight White begged his doctors to let him out of the hospital. He was down to 220 pounds. Perles had told him he wasn't going to play. Noll had told White's backup, Steve Furness, he'd be starting. White was desperate to at least be in uniform, to be introduced. "Dwight White on Super Bowl Sunday called me and said, 'Come get me,'" says Berlin. "He said to the team doc, 'I want to dress, just let me dress.' The doctor, whose name was John Best—players called him John Wayne because he was big and looked like the actor—said to me, 'Let him get dressed. What can happen? He'll play three or four plays and we'll take him back to the hospital.'"

After watching White struggle to get his jersey over his shoulder pads and pull on pants that sagged like potato sacks, the Steelers roared out of the locker room. By a quirk of scheduling, both Pittsburgh and Minnesota lined up outside the Tulane Stadium tunnel, on the turf that ringed the field, at the same time, waiting to be introduced. An alley of fans held back by rope lined up on both sides of the teams, taking pictures, cheering, screaming. The Steelers were rowdy and laughing and couldn't wait to play football. At one point Steelers safety Glen Edwards saw the Vikings All-Pro defensive tackles, Carl Eller and Alan Page. "Edwards is being funny and shouting and people are taking pictures of us and the Vikes seem uptight," says Russell. "Glen sees Eller and Page and says, 'Hey bub, what's up?' They're stone-faced, refusing to acknowledge him. So he says it again. Still nothing. So Glen gets himself in between these two big Vikings and stares and says, 'Hey man, I am talking to you.' Nothing. So finally he just looks at them and says, 'You dudes better buckle up.' They didn't even respond."

At one point, while awaiting the team introductions, a shirtless Viking fan in a set of plastic horns collapsed right next to the Steelers, who were herded in their pen. "I was right there, he was turning blue," says Mullins. "We look down and there is a guy just laying on the ground. I think he died. Right there."

People in the crowd ran over to help. "But he hit the ground and never moved," Bradshaw wrote in *It's Only a Game*. "The man dropped dead right in front of me! He died with his horns on. And it didn't stop the program for one second."

There were more than eighty thousand fans waiting for the game to start.

And the moment it did, the game perfectly reflected the weather: dreary, harsh, unforgiving. The first quarter was played to a scoreless tie, with Bradshaw and the Steelers offense doing the smartest thing they could—staying out of the way of their defense. Greene and Co. befuddled the Vikings All-Pro scrambling quarterback, Fran Tarkenton. It wasn't until the second quarter that the first points were scored. Appropriately, it was a safety by the Steelers defense. With the Vikings backed up deep in their territory, Tarkenton wheeled around to hand the ball off. But it slipped from his grip and rolled toward the goal line. In the mad scramble, Tarkenton beat four other Steelers to the ball, landing on it in the end zone. The first player to tap a finger on Tarkenton and get credit for the safety was Dwight White.

The Steelers went into halftime ahead by those two points, then pulled ahead early in the third on a short drive capped by a Harris touchdown. But in the fourth, with the Steelers still up 9–0, the Vikings were at the Steelers' five and threatening to score. Until Greene, who had already picked off one of Tarkenton's passes, stripped running back Chuck Foreman and recovered the fumble. The Vikings would score on a blocked punt later in the quarter, but on the next drive the Steelers rushed down the field. The game-winning score, a four-yard touchdown pass from Bradshaw to tight end Larry Brown, was a play called by Joe Gilliam.

"Honestly, for me it was anticlimactic," says Ham. "The front four was so dominant that game that you could have taken off my uniform and put it back on a hanger." The Steelers limited the Vikings to just seventeen yards on the ground. Tarkenton threw twenty-seven times, completing just eleven while getting picked off three times and having four passes knocked down.

In the locker room afterward, Russell, the team captain, stood on a podium with one of the game balls in his hand. He was prepared to make a speech about the defense, about how Greene's play that day epitomized this team's rise from also-ran to Super Bowl champ, and then hand the ball to the All-Pro defensive tackle. But at the last second, just before he spoke, he spotted the Chief standing in the corner. He bagged his speech and yelled, "Chief, come up here. This is your ball."

With tears in his eyes and a stogie in his mouth, Art Rooney wrapped his hands tightly around the ball.

FOURTH
QUARTER

1975–1977

37

NOLL DIDN'T CHANGE HIS GRUMPY, PRAGMATIC APPROACH just because the Steelers had won the Super Bowl. "When we opened camp in 1975, the message was, first of all, win the battle of the hitting," says Greene. "Win that battle. Then you have to protect the quarterback, which means receivers block; the defensive line has to protect against the run and put yourself in a position to rush the passer and give D-backs time to cover. Everyone had to utilize techniques that were taught to them in individual positions. The same things we were doing when we were 1-13 were the same things we were doing in 1975. But with much better players."

They were more talented, and more motivated. Tim Rooney, one of Art's nephews, timed all the veterans in the 40-yard dash when they first checked into St. Vincent's that summer. And almost to a man, their times were faster than the year before. "We were all shocked," says Wagner. "After practice that night a bunch of us went back out to the fields just to make sure they hadn't shortened the sprint."

But more than anything, they were confident, carrying themselves with the bravado and swagger of kingpins, no one more so than Lambert. The prickly middle linebacker once stopped first-round draft pick Lynn Swann in the locker room and said, "You should have been number two, I should have been number one."

Lambert played at a controlled sizzle that entire 1974 season. Calling plays from his middle linebacker position, telling even Joe Greene when he was out of position, and hitting with anger. *Sports Illustrated* wrote, "He's meaner than Greene." While Greene himself said, "Jack Lambert is so mean that he doesn't even like himself." The only thing that seemed to make his jack-o'-lantern grin glow was winning. And by the end of his first season, to go along with Pittsburgh's W in Super Bowl IX, Lambert was named the NFL's Defensive Rookie of the Year.

Like Noll, Lambert both seized on and was seized by the moment. He fell into a defense that catered to his skills, emphasizing geometry and angles over brute strength. As mean as he was, as intimidating as that face could be, he was never the biggest man on the field. At 6'4" and just 218 pounds, he barely outweighed some receivers. "I give away twenty pounds whenever I step on the field," Lambert once said. "So I have to be twenty pounds more aggressive."

"Smilin' Jack," as Lambert was called, was a natural heir to the middle-linebacking legends who defined intimidation in pro football. The Giants' Sam Huff, another toothless hitter, the Packers' Ray Nitschke, the Bears' Dick Butkus. It didn't matter that Lambert's bookshelves were lined with Updike and Kafka and Joseph Heller. Or that his favorite hobby was playing Taso, a high-speed, highly complex version of chess. Or that, as a kid working on his family farm on Ohio, all he dreamed about was living on a beach, bodysurfing in the ocean, and fishing for his supper. Or that his teeth weren't lost in a barroom brawl or from hitting bone after biting an opponent. Instead they were the victims of a hard pick set by a teammate during a high school basketball practice. Lambert was so self-conscious about his smile at the time that, after losing his false set while swimming in a quarry as a teenager, he wouldn't go back to school for a week, until the dentist had made him a new bridge.

Of course almost no one knew any of these things. Lambert was most effective when opponents worried about—and fans lustily cheered for—the guy whose feet pumped like pistons before every snap. "Jack Lambert wasn't great because of his tough-guy attitude," says Russell. "He was a great player because he was very, very smart. He never made a mistake and his techniques were excellent. It had nothing to do with his personality, but the fans loved him for that."

Of course inside the Steelers locker room, his penchant for scowling and blowing up made him a favorite target. Nothing was sacred on this team. Egos were constantly kept in check. Says Grossman: "If anyone thought they were going to promote themselves, they would have been beat down so fast and thrown out of the locker room. "

Grossman, a nice Jewish kid from Philly, was mockingly called Rabbi. Bleier's constant talking often led to his being taped to the goal posts or stuffed in a tub of ice. Bradshaw's acting—he often rolled around the turf like he'd been shot after taking a sack, only to bounce back onto the field a play later—garnered him a faux Academy Award.

The merry prankster on the Steelers had always been Hanratty. He was so affable and self-assured, even as a backup, that he could get away with anything. "The only guy I never screwed with was Ernie [Holmes]," he says. On the practice field he'd amble up to Lambert, whose long blond locks always peeked from under his helmet, and say, "What's up, Straw-head? I need a guy for Halloween. What are you doing? What do you charge?" Once, he started blowing him kisses, at which point Lambert yelled at Noll, "Get Hanratty over here to stop blowing me kisses," which led to convulsive laughter from the rest of the defense.

But mostly, Hanratty toyed with Lambert at his locker. He'd fill a cup with water and hide it underneath Lambert's shoulder pads, which were propped on the top the locker. When Lambert pulled down the pads, the water would drop onto his head. "I got him once. And the next morning he walks in. I'm at my locker and we nod at each other. Then he pulls down the pads and the same thing happens again. Next day, same thing. Finally I say, 'You dumb bastard, get on a stool and check for water before you pull your pads down.' He does that the next day. Then the day after that, I get him again."

During practice one week leading up to a game against the Broncos and their star linebacker Randy Gradishar, who had played at Ohio State, Hanratty kept poking Lambert. He'd tell him how good Gradishar was, that he was the best linebacker that Ohio had ever produced, and that if

Lambert hadn't been such a screwup he would have been a first-round pick, too, just like Gradishar. When the two Ohioans finally met on the field before the game, Gradishar stuck out his hand and said, "Hi, I'm Randy Gradishar." Lambert's response was simply, "Who gives a fuck?"

Some players were too relaxed to screw with—there was no payoff in their reaction. Jack Ham was one of those guys. Icicles ran hotter than Ham. He had thighs as big as an offensive guard's, the first step of a wide receiver, and the technique of a coach. "Ham was a better linebacker than Lambert," says Russell. "The best I ever saw. He was Mr. Cool. He never tried to be macho or get in a fight. He would say something funny to defuse a situation. They had two totally different styles."

"When Ham showed up, Art Rooney thought the guy was a delivery boy because he was such an unimposing figure," says Vito Stellino, who covered the Steelers for the *Post-Gazette* in the 1970s. "But he had such quickness when he diagnosed plays. That left side—with Greene and Greenwood, Ham and Blount—was unbelievable."

Ham's greatest gift was his reaction to the ball. With the front four occupying blockers he was always able to get a clean jump on a short pass or a sweep to his side. Those ham hock–size legs churned through the patch of field he covered and made it a total dead zone for the offense. "I remember not being timed all that great in the 40 at Penn State," says Ham. "But we were also clocked at ten yards, and at that I was very good."

Ham's game was effortless, which freed his mind. During the end of the Steelers' 1975 season-opening blowout win over the Chargers, Ham and Russell had been taken out. Along the sidelines, as the reserves finished out the game, Ham asked Russell how his investment-banking business was going. Russell, trying to watch the game, blew him off. So Ham started talking about the coal brokerage business he had started during the off-season. "There are so many different types of coal," he started and then continued to describe them in detail. The Chargers punted. The Steelers took over. Franco Harris fell at Russell and Ham's feet, but Ham kept on talking about coal.

FOURTH QUARTER | 215

Then Bradshaw threw a pick and the linebackers coach put Ham back in the game. He ran onto the field, caused a fumble on the first play, ran back to Russell, took a knee, and picked up the conversation right where he had left off.

That 1975 season, the Steelers did the same thing. The Super Bowl against the Vikings was just the beginning of the team's ascent. After starting 1-1 in '75, they went on an eleven-game win streak, not losing again until the last game of the season, when they already had the AFC Central title locked up. Through the first six games that season, Pittsburgh went 5-1 and the defense gave up more than a hundred yards passing just twice. They didn't just win those first few weeks, they embarrassed teams. 37–0. 42–6. 34–3. The Steel Curtain was so unlike anything pro football had ever seen that *Time* magazine put Greene, Greenwood, White, and Holmes on the cover, calling them "Half a Ton of Trouble."

It wasn't just the Steelers defense that dominated. Beginning with a 16–13 win over the Packers in the sixth week of the season, the Steelers went on a stretch where they gained more than two hundred yards on the ground in five of six games. The one time they fell short, they gained 183. Bleier, who had become a starter at fullback midway through the 1974 season, was the perfect blocking, battering, inside-running complement to Harris. He picked up yards in small bites, while Harris, with his long strides, ate them whole.

They were helped along by some radical changes in the offensive line, beginning with the coach—Bad Rad. In January 1974, after two seasons at Colorado, Radakovich and the rest of the staff were canned. Looking for a job, he went down to the Senior Bowl, where he saw Noll in the lobby of a hotel. Radakovich told his old boss he needed work. Right there, Noll said, "You wanna coach our offensive line?"

"I thought about it for thirty seconds," says Radakovich. "Then I said, 'Sure.' I had played both ways in college. I knew I'd figure it out."

That first Super Bowl year the offense rarely found its rhythm. But in 1975, especially during its streak of two-hundred-yard rushing games, the Steelers offensive line provided protection worthy of the Secret Service. It wasn't just the trap that helped the unit elevate its game. Or the installation of new personnel—Webster and Mansfield, for example, split duties at center. It was the techniques and tricks that Radakovich was teaching.

One day during a film session, Radakovich noticed his linemen's jerseys being held and tugged by defensive linemen. It reminded him that when he coached the defensive line he had taught his players to pull on players' sleeves. To combat that, he asked Tony Parisi, the equipment manager, to tailor all of the offensive linemen's shirtsleeves, making them as tight as possible around the chest and biceps. Parisi enlisted his wife to do all the sewing. Then Radakovich's wife bought roll after roll of two-sided tape and before games any slack left over in the jerseys was taped down.

Another innovation was making his players buy the padded gloves, at $100 a pop, that boxers wore when they were in training. The most important move for an offensive linemen is that first explosion off the ball and the pop with his hands into the opponent's chest. That turned palms into hamburger. And if players compensated by using their fists instead, they'd find their knuckles breaking against shoulder pads and helmets. "He was ahead of his time and made us feel like the aggressors," says Mullins. "That and the fact that Bad Rad was a maniac. He made me stay after practice once and he was holding these pads, like gladiator shields, but he didn't have any pads on himself. He was making me hit him and we went for half an hour nonstop. I was just trying to knock his ass off and he kept goading me. Finally, I stepped in a hole and fell and he was bragging that he put me down. Two days later he showed me his body and it was black and blue all over. He said his wife was going to kill me for beating him up."

By the middle of 1975, the Steelers offense had become the defense's equivalent. In early November, at 6-1, the team was still in a three-way tie for first with the Bengals and the Oilers, and Houston was up next at

Three Rivers. Joe Greene was out with an injury. L. C. Greenwood would leave the game with a sprained ankle. And with less than a minute remaining, the two teams were tied at seventeen, after the Steelers blew a ten-point lead.

Pittsburgh had the ball on its own twenty-two, nearly the length of the field ahead of it. These were the moments that sent Noll into an empty place. For all the reserve and calm and intellect he displayed during practice, his lack of control of the games—the time when he knew it was all up to the players—forced him to actually lose it. Players often heard him muttering to himself. Especially when the game was in Bradshaw's hands. But that season, Bradshaw seemed more at ease than ever before. Winning a Super Bowl had helped. "There was nothing anyone could say about him anymore," says Greene. Some players also believed that being forced to sit and watch and earn back his job during the switcheroo with Gilliam had helped Bradshaw, too. "His biggest advantage was when he was forced to come back," says Bleier. "He was a tall, strapping good-looking guy, always a great athlete, so natural it all came easy, he was never short, never fat, never second-guessed himself. He became one of the guys sitting on the bench in the locker room, he sat around and bullshitted with us."

The Steeler huddles, which had been a raucous affair, with Stallworth and Swann screaming that they were open and Mansfield and Webster trying to dictate what plays to call, became more focused and directed. "They were Brad's," says Mullins. "He was in control."

As he was that day against Houston. Calmly, methodically, Bradshaw moved the Steelers down the field. He ran once for eight yards. He threw it three more times for sixty-eight yards. That included a twenty-one-yard, game-winning touchdown pass to Stallworth. For the day he completed 17 of 28 passes for 219 yards and three touchdowns. For the season, at that point, he had ten touchdowns and just four interceptions. It was the fiftieth win of Chuck Noll's career, and it put the Steelers on the path to another AFC Central title.

38

BEFORE HE RETIRED AT THE END OF 1976, I. W. ABEL COMMIT-
ted to securing his legacy. And to get through the rough patch the steel
industry was experiencing, he felt it was more important than ever to keep
in close contact with the manufacturers.

Abel could see the inevitable necessity of giving back some of the
wage and benefit guarantees he'd gained. The USWA's own in-house economic advisor, Edward Ayoub, estimated that the costs of labor (hourly
wage, plus health plan, plus pension) would reach $22 to $25 per hour in
1982. The day was rapidly approaching when the steel companies would
revert to Henry Clay Frick tactics—give us concessions or we'll shut down
the plant. What the USWA needed was unity, not internal bad blood. Its
new president had to be pragmatic, or the entire U.S. Steel industry would
be exported to Germany and Japan.

While Ed Sadlowski was a pain in his ass, Abel couldn't deny that he
was reaching the rank and file. His "Steelworkers Fight Back!" campaign
gave the out-of-work a chance to vent a lot of pent-up frustration. But it
wasn't pleasant to be vilified—Abel had been just like Sadlowski in 1936
and 1965—and he certainly didn't like Sadlowski's rhetoric, or the fact
that he made his name by attacking Abel's leadership. He claimed that
Abel was so in bed with the steel manufacturers—eating expensive lunches
at the Duquesne Club and sharing limousines in Washington—that Big
Steel had rendered the USWA powerless. Sadlowski charged that Abel
couldn't care less about the man on the shop floor. In his ten years as president, Abel had hiked up union dues but had never given the man on the
job the right to even ratify his own contract.

The USWA scheduled an executive meeting in upstate New York just prior to the 1976 national convention. Nominations for a new administration had to be decided. If it would bring the old-timers and the upstarts together, Abel would reach out to Sadlowski and get him into what Abel's men referred to as the union's "official family." Abel was looking at fellow 1936 SWOC veteran Lloyd McBride for the top spot. Maybe, he thought, he should put Sadlowski on the ticket as vice president.

But before he did anything, he was going to extract a little public blood from the kid. "The second afternoon of the meetings Abel pulls out this big file of papers and starts reading insulting stuff I had said about him. He developed this theme of one big lie, saying I said stuff so often that people were believing it, like Hitler," Sadlowski remembers, "I said, 'Well, the things I've been saying are not lies.'

"Then Abel shifted gears and started saying there had been too much divisiveness and we ought to close ranks," Sadlowski recalled, "For two more days they were feeding me, softening me up, shaking my hand and then offering to let bygones be bygones and have me join the club." The whole time Sadlowski considered his supporters, laid-off workers desperate to stand toe-to-toe with the corporations that held their fate in their hands. He thought of Local 1397 president Ronnie Weisen in Homestead, who led a group of Sadlowski's supporters into a downtown Mellon bank with a load of fish. They stuffed them in strongboxes to protest a source of U.S. Steel's capital and the anything-for-a-buck attitude of Big Steel.

And then there was Pat Coyne. Coyne was still an employed USWA staff rep, but he'd made so many enemies at work supporting Sadlowski that no one would get in an elevator with him. He stopped going into the office and was spending more time at confession than he did at Five Gateway Center. At that moment, he was talking with a concert promoter in New York to bring folk-singer activist Pete Seeger into Homestead for a Fight Back! benefit. If Sadlowski abandoned the movement, Coyne would be out of work with a wife and four kids to support and probably blackballed from the unions.

After another make-nice session, Sadlowski stood and looked Abel directly in the eye. "I've listened," he said. "Now it's my turn. I don't want things to continue the way they've been either. But let's go back to day one. You've lied, cheated, deceived, connived, stuffed ballot boxes . . ." Abel's eyes glazed over. The rest of the board sighed as Sadlowski ranted. Then a Canadian representative turned red. "It's obvious, Sadlowski, that President Abel threw out the olive branch and you stuck it up his ass."

That was the end of the peace process. In September 1976, Sadlowski announced his candidacy for USWA President.

39

AS THE PLAYOFFS BEGAN, THE STEELERS WERE NOT NEARLY the same team that, a year before, had been expected to lose its opening-round playoff game. They scored more points and gave up fewer points than in 1974. Lynn Swann, who had just eleven catches as a rookie, had eleven touchdowns in his second year. The D-line led a team that recorded a league-high forty sacks. Eight of eleven starters on defense went to the Pro Bowl. That opening-round game, a ho-hum, exactly-what-was-expected 28–10 win over the Colts, was actually memorable for just one thing: the invention of the Terrible Towel.

It was radio announcer Myron Cope who thought of the idea. Once upon a time, before becoming the man who was as associated with the Steelers as any Rooney, Cope had been one of the nation's most glorious sportswriters. His writing was no different than his talking, full of humor and insight that pulled on your eyelids and gave you no choice but to pay attention. He wrote for the papers in Pittsburgh and for *Sports Illustrated,* and he wrote books. In 1963 his magazine profile of Cassius Clay was named the nation's best. But at heart he was a lifelong Pittsburgh guy who loved the Steelers. He was the high-pitched, record-scratching voice of the team, shouting out "Yoi" and "Double Yoi" with every big run or dropped ball. His game calls were stream-of-consciousness poetry—fueled by the cigarette hanging between his fingers.

The towel wasn't born from in-the-booth inspiration, though. It was plain old duty. His radio bosses told him to think of a gimmick for the upcoming playoff game with the Colts. "I don't do gimmicks," Cope told them.

"Your contract is up in three months," they responded.

"I love gimmicks," said Cope.

On his nightly sports broadcast, he told fans to bring yellow dish towels to the game. "The Terrible Towel is poised to strike," he said. "If you don't have one, buy one, and if you don't want to buy one, dye one!" Then he threw towels at the faces of the weatherman and the two anchors sharing his desk.

The power of Cope's voice was such that, on a wet Sunday afternoon, more than thirty thousand Steelers fans carried Terrible Towels into Three Rivers for the game against the Colts. But after the easy win, everyone—fans, players, Cope—knew it would take more than towels to win the AFC Championship. That's because the Steelers were playing a familiar foe: the Raiders.

For years there had been rumors circulating around the NFL that Al Davis, in order to give his plodding running backs an advantage over speedier teams, had instructed his grounds crew to soak the Raiders' home field the night before games. Come Sunday, even with a bright northern California sun burning high in the sky, football would be played on a slow, sloppy track. No one ever proved it. But the conspiratorial Davis remained convinced that teams were always looking to retaliate. Teams, for example, like the Steelers.

The night before the Steelers-Raiders AFC title game, Dan Rooney was at an NFL-hosted party inside a fancy club at Three Rivers. The club had picture windows with a great view of the field below and, on this wintry night, it was easy to see the sleet being blown sideways by the Ohio River–driven wind swirling around the inside of the stadium. Rooney became so worried the turf would freeze over that he called his grounds crew and had them put a tarp on the field in the dark of night, as well as high-powered heaters to keep ice from forming.

Problem was, the wind ripped the tarp in half long after the party had ended and the crew had gone home. Water seeped in and collected along the sidelines, where it froze into skid-friendly slicks of ice. Those happened to be the spots where the Raiders receivers, who loved running sideline patterns, spent most of the game. "Our game was to throw the deep ball," Davis once told NFL Films. "With that ice we had to narrow the field. I'll never forget Pete Rozelle saying to me, 'Well it's the same for both sides.' And I said, 'Goddammit, Pete, you don't know what you are talking about—it's not the same for both sides'."

This was the fourth consecutive year that these two teams had met in the playoffs, and the second straight time the winner would play in the Super Bowl. And the Raiders were feeling confident—if not in themselves, then in the fact that Joe Greene was expected to see limited time because of a pinched nerve. "We saw *Jaws* on our flight from the coast," John Madden said before the game. "And that shark reminded me of Mean Joe."

But the two teams' familiarity with each other, as well their shared contempt, combined with the subzero temperature, made for an ugly game. "You couldn't play perfect football," Noll said afterward.

They could barely play good football. There were nine fumbles in the game, including four in the span of eight plays. Three of those were recovered by the defense. Five other times quarterbacks threw interceptions—and one of those was fumbled, too. Through three quarters the score was 3–0 Steelers.

What the game lacked in skill it made up for in violence. "The hardest hitting I've seen all season," Noll said after the game. As hard as Lambert and Greene hit players, the Raiders secondary, led by safeties George Atkinson and Jack Tatum hit harder. One of Atkinson's favorite maneuvers was something he named "The Hook." As a receiver ran by, Atkinson would wrap his arm around the pass-catcher's neck and fling him to the ground. And the elegant Lynn Swann had a neck that Atkinson was particularly fond of flinging.

Swann was nettlesome to a defense. He wasn't very big and he played with the grace of a dancer. But he spent much of his time careening through the middle of the field, making catches, getting pummeled, and then bouncing back up as though he were a cartoon character. That day against the Raiders he hadn't been remarkably effective, catching just two passes. On the second one, as he drifted across the middle and caught the ball, Atkinson applied The Hook, throwing Swann to the turf, knocking him out cold and forcing yet another fumble. "I was out of the ball game and later on in an ambulance going to the hospital," Swann once told NFL Films.

But in that moment, he was unconscious on the frozen Three Rivers turf. And from the sidelines ran Joe Greene. He scooped Swann up in both arms like he would a sleeping child. But because of Greene's pinched nerve, he struggled for a grip. Swann's neck was exposed as his head lay back and one of his legs dangled freely while Greene struggled to maintain his hold. As he reached the sideline, teammates came to Greene's and Swann's aid, as Greene's arm went dead and the limp Swann nearly tumbled back onto the field. Years later, Swann would give Greene an autographed copy of that picture saying, "Thank you." Greene told him, "I appreciate it, but really, I just didn't want the team to waste a time-out."

The game was in question until the final play, even though the Steelers had a 16–7 lead and the ball with less than two minutes to go. But with Bradshaw foggy from a hit to the head, Hanratty took the snap and fumbled. The Raiders recovered and, with seventeen seconds left, kicked a field goal to make it 16–10. Even worse for Pittsburgh, John Stallworth bobbled the ensuing onside kick and the Raiders had one last shot. But a Stabler completion to Cliff Branch fell short of the end zone, after the Raiders receiver slipped on the ice and was tackled trying to get out of bounds before the clock hit zero. For the second straight season, the Steelers were headed to the Super Bowl.

"We'll be bringing our golf shoes," Ray Mansfield said of the impending trip to Miami. "Not our ice skates."

40

SUPER BOWLS ARE BUILT ON HYPE. THERE HAS TO BE GLAM-our. There has to be trash talking. There has to be inherent drama. And this one, featuring America's Team versus the defending champs, the so-phisticated oil barons versus the Imp-and-Iron (a Pittsburgh staple—it's a shot of Imperial whiskey chased down by an Iron City beer) steelwork-ers, checked all the boxes. And the trash being spewed was especially inspiring. Swann hadn't been out of the hospital more than a couple of days after getting hit by Atkinson when Cowboys safety Cliff Harris is-sued this backhanded warning: "I'm not going to hurt anyone intention-ally. But getting hit again while he's running a pass route must be in the back of Swann's mind. I know it would be in the back of my mind."

This was no idle threat. Cowboys players had nicknamed Harris "Captain Crash." They often worried that the free-hitting safety did not distinguish between friend and foe when someone was roaming in his area. He was so committed to the law of speed times mass equals power that he shed the standard pads safeties wore and replaced them with the lighter, smaller pads worn by kickers.

"I read what Harris said," Swann said in response. "He was trying to intimidate me. He needn't worry. He doesn't know Lynn Swann. He can't scare me or the team. I said to myself, 'The hell with it, I'm gonna play.'"

Swann had been wobbly in the days leading up to the game. Doctors had told him they weren't sure he'd recover in time to play, and they warned him that the effects of another hit like the one Atkinson delivered could turn his brain into mush. Noll didn't even let him practice and listed him as doubtful on the injury report.

But there were broader factors contributing to the animus between the two teams. As much as they had dominated that year, and even though they were the defending champs, the Steelers felt very much like the enemy. The Cowboys had started the year 4-0. They made the postseason for the ninth time in ten seasons, including two recent trips to the Super Bowl. They won some games by scoring loads of points. And others by stopping those who could. They had an All-American, Heisman-winning, Naval Academy–graduating pitchman of a quarterback, Roger Staubach, lofting bombs to a receiver whose first name was Golden. Even their cheerleaders had fans.

The Steelers' version of football was modern, but not all that far removed from the blood battles that had been taking place for the previous thirty years. See something, hit something—whether it was an opposing player or a hole in the offensive line. Noll used to preach not letting paralysis by analysis be your undoing. But the Cowboys were all about analysis.

And the coach couldn't have asked the engineers at Texas Instruments to create a better vessel to execute his plans than Roger Staubach. No. 12 was efficient, not flashy. Accurate, cool, calm, and collected. He didn't just run plays, he perfected them. And people revered him for it. The Cowboys offense was an aerodynamic masterpiece.

The saying was that Texas Stadium, home of the Cowboys, had a hole in the roof so God could watch his favorite team play. No one said that about Three Rivers, home to the Terrible Towel and ashen skies and sleet that stung the face like a hatpin. No one dreamed of growing up to work in a steel mill; everyone dreamed of being a Cowboy. "We took it personally that they were called America's Team," Mel Blount told NFL Films. "Who granted them that?"

"The fans and media hype of that America's Team is something we resented," Bradshaw once said.

None of the nine Super Bowls before had been as intense or full of hatred. To those watching and to those playing, this game felt more like a gang war, and it had all the vitriol that comes with it. The Cowboys thought they were superior to the Steelers. And the Steelers, even while defending the Lombardi Trophy, felt aggrieved. The game wasn't just about winning or losing a title. It was about proving whose way was better. "They mess up your head too much," Lambert had said before the game. "If they beat you, you feel like you've been tricked instead of whipped. I hate teams like that." Lambert was even ticked about the Steelers' standard accommodations in Miami—chosen by the NFL—compared to the Cowboys' glamorous beachfront hotel in Fort Lauderdale. "I hope Staubach is eaten by sharks," he told reporters during the week. All that turned it into a happening. The price for scalped tickets was the highest for any Super Bowl. The NFL granted more press credentials than it ever had. The cost of commercial time reached its all-time high, $110,000 for a sixty-second spot. Even Hollywood cashed in, using the game as the backdrop for scenes in the movie *Black Sunday,* in which terrorists blow up a blimp over the Super Bowl. "I remember walking out of the tunnel and seeing Robert Shaw, who starred in the movie, standing on the sideline, and I thought, oh man, the stars are even here," says Bleier. "I had no idea they were shooting a movie that day."

The pregame warm-ups were pandemonium. The movie was shooting. The halftime act, Up With People, warmed up the Orange Bowl crowd of more than eighty thousand people. Someone had forgotten to put up the net behind the goalposts that Steelers kicker Roy Gerela was using for his practice kicks, so all of his balls kept drifting into the stands, where fans would run away with them. At one point he became so frustrated that he walked into the stands, in uniform, and grabbed a ball from a spectator. Other fans started shoving the kicker and security had to escort him back down to the field.

It would get worse for Gerela.

On the game's opening kickoff, the Steelers kicker lofted the ball to Preston Pearson, the former Steeler who had signed with the Cowboys during the off-season. Pearson cradled it and then, using the trickery the

Steelers so despised, handed the ball off to Thomas "Hollywood" Henderson, the Cowboys first-round pick that year as a linebacker. At Henderson's first press conference, reporters made the mistake of calling him Tom several times. Henderson stopped the session and said, "My name is Thomas. If my sister has a daughter, I don't want her growing up to call me Uncle Tom."

He was brash and full of attitude and as fast as a sagebrush fire. Even though he barely played defense that rookie season, Henderson's impact was felt on special teams, where he was split out wide on punt coverages. And he was the only linebacker in the league running the reverse on a kickoff. Which is how he scampered forty-eight yards, then a Super Bowl record, before being tackled by Gerela at the Steelers' forty-four. Poor Gerela. On the play he injured his rib cage, which, along with his lack of quality practice time, affected him for the rest of the day.

The Cowboys stalled, but on the next drive, following a blocked Steeler punt, Staubach connected with Drew Pearson on a twenty-nine-yard pass for the game's first score. Standing on the sidelines, Bradshaw thought to himself, "We're going to lose."

But in the following Steelers series, on his first pass of the game, Swann offered Bradshaw some confidence. "I decided if I was going to play I had to make the first catch," Swann once told NFL Films. "I didn't care where it was going to be, I had to make the first catch." Even if it was practically uncatchable. From midfield, Bradshaw dropped back. Swann, lined up wide on the right side, was bumped toward the sideline by corner Mark Washington. Bradshaw lofted a deep, parabolic ball that looked like it was going to sail out of bounds. Swann tiptoed along the green turf, treading close to the white paint, perilously close to falling out of play. At the last possible moment he leapt into the air, let Washington run by him as he reached back, and then grabbed the ball, which was about four feet out of bounds, back into play with his fingertips. He landed with a couple of toe taps and fell out of bounds for a thirty-two-yard gain. "Andy and I were kneeling down, and when Bradshaw threw that pass, it looked like he was just throwing it away," says Ham. "Everything except Lynn's two feet were out of bounds, and he twisted to bring it back in. Andy and I just looked at each other as if to say, 'How did he do that?'"

More important is what he did: He caught that first pass. And set up the Steelers' game-tying touchdown, a Bradshaw-to-Grossman throw three plays later.

The Cowboys answered with a field goal, and then the two teams settled into a slugfest. The Steelers drove toward midfield, and then Bradshaw was sacked. The Cowboys drove inside the Steelers' twenty, and two sacks of Staubach pushed them back to midfield. Lambert was so caught up in the game that he ripped off his elbow pads and screamed that he wanted to hurt someone.

Then, with a little more than three minutes left in the half, Bradshaw dropped back to his own goal line. Swann was sprinting on a fly pattern down the middle of the field, again with Washington trailing. At midfield Swann tipped the ball and jumped into the air. As Washington fell, grasping at Swann's waist, Swann tracked the ball. He was parallel to the ground with his neck stretched toward the sky, and he put his hands up to his shoulders and, just before landing, cradled the ball into his chest. It was his second catch of the game.

Unfortunately, this brilliant effort, unlike the first, would be wasted, as Gerela, fighting his rib injury, couldn't get much lift on a thirty-six-yard field goal try with twenty seconds left and hooked a line drive to the left. At the half, the Cowboys led, 10–7.

And the score stayed that way into the third, as Gerela lined up for another game-tying kick from the thirty-three-yard line. Before the play, on the sidelines, he had been grabbing his left side, trying to stretch it out. On the field, as he lined up the kick, he shielded his eyes from the glaring sun. And again, he missed. As Gerela hung his head, Cliff Harris, Captain Crash, tapped the kicker on the head and yelled into his face mask, "Nice going, that really helps us." Lambert saw Harris taunting his kicker and, from behind, grabbed Harris by his shoulder pads and whipped him to the ground. "The ref said to me, 'You're out, Lambert. You're out of this game,'" Lambert told NFL Films. "And I said, 'Wait a minute, this is the Super Bowl—you can't throw me out.' He said, 'Well, then, you get back in the huddle and just shut up.' I said, 'Yessir.'"

"When he threw Cliff Harris down I ran on the field and chewed him out," says Russell. "I was like, what are you doing, that's stupid, you can't do that or you'll get thrown out of the game. I know the announcers said that turned us around. No it didn't. He was being stupid."

But in the fourth quarter, the Steelers did chip away. First it was a safety off a blocked punt. Then a Gerela field goal. Then another field goal. And finally, up 15–10 with a little more than three minutes left in the game, the Steelers had the ball on their thirty-six-yard line. It was third and four, and the Steelers, with the most dominant rushing attack of the era, needed a first down to eat up more clock and seal a win. But in the huddle, Bradshaw called 69 Maximum Flanker Post. In other words: Go deep, Lynn Swann.

Bradshaw, as he had been the Super Bowl before, as he had been during his entire career up to this point, was pestered with questions about his intelligence. No one made note of the fact that he called his own plays, while Navy genius Staubach only followed Landry's orders. This game, this play, being better than Staubach when it mattered most, meant something to him.

The Cowboys had the play read perfectly and Cliff Harris came screaming through a hole in the offensive line on a blitz. Just before he leveled his helmet into Bradshaw's left cheek, the quarterback unloaded a ball that traveled seventy yards in the air. Waiting at the other end, on the Cowboys' five-yard line, was Swann, who sauntered in for a touchdown.

Bradshaw never saw it. He was severely concussed. "I was in the locker room and the game was just about over when I finally understood what happened," he said afterward.

The Cowboys didn't quit, scoring on the next drive to make it 21–17. And then, with Hanratty playing in place of Bradshaw, and his team facing a fourth down and nine near midfield and a little more than a minute left, Chuck Noll decided to go for it and try to ice the game, rather than punt. His theory was simple: The Cowboys had already blocked a punt. But his defense was on the way to setting a Super Bowl record with seven sacks. He trusted his defense.

He was right. When Staubach's last Hail Mary pass fell incomplete, the Steelers were Super Bowl champs.

Swann, who had been lying in a hospital bed pondering whether his days in football were over when the Super Bowl hype began, finished the day with four receptions, 161 yards, a touchdown, the game's MVP and two career-defining catches. "I don't care what kind of catch a guy makes if he beats me," said his most frequent victim that day, Cowboys corner Mark Washington. "Swann just beat me one time too many."

"It was Camelot," says then *Post-Gazette* Steelers beat writer Vito Stellino. "All they cared about was winning."

And that's all they did.

41

THERE WAS LIGHTNESS DEEP WITHIN CHUCK NOLL. THERE was civility and etiquette and appreciation, too, all of it revealed in waves, when the consumption of football and practice had ended. His wife saw it. Their son did, too. It was evidence that he believed it when he told his players their existence after football would matter more than their existence during football, that he meant it when, as he cut them, he said, "It's time to do your life's work."

"After every Super Bowl he took all the coaches somewhere. We went to a place called Walker's Cay in the Bahamas, and to Acapulco. He treated the whole staff and our wives," says Dick Hoak. "We would go for a week. He was the boss but he was different there. He had this place on top of a hill in Acapulco and we would go up for cocktails at five o'clock and then go to dinner somewhere. He treated the wives like, wow, it was amazing. People called him Chuck Knox, he never wanted any fame, didn't care who knew him other than what they knew about him as a coach. American Express wanted him to do something after the second Super Bowl and he said go get the players. His only motivation was to win football games. The only promotion he ever did was a billboard for a friend who worked at a local bank.

"Every year before training he would have a party at his house and he would do all the cooking: steaks on the grill, chicken, pork, everything, and then all these bottles of wine, and we would all be there until two or three o'clock in the morning. He was so warm and intelligent. He was always teaching. When we would go scouting he would take us up in his plane and show us around. You'd go play golf with him, and he used to tell me what I was doing, coaching me around the golf course, and I would look at him and say, 'Chuck, I'm shooting about 78 and you're shooting a 92.' But that's the way he was.

"He had built a home in Hilton Head and had some other properties in the area, so one year in March we were all working on the playbook and he says, 'Come on, let's go, we're all going to Hilton Head. I got places for you to stay and we'll work on the playbook there'. But we never worked on the playbook. We played golf every day and he would take us out on his boat.

"We'd go to the Senior Bowl and he'd take us driving and sightseeing. The year we went to Palm Springs to practice for the last game of the year against San Diego, in 1972, he took us to dinner every night, and then he'd drive the car into the mountains and park the car and say, 'Let's look at the sky and at the stars.' Then he would point out all the different things that were up there. If you got to know Chuck a little bit he was a really comfortable guy.

"Really, he was the kind of guy who, if something happened to you and you had to give your kids to somebody, you'd give them to him."

It may have been a new year, but Lynn Swann, now a Super Bowl MVP, was still a target. It took less than two quarters of the 1976 season for him, and the rest of the Steelers, to be reminded of that.

They played their home opener against the Raiders in Oakland. As Bradshaw dropped back to pass, Swann sprinted down the right sideline, covered by his old pal George Atkinson, and then cut toward the middle of the field. Bradshaw unleashed a pass for Franco Harris. But, fifteen yards away from the play, Atkinson took a forearm to the back of Swann's head. The receiver crumbled to the ground, unconscious, with a concussion. The Steelers lost the game, Swann went on the disabled list. But what lingered were Chuck Noll's comments after the game. "You have a criminal element in all aspects of society. Apparently we have it in the NFL, too. Maybe we have a law-and-order problem."

For his hit, Atkinson was fined $1,500. For his reaction to the hit, Noll was fined $1,000.

Things would get so much worse. The team started just 1-4, including falling to the Browns for their third straight loss. During the game, and again after the play, one of the Browns lifted Bradshaw, flung him over his hip, and planted the quarterback into the turf on top of his head. He'd miss four games and half of four others. The backup quarterback—replacing Terry Hanratty, who had been picked up by the Bucs in the expansion draft, and Joe Gilliam, who had been released—was a rookie, Mike Kruczek. "If we have to be in this position," Joe Greene said after the loss to the Browns. "I'd rather be in it with this team, with these people, and particularly with the man running it."

Noll treated his team the same way he did his squads of the early seventies: Run the ball, play good defense, don't lose games with mistakes. Only, instead of teaching young talent to do all that, he just unleashed it. After losing to the Browns, the Steelers D held the Bengals to 171 total yards in a 23–6 win. It was vintage Steelers. Kruczek threw the ball just twelve times, while Harris ran it forty-one times for 143 yards and two touchdowns.

Then the Steelers got serious. The next week they shut out the Giants 27–0, limiting New York's offense to 151 total yards. The next week: another shutout, this one 23–0 against the Chargers, who gained just 134 total yards and had nearly as many turnovers, five, as first downs, seven. They did it one more time the following game against the Chiefs, blanking them 45–0 as both Harris and Bleier rushed for more than a hundred yards. The Steelers won the next three games, too, but were disappointed with their performances. After all, they gave up three points to the Dolphins, sixteen to the Oilers, and then three to the Bengals. Following one more shutout in the penultimate game of the season, a 42–0 win over

Tampa Bay, the Steelers had an eight-game win streak, had given up just 28 points during that span, at one point had not allowed a touchdown in twenty-two straight quarters, and needed to beat Houston in the season finale to win the AFC Central. And they did that in style, pitching a 21–0 shutout. The Oilers had eleven punts and only nine first downs.

The defense was so dominant, and the offense so bland, that both Harris and Bleier rushed for a thousand yards that year. Passes were so rare that Stallworth and Swann once stood up and clapped during a film session when a scene of Swann catching the ball flickered across the screen.

But during a first-round thrashing of the Colts, both Harris and Bleier were injured. The Steelers went into the AFC Championship against the Raiders, for the third year in a row, playing a rookie quarterback and a third-string running back, and they lost 24–7 in a game that was never close. Lambert called it the most heartbreaking loss of his career. "Give me a six-pack and an hour's rest and let's go again," he said after the game. "Because I think we can beat them."

Russell and Mansfield, wouldn't get the chance. The two men—partners in fun and football from the Steelers' most hapless days to their brightest—had decided to retire, together. "I never wanted Chuck Noll to come to me and say, 'It's time to seek your life's work,'" says Russell. "I decided I would be the one that told him."

42

FOR A FEW DAYS IN OCTOBER 1976, PAT COYNE CHECKED OUT of the Sadlowski campaign. He had to bury his mother.

Mass cards from steelworkers in Clairton, Braddock, Homestead, the South Side, Aliquippa, Ambridge, and Chicago were stacked by the open casket. Laid-off McKeesport National Tube worker Ronnie Demarkski, dressed in his best flannel shirt and dungarees, brought two sacks of homemade pierogis to Pat's wife. Retired rigger Tony Franchini had two gallons of what Coyne called his "dago red" in the trunk of his Galaxy 500. They'd all end up at Coyne's house after the viewing for a proper Irish wake. Uncomfortable in situations that required restraint, Coyne did his best to shake every gnarled hand extended to him. He made small talk: "Yeah, that Lambert's a mean son of a bitch." It would all be over soon.

The viewing was at Laughlin Funeral Home in Pittsburgh's South Hills, just six miles from 940 North Lincoln Avenue on the North Side. But for a seventy-one-year-old man with Coke-bottle glasses, it's a bleary hump. Pittsburgh's streets were known for axle-snapping potholes, and the day's ash and soot from the mills in the air blocked out any moon or starlight. The only evening glow came from the few blast furnaces that hadn't gone cold during the current wave of layoffs.

The old man drove across the Allegheny River on the Fort Duquesne Bridge, which had only recently been completed. It used to be called "the bridge to nowhere," a jagged mess constructed by the Pennsylvania Department of Transportation. It took PennDot five years to figure out that no one ever bothered to clear the rights to the land for the access ramps on the North Side, so the bridge literally stopped in midair for another six years until they got it back to earth.

Once he made it over the Fort Duquesne, he stayed in the right-hand lane to exit onto another bridge, the Fort Pitt. It would take him over the Monongahela and into a tunnel dynamited out of Mount Washington. On the other side, he followed Route 19 a few miles on Banksville Road, then turned left onto Potomac Avenue, and then right onto West Liberty Avenue. He took West Liberty until it changed into Washington Road and tried to find a parking space at number 222, but the lot was a sea of pickup trucks and battered Chevrolets. He pulled up to the curb next to the funeral home's awning and shut off the engine. A man from the home came out to tell the old man he couldn't park there, but instead offered a pleasant, "Good evening, Mr. Rooney."

Art Rooney Sr. didn't mind the drive. He always had time to share with the people he cared about. When he arrived at the Steelers offices in the morning, one of the staff would have already prepared a list of wakes or funerals for that day. And when the offices closed, he'd be off on his rounds.

He liked people, wanted to know more about them. Rooney would remember the name of a cab driver and the kind of cigarette he smoked if he met him twice. He treated Dirt Denardo, the head of Three Rivers Stadium's ground crew, with as much respect as the president of the United States.

In the casket that night was the niece of one of Rooney's mentors, State Senator James "Jimmy" Coyne. It was Jimmy Coyne who had once made Rooney a ward boss. Rooney knew Pat Coyne, too. Rooney's father's family had roots in the puddling era, and on his mother's side in Pittsburgh's coal seam. Whenever he was asked where he came from, Rooney would proudly say, "My mother's people were all coal miners and my father's people were all steelworkers." He liked to talk to the guys in the hard hats singing "Here we go Steelers, here we go!" at home games. Rooney read the paper. He knew how dire the straits were for the rank and file.

Rooney made his way into the foyer. All of the long faces at Laughlin Funeral Home livened. He went directly to a corner by the casket where Coyne's children sat vigil. Someone said, "Hey the Chief's here. He's giving tickets to the kids!"

It was the only time that day Pat Coyne smiled.

43

AT PITTSBURGH'S 1977 DAPPER DAN BANQUET, AN ANNUAL celebration of the best of the previous sports year, Tony Dorsett was named the top football player in the state of Pennsylvania. He caught Steelers president Dan Rooney's eye and joked, "Don't let me go! Make me a member of the Pittsburgh Steelers. You won't be sorry." Rooney laughed but knew what he was missing. The Steelers had just lost the 1976 AFC Championship to the Raiders, due in no small part to the fact that star running backs Franco Harris and Rocky Bleier had missed the play-offs with injuries. But with the twenty-first pick in the draft, the Steelers had little chance to claim the Heisman Trophy winner.

Two expansion teams in their second year of operation held the top two picks—Tampa Bay and Seattle. Dorsett had no intention of playing for either of them. Tampa Bay made it clear that they were picking the University of Southern California's Ricky Bell as number one. Bell had played for Tampa Bay's head coach John McKay when McKay coached the Trojans. Dorsett hired agent Mike Trope, who threatened Seattle with a Dorsett defection to the Canadian Football League should they draft him. Not only would Seattle not get the prize back, but they would lose the coveted draft selection, too. Trope had taken two of his clients— Johnny Rodgers and Anthony Davis—to the Great White North before, so it was no idle threat. Seattle was open to trading its pick to the best bidder.

Gil Brandt conferred with Tex Schramm and Tom Landry. They gave Seattle their number-one pick (the twenty-fourth overall) and their three second-round picks in exchange for Seattle's first-rounder. On May 3,

1977, Tony Dorsett was drafted by the Dallas Cowboys. After making a statement to reporters, "We realized we were never going to win the big games without a great tailback. Finally, now, all of the pieces are really set in place. We're going ahead and booking our rooms for the Super Bowl," said Brandt.

He sent a private jet to Pittsburgh International Airport to pick up the missing piece. Dorsett landed and posed in his new Dallas jersey, number 33, and humbly thanked Dallas for the opportunity.

His contract was remarkable. The Cowboys' 1970 number-one draft pick (Duane Thomas) received a three-year deal worth $87,000, $25,000 of that in a signing bonus. Just seven years later, the beneficiary of labor progress and a huge growth in NFL revenue, Dorsett signed a $1,600,000 three-year deal, with $600,000 on signing. Before playing one NFL down, he was one of the highest-paid players in the league, better paid than Pro Bowlers and future Hall of Famers on his own team.

Dorsett moved his mother and father out of Aliquippa's Plan Eleven and bought them a brand-new home. "My mom and dad were the first black family in the neighborhood," Dorsett remembered. But Wesley Dorsett refused to leave the mill. He was proud of his son, but he would not have him put food on his table. He continued the daily trek to one of J&L's basic-oxygen furnaces, donned his green asbestos pants and jacket, and weathered the heat from tap after tap of 3,000-degree steel.

After the fanfare and jubilation, Tony Dorsett proceeded to alienate the entire Dallas metropolitan area. Mel Renfro and Rayfield Wright gave Dorsett the compete lowdown about what he was walking into. The city had more than its share of citizens who still referred to black men as "boy" and "nigger." North Dallas continued to be white and South Dallas black. The Cowboy organization was built on clean-cut, deferential players, especially black players, and he would be expected to keep his mouth shut, learn Landry's system, and defer to the Cowboys' front office.

But after all the sweat and pain it took him to reach the top of his profession, Dorsett had little interest in toeing the line. He bought the obligatory nouveau-riche toys—the big house with the Jacuzzi, the motorcycle, the custom van (the thing to have in 1977) and a dove-gray Lincoln Continental with "TD" engraved on every door. And he would enjoy the bachelor life as much as he pleased. He also announced that he would prefer that people pronounce his last name "Dor-SETT," rather than the Pittsburgh pronunciation, "DOR-sitt." "The name is French, and I liked the sound of it that way. It wasn't as if I had changed my name to some exotic African name. I just wanted it pronounced the way I liked it pronounced," said Dorsett.

In his very first week in Dallas, Dorsett got into a fight at a disco. Harassed at the door and made to wait while white men and women brushed by him, he steamed. When he was finally admitted, he approached a woman to dance, she accepted, and after the song ended he took her to the bar for a drink. The bartender served him then asked him to take his companion and drinks elsewhere. Dorsett refused. The bartender called him a "nigger son of a bitch" and the two men squared off. The disco's manager eventually intervened, the police were called, and Dorsett was charged with two counts of assault. The charges were later dropped.

Dorsett continued to be in the wrong place at the wrong time. "Whenever a fight broke out around town," he once said, "it seemed that I happened to wind up in the middle of it all." Tex Schramm called him into his office for a talk. But to little avail. When asked about Dorsett's troubles, quarterback Roger Staubach recalled that "being an outspoken black man in Dallas wasn't easy then. If he had been white, perhaps a lot of what happened would have been overlooked."

When the 1977 training camp opened, Dorsett was shocked to find a distinct separation between white and black players. "All through high school and at the University of Pittsburgh, all the black and white guys hung around together. We partied like friends. We liked each other. On the Cowboys there were black and white cliques." Landry's system added to his discomfort. At the most basic level, it was counterintuitive to him.

"As you're coming up in football as a kid, 'even' is to the right and 'odd' is to the left," he once said, "there were times in those workouts when I was tired and my concentration lapsed, and I'd find myself going back to my old ways." Dorsett didn't like all of the contact in practice either. He was used to walking through plays at Hopewell and Pitt without being hit, but at camp he took a beating and for the first time suffered an injury that kept him off the field. He missed the entire preseason.

The put-on seriousness turned him off, too. Dorsett like to goof around with one of his fellow rookies, wide receiver Tony Hill. They were quickly dressed down by a veteran: "This is football, not kindergarten." For Dorsett, treating the game as business took the heart and fun out of the team equation. Every player was so intent on making sure his individual performance satisfied the computer that there was little chance of guys joining together and being better than the sum of their parts. The Cowboys were sterile. The one exception was the receiver coach, former Cowboys tight end Mike Ditka. "In a game in Pittsburgh, one of our receivers was bumped out on the sidelines," said Dorsett. "One of the Steelers piled on with a late hit. Although a flag was thrown and Pittsburgh was penalized, it didn't calm Mike Ditka down much. He picked up the football and fired it at the head of the guy who had made the late hit. Coach Landry didn't appreciate that show of emotion."

Dorsett didn't fit in, and Landry had no intention of bending the rules to accommodate him. He'd done that with Duane Thomas. Preston Pearson, the former Steeler who'd passed on Dorsett when he was scouting him as a possible recruit for Pearson's alma mater, the University of Illinois, was awarded the starting tailback position at the beginning of the season. Dorsett was put in sporadically, and in the first three games of the year, he'd only been given the ball twenty-one times. But the Cowboys were winning, and Landry seemed intractable about giving Dorsett more opportunities.

Dorsett's off-field troubles continued. He was stopped by the highway patrol, which discovered that a woman sitting in his passenger seat had a stash of cocaine in her purse. And there were many incidents that Cowboys management kept quiet. Gil Brandt let him know that he was being monitored: "Tony, I hear you were at [such and such a place] last night." Eventually, Schramm sent Dorsett to New York to have a sit-down with Pete Rozelle. The commissioner diplomatically warned him about the risk to his career if he continued his path. Dorsett ignored all of it. As far as he was concerned, if the Cowboys wanted him to sit on the bench and rob him of the satisfaction he felt on the field, he was at least going to have a good time in his off-hours.

Realizing that his icy approach wasn't working, Landry finally called Dorsett into his office in the middle of the season and dressed him down. He told his troubled number-one pick that he was disappointed in the way he was working out. Dorsett was unmoved and told him he had decided to ride out the season and think about next year. Landry needed Dorsett to hit his stride going into the playoffs. Preston Pearson was still starting, and would prove to be a talented third-down specialist, but there was little doubt that his best years running the ball were behind him. Landry's strategy of keeping his cocky rookie down to break him into the Cowboy mold had backfired. He knew that his best hope for another Super Bowl was an age-old coach-player deal: "If you showed some intensity in practice, some more hard work, it might be different." Dorsett got the message. "After that conversation with Tom, I decided to run my butt off all the time in practice and show him and the other coaches and players that I meant business." This gave Landry an excuse to bench the hard-working Preston Pearson.

Dorsett's first professional start was in Pittsburgh against the Steelers in the tenth game of the 1977 season. He ran for seventy-three yards and a touchdown and caught four passes for thirty-seven yards. But the Steelers beat the Cowboys 28–13. Two weeks later, Landry called Dorsett's number twenty-three times against the Philadelphia Eagles. The critics were finally silenced. Dorsett ran for a Cowboys-record 206 yards, including an eighty-four-yard touchdown. Roger Staubach admitted, "If it hadn't been for Tony Dorsett, we would have lost. A couple of years earlier we lost games like that. It showed the Cowboys that when the rest of the team was not playing particularly well, we could still win because we had Tony Dorsett as a weapon."

Dorsett finished the regular season with 1,007 yards and was named the NFL's Rookie of the Year. After nine games on the bench to begin the year and below-average carries for a featured running back (the Steelers' Franco Harris was handed the ball more than three hundred times, while Dorsett had just over two hundred carries), his production exceeded everyone's expectations. Dorsett and Landry had reached a détente. As long as he performed on the field, his head coach would look the other way. Landry had learned the hard lesson with Duane Thomas. Sometimes you have to leave the gifted alone.

A former Cowboy had been watching Dorsett's career with keen interest. "One night I was having a party," Dorsett remembered, "and all of the sudden the doorbell rang. We wondered who could be calling at that hour of the night. I went to answer the door. There was Duane Thomas, standing all alone in the darkness."

44

EDWARD SADLOWSKI'S USWA TICKET WAS A RAINBOW coalition—Ignacio "Nash" Rodriguez for secretary, Andy Kmec for treasurer, Oliver Montgomery for vice president of human affairs, and Marvin Weinstock for vice president of administration. While their multicultural Fight Back! message appealed to the national media, it was the black and white campaign poster that brought film crews, magazine profilers, and television cameras on the campaign trail.

The poster featured Sadlowski on the left side of the frame. Wearing a white crewneck T-shirt beneath a blue open-at-the-collar work shirt, and covered by a worn dungaree coat, he looked liked he'd just gotten home from the blast-furnace graveyard shift. His eyes were a thousand miles away and a five o'clock shadow covered his neck and jaw. The right side of the frame was the grim yet comforting view of a mill. Smokestacks rising out of tin sheet–covered rolling mills on the banks of a steel-gray river. The photograph could have been taken in Chicago, Gary, Youngstown, Pittsburgh, or Baltimore. Sadlowski looked like a man with a vision, ready to put the industry on his back and take it to new heights. The subtext was, *I'm one of you, and I've got a mission.*

Sadlowski wanted to bring democracy to the USWA. He'd change the union's bylaws so that the rank and file could ratify the USWA contract. The local union elections, which had long ago become as fixed as a banana republic's, would mean something under Sadlowski, too. They had always been treated as lifetime-achievement awards for guys who hadn't been inside a mill for years. He wanted the local leaders to come directly from the shop floor. Sadlowski would kick out the 600 USWA staff reps who colonized Five Gateway Center in favor of new blood from the locals. Those would be the guys invading Pittsburgh for executive board meetings. Not the lawyers and stuffed suits that McBride favored. There would be lively debate and communication between the leaders and the workforce, not decrees issued from a corporate tower. And most of all, Sadlowski would give the men back the only tool they had to confront their bosses—the strike.

The New York Times Magazine characterized Sadlowski as "a rebel candidate for president of the steelworkers (that) wants to take his union— and the whole labor movement—back to the class struggle." *Meet the Press* interviewed him, as did Phil Donahue and Mike Wallace for *60 Minutes.* Sadlowski attracted liberal icons to his cause. Jane Fonda, Tom Hayden, Kennedy advisors Theodore Sorensen and Harvard economist John Kenneth Galbraith were identified as supporters of his campaign. Momentum was building.

Pete Seeger waived his fee and agreed to come to Homestead for a concert to support Sadlowski's campaign. On a frigid January night in 1977, Seeger took the stage at Homestead's dilapidated Leona Theater. Behind him was a mural of the 1892 Homestead Strike. There were so many steelworkers jumping up and down with Imp and Iron–fueled joy that Pat Coyne worried that the balcony would fall. *Rolling Stone's* Joe Klein covered the concert and rhetorically wondered if it might be "the beginning of a new era in trade union activism, or just a momentary indulgence in nostalgia?"

But all was not rosy for Sadlowski. A supporter in Texas was shot in the neck distributing his literature, and Sadlowski's opponent, Lloyd McBride, accused him of being a communist posing as a steelworker to overthrow the union. The old guard wasn't pulling any punches, and tension in Pittsburgh rose to new heights. Lawyer Tom Geoghegan, a volunteer consultant, was in a clubby businessman's bar one night near U.S. Steel headquarters with a bunch of Sadlowski people, "not socializing with them, just in the same bar with them." Geoghegan recalled, "I turned to my friend Betsy, but she was just watching as Pat Coyne over at the bar was picking up people by the hair."

The USWA's 1977 election held no less than the future of industrial America in its hands. Sadlowski's people believed that if the steelworkers didn't get one of their own in the top spot, their USWA leadership would blindly lead them to the slaughterhouse. A. H. Raskin, the assistant editor of *The New York Times*' editorial page, presciently commented in 1972, "The basic membership re-education essential to thoroughgoing changes remains undone. It is easier to keep doing things the familiar way, even if the end of the road is economic suicide."

The Steelworkers Fight Back! movement wasn't interested in suicide. If their jobs were going to be killed, they would hit Big Steel with everything they had before going down—maybe even take over the mills themselves.

But even with across-the-board liberal support, Sadlowski's campaign was a huge Hail Mary. With Abel's aggressive recruitment of other trade unions into the USWA fold, steelworkers accounted for only 40 percent of the dues-paying membership. Just to have a chance, Sadlowski would have to take all of the basic steel membership ballots and hope for a low turnout among the USWA's "Chock full o'Nuts" waitress rank-and-file crowd.

McBride's men could do the math, too—1.5 million dues-paying USWA members minus 400,000 actual steelworkers did not add up to zero. Even if the entire steel industry went under, there would still be enough income for the USWA to soldier on. While the staff reps at Five Gateway Center were sympathetic to the rank and file, they had families, too. They had bills to pay and wives and kids who depended on them to provide. The entire U.S. economy was in freefall. If Sadlowski won, they had no doubt he'd fire them. If McBride won, their jobs were secure. Whether or not the United Steelworkers of America had any steelworkers made little difference anymore. It was every man for himself.

A month before the election, a four-color photo of an exhausted Ed

Sadlowski along with an eight-page interview appeared in the January 1977 issue of *Penthouse*. He didn't look like his campaign poster. He was in a garish paisley shirt and an ill-fitting leisure suit, and his expression was no longer rugged confidence—he was no longer looking into the far distance. He seemed to be lost, looking directly into the camera, overwhelmed by the magnitude of the moment. It wasn't until after Pat Coyne read the interview that he realized that Ed Sadlowski was not afraid of losing, but rather terrified he'd win.

Sadlowski attacked America's manufacturing economy. "First of all, to start an industrial society, you have to capture people," he explained. "You get a bunch of immigrants without any legal resources and you put them in plants. You make language a barrier. If they strike, you beat their heads in. Or you try psychic blackmail, coming up with some Calvinistic scheme whereby the worker will think he's saving his soul by becoming an ox who works from sunrise to sundown . . . you make propaganda about the moral stamina involved in becoming a slave. You surround it with the glamour of the American dream." After referring to steelworkers as slaves, he did something worse. He pitied them. "The poor motherfucker who works for forty years and has nothing to show for it, who feels his whole life has been wasted—he'll disprove that bullshit in forty seconds." Asked how he would change the union, he argued for the same thing Big Steel thought would solve all the problems: technology. "With technology, the ultimate goal of organized labor is for no man to have to go down into the bowels of the earth and dig coal. No man will have to be subjected to the blast furnace. We've reduced labor forces from 520,000 fifteen years ago to 400,000 today. Let's reduce them to 100,000."

Coyne couldn't believe what he was reading. To Ed Sadlowski, being a steelworker was the equivalent of being an ox? He wanted to shed jobs? What kind of message was that? They were going to take Gateway Center and knock some heads together, bring the union to the membership, what happened to that? Coyne couldn't help but think that "the poor motherfucker wasting forty years of his life with nothing to show for it" would be him. Mike Olszanski, an Inland Steel vet and coeditor at *Steel Shavings* magazine, remembered how Sadlowski faced the criticism: "You know, I was half asleep, riding on a plane, this guy's got me pumped full of booze, and I don't remember what I said." Coyne had heard the same thing from Ed, but he never forgot the Latin that the brothers at Central Catholic had pounded into his head: *in vino veritas.*

Coyne pushed hard in the final months of the campaign, the tension in his blood rising. It culminated at a local union hall in late November. A couple of Fight Back! supporters weren't being let in to their own building. They called Coyne, who got out of bed and drove six miles to the hall on Carson Street. A friend named Pete Mamula met him there and covered Coyne's back as he let loose on the McBride men barring the door. Pittsburgh police came with their attack dogs, and then Coyne got into a Jack Lambert linebacker crouch, inviting the dogs to come and get him. He let loose a primal growl fed by the years of hard work he feared would amount to nothing. The German Shepherds didn't even sniff him. His wife's alarm clicked on at 6:00 A.M. with KDKA's top news story—a wild man raising hell at a union hall. She grabbed her purse, put on her coat, and was out the door before the traffic and weather.

On February 10, 1977, *The New York Times* reported that Sadlowski had gotten 44.6 percent of the 600,000 ballots cast. The fight had been lost.

45

THE RAIDERS WEREN'T DONE PILING ON THE STEELERS. Knocking Swann unconscious wasn't enough. Ending their season wasn't enough. The words "criminal element" lingered long after Noll said them in reference to Atkinson. In December 1976, Atkinson, with the support of Davis, filed a $3 million lawsuit against Noll for slander, saying in the suit that the remarks were made "for the sole purpose of causing him punishment, embarrassment, and disgrace." Depositions were taken that April, and Dan Rooney was told by his insurance company to just settle the whole mess for $50,000. He refused. They'd go to trial that July in San Francisco, just as training camp was about to start.

The Steelers had other troubles. Mel Blount, the 1975 defensive player of the year and 1976 Pro Bowl MVP, announced before camp that he was holding out for a new contract. Lambert held out, too. And then the lawsuit went to trial. On the witness list: Chuck Noll, Terry Bradshaw, Jack Ham, and Rocky Bleier. In other words, more players missing more camp.

It was a fiasco, and not just because of the lost practice. During his cross-examination, Noll was forced to admit that players like Joe Greene, Blount, and Glen Edwards were part of the criminal element, too, because of their dirty play. Upon hearing that while holding out in his native Georgia, Blount announced he was going to sue Noll for $5 million. Even when Noll won, he lost. In late July, after a two-week trial, a jury dismissed Atkinson's suit. Later that day, Edwards announced he was unhappy with his contract. A week later, Lambert's agent declared that his client "wants to be traded." The war of words escalated in late August, when Noll announced his team captains and didn't include Lambert on the list. The capricious middle linebacker blasted his coach in the papers, who returned fire by saying Lambert didn't deserve to be a captain because he was a holdout.

The careful, egoless ecosystem that Noll had built had been pierced. And even though Lambert and Blount reported to camp just before the season began, and the disgruntled Blount agreed to drop his lawsuit, the team was fractured. It was so obvious that the Chief felt it necessary to come down from the mount and make a case for unity. "This isn't like baseball," said Art Rooney Sr. "Baseball is an individual game. You can have eight players who dislike each other and the management, and they can still go up to the plate and hit. But this is a team game. Everybody has to work together."

The Chief's speech didn't help. The Raiders came into Three Rivers the second week of the season and beat up the home team, forcing five turnovers in a 16–7 win. A few weeks later, Bradshaw broke his wrist and would spend most of the season playing in a cast. Edwards, who signed a new deal, decided he was still unhappy with his contract and left the team just days before a November loss to the Broncos. In December, the night before a game with the Bengals, Noll slipped on a patch of ice and broke his arm. The next day, the Steelers lost. For those who didn't know any better, who hadn't seen up close what a fortress of unity the Steelers had once been, it seemed like the sky was falling, literally. "Honestly," says Ted Petersen, a rookie offensive lineman that season. "I didn't want to practice because there was black soot raining down."

The vibe on the team was different, more ornery and businesslike than it had ever been during Noll's era. Big personalities on the team, the throwbacks who treated the game like, well, a game, were disappearing. Hanratty went to Tampa Bay in the 1976 expansion draft. Mansfield and Russell were gone, too. But the Blount holdout, the Lambert holdout, and the fact that rookies like Tony Dorsett were getting million-dollar contracts while the veterans—three years after the strike—had to now fight well-heeled rookies for their jobs and management for every last dollar they felt they were due put a spotlight on issues that had been festering for years. Issues that were easy for coaches to squelch when Super Bowls were being won and parades were being held and rings were being handed out. But less so when players were losing and underpaid.

As the stakes grew, so did the pressure to perform. And players looked for every advantage. There was a long tradition of players using amphetamines before games to, the players presumed, make themselves more alert and move faster. In locker rooms all over the NFL there were bowls of them, available to be gulped by the handful. The Steelers were no different. "I used them," says Russell. "I thought they would make me better." But when Noll took over the team in 1969, he discouraged players from taking speed. "He thought the pills made you play bad and kept you from using your brain," says Russell. "And he was right—I was much better player without them."

Noll knew his players were using steroids, too. He wasn't unfamiliar with the drug. He had been a coach with the Chargers in 1963, when former U.S. weight-lifting coach Alvin Roy became the team's strength coach and introduced Dianabol to the team, the first evidence of its use in professional football. But he was suspicious of its usefulness. "He didn't know why players would use it," says Art Rooney Jr. "He thought it would make your nuts shrink."

Still, unlike the shakiness and hyperactivity that came with amphetamines, it was harder to see the negative impacts of steroids. Players got bigger, they got stronger, they got better. "Chuck was a disciplinarian on the important things, meetings, practice, travel," says Mike Wagner. "But at times he kind of hid in his room, hoping no one was misbehaving. He wasn't always looking to enforce the rules."

In the mid to late 1970s, as Arnold Schwarzenegger propelled the Mr. Universe contest into the mainstream and weight training became more popular, NFL players became more dedicated to weight lifting. It became a year-round commitment—training camps were no longer for getting in shape but for showing how hard you had worked out during the off-season. The Steelers were no different. While they had a weight room in the bowels of Three Rivers, a lot of guys trained on their own, in the back room of a restaurant called the Red Bull Inn, on the side of the road in the middle of Pennsylvania deer country. "Believe it or not, our facility wasn't as well outfitted as the Red Bull," remembers Petersen. "And since it wasn't downtown, we didn't have to fight traffic to get there."

Jon Kolb worked out there. Mike Webster did, too. The smell of sweat mixed with the aroma of the steaks and chops coming from the Red Bull's kitchen. By 1977, with Ray Mansfield retired, Webster was now the Steelers' unchallenged starting center. And he was obsessive about his training, as he had always been. Growing up on a farm in Wisconsin, Webster had pushed a plow through potato fields. It taught him to get low, use his leverage, and drive his legs. And to work. When he was drafted by the Steelers in 1974, he was an undersized 225 pounds. But he was in the weight room every day, sometimes two hours before a game, pumping iron. Even when he became a perennial Pro Bowler, he'd come back from the game in Hawaii and coaches would find him running the steps in Three Rivers Stadium. "He was a compulsive individual," says Petersen. "No one out-trained him, no one outworked him."

Every season, Webster seemed to get bigger. His biceps bulged against his tapered Steelers jersey. Soon, he had morphed from a proportioned 225-pound center into a hulking 255-pound specimen. Years later, espn .com reported. Webster admitted to physicians that he had used steroids. "We used to call it the scholarship program," says one former Steelers beat writer. "Before guys started using steroids they'd be 230 pounds. A year later they'd be 260 and chiseled."

Still, who was using was rarely openly discussed. "It wasn't like they were handing them out in the locker room," says Moon Mullins. "You would look at people and wonder if they were 300 pounds and solid muscle, what was up. But it was a different era, it was more footloose and fancy free."

"Here's an example of how little we knew about anything," says Petersen. "I remember looking at *Time* magazine as a rookie and it had a big article on cocaine and how it was a rich man's drug and that it was harmless. A buddy called and asked me if I was taking it, because he thought I had so much money."

Into this disarray on the team that season entered Steve Courson, a fifth-round pick out of the University of South Carolina. Courson had been a dominant athlete at his Pennsylvania high school as both a linebacker and offensive lineman. But once he got to college, he found himself falling behind. He had heard about steroids while in high school, and during his freshman year at South Carolina, he began to take them regularly. "The team doctor just handed me a prescription," Courson wrote in his book, *False Glory*.

Within a month of first trying them, the 6'5" Courson had pumped up from 232 pounds to 260, his bench press had increased from 400 pounds to 450, and he was running faster 40s than he ever had. He soon fell into a cycle that would continue throughout college. By the time he was drafted and heading to his first training camp with the Steelers, Courson was taking triple the amount he had used as a freshman. And he punctured the cloistered culture that had existed around the drug. "I am sure there were other guys on that team that used them," says Mullins. "But Steve was just so open about it. He was a hulking person with huge arms and huge chest, and you looked at him and [figured that] if he [was] that big, he must be experimenting with gorilla hormones. He was a student of this stuff—he did a lot of reading, and he had patterned some of the things that had been done in the 1950s with the weight lifters in the Olympics. That was his model."

There were times that Courson's strength worked against him. On drive blocks for running plays, rather than pancaking defenders, Courson was so strong that opponents bounced off his hands, enabling them to keep their feet and slide back into the play. On more than one occasion, Bad Rad kicked him out of practice and told him to stop bench-pressing.

"He was running faster and jumping higher and yet he wasn't the athlete the Kolb and Webster were," says Radakovich. "But we didn't know if what he was doing was good or bad or what the hell it did."

No one did. Roy, the Chargers strength coach, went on to jobs with the Chiefs, Raiders and, from 1973 to 1975, the Cowboys. His successor in Dallas, Bob Ward, once estimated that 25 percent of his team, "maybe more," used steroids. But eventually, they'd all learn. Webster died of a heart attack at fifty. Jim Clack died of a heart attack at fifty-eight. Steelers defensive lineman Steve Furness, a suspected user, died of a heart attack at forty-nine. There were other players, on other teams—known steroid users—whose lives ended just as quickly and tragically. Ex-Raider Lyle Alzado believed his steroid use caused the brain tumors that eventually killed him. Bob Young, an All-Pro lineman with the Cardinals in the 1970s and an admitted user, collapsed from a heart attack at fifty-two. Courson, who bench-pressed 600 pounds at his strongest, was diagnosed with a heart ailment at the end of his career and became a staunch opponent of the drug. He wrote a tell-all about his use, testified before Congress, and did hundreds of presentations to high schools and colleges every year. Right up until he was killed at fifty, crushed while trying to save his dog from a falling tree that he had just chopped down.

But even amidst the confusion, there were moments to build on. That year the Steelers drafted a quarterback from the University of Minnesota named Tony Dungy, whom they had decided to convert to safety. The day he got off the shuttle bus and arrived at the William Penn Hotel for team meetings that spring, he ran into a guy in a cowboy hat who sized him up and said, "You look like a rookie."

"I am," Dungy responded.

"I'm Mel Blount," the Pro Bowl corner said. "Let me know if you need anything."

During camp Dungy backed up Donnie Shell, who, rather than shun the competition, invited the rook into his dorm room to talk about that day's practice. "I would sit there at night and ask questions," says Dungy.

"He was explaining what you should do, and no one was worried about losing their job. They all wanted to get everyone ready to play because anyone might help. The offensive guys would come up after a play in practice and tell you how to line up."

Dungy took note of the way Noll managed his practices and his players. "We had a wide variety of personalities on that team," says Dungy. "And that was his thing—he wanted you to be an individual as long as you functioned within the team concept. He didn't try to pigeonhole everyone. You could do it in your own way with flair as long it worked with the team."

The teaching was constant, even for a sub like Dungy, a converted offensive player who made more mistakes than plays. "I would come off the field and he would ask me where my eyes were, and what was I thinking, and I know you know what to do but why didn't you get it done," says Dungy. "There was nothing accusatory, just questions to make me think about how to improve."

The Steelers did win their division again, but had the AFC's fourth-best record. And it was indicative of their season that the historical footnote that emerged from that season was this: On October 30 against the Oilers, after Bradshaw and Kruczek were injured, Dungy was called upon to be the emergency quarterback. He already had an interception in the game as a backup safety. Then he threw one, too, becoming the only player since the AFL-NFL merger to accomplish that feat.

46

ON CHRISTMAS EVE 1977, ALMOST A YEAR AFTER ED SAD-
lowski lost the USWA election, Pat Coyne was out of a job. While Sadlowski settled back into a position as a rep for District 31, Coyne relied on
his wife's salary as a grade-school music teacher. It was enough to pay the
utilities and put tuna casserole on the table for his four kids. But his oldest daughter was a senior in high school and applying to the most expensive private colleges in the country. And she was smart enough to get
accepted. How was he going to tell her she couldn't go? He had to keep it
together not only for his family, but the steelworkers who kept showing
up asking, "What am I going to do now, Pat?"

Pittsburgh's steelworkers were barely hanging on. In October, USWA
president Lloyd McBride went to Washington to meet with Jimmy Carter
and his administration to complain about foreign imports. At a press
conference prior to the meeting, McBride described Carter's attitude toward the steelworkers as "aloof." Carter wasn't all that interested in meeting with him in the first place, but relented after McBride reminded him
that his union helped put him in office. "Our union has been suffering the
most dramatic loss of jobs in the union's history," McBride told the press
afterward. Asked to be more specific, he added, "Sixty thousand members of the union are receiving assistance from the federal government,"
a polite way of saying food stamps.

Steelworkers would come by the Coyne's at all hours of the day and
night, half in the bag and weepy. Ever the big wheel, Coyne would lend
them money he couldn't spare.

On Sundays, Coyne's house would fill with guys from all over western Pennsylvania. They'd bring Mickey's wide-mouth malt liquor and cheap potato chips, smoke nasty cigars, and watch Coyne rage at Terry Bradshaw on the console color television in the basement. One of the regulars, Pete Mamula, never tired of telling the story of when he and Coyne first met at the downtown Oyster House. "We're all sitting there and this huge figure steps up to the bar and lines up five shots of John Jameson whiskey. He takes out his Zippo and lights them, then knocks 'em back one after the other. The whole joint loved it! Coyne's drinking fire!"

If it was a 1:00 kickoff, Coyne's wife would make chipped-ham sandwiches for halftime and the guys would be out by 5:00. But late games were a problem. The 4:00 kickoffs tended to push into the dinner hour. Coyne insisted that his family eat together every evening, so he'd pull an old black-and-white set into the dining room and everyone would watch the game from there.

With its struggles and a 9-5 record, the 1977 Pittsburgh Steeler season did not lighten Coyne's load. But somehow the team scratched and clawed its way to an AFC Central title. The Steelers flew to Denver to play the Broncos in the divisional playoffs. But the game would be played at 4:00 on Christmas Eve. In a rare moment of reason when it came to the Steelers, Coyne suggested that they have dinner afterward, a few hours before midnight mass.

Coyne slapped his hands together and led a round of "Here we go, Steelers, here we go!" right before kickoff. His face flushed red throughout the back and forth battle, his blood pressure rising and falling with every series of downs. Franco ran for a touchdown and even Bradshaw got over the one-yard line. To the guys in the basement, the Broncos were a soft team built on "Orange Crush" marketing hype. They weren't as supercilious as the Miami Dolphins or as purely evil as the Dallas Cowboys, they were simply vacuous.

The score was tied deep into the game. The steelworkers had faith that the Steelers would pull through. But then Bradshaw threw an interception. And then another. Broncos 34, Steelers 21. Like the blast furnaces along the Monongahela, the men in Coyne's house, the out-of-work fans wasting away in the Iron City, wondered if the Steelers had lost their fire.

It made Pat Coyne tremble with rage. His town was desperate for winners.

47

WITH DORSETT, THE COWBOYS OFFENSE WAS UNSTOPPABLE. Opposing defenses that committed to stopping him put a man in every rushing hole. They might slow him down, but it would leave opponents susceptible to Roger Staubach and his fleet cadre of receivers—Drew Pearson, Golden Richards, Tony Hill, Butch Johnson, and tight end Billy Joe Dupree. With play-action-fake handoffs to Dorsett, the defense would attack the line of scrimmage, freeing up receivers downfield and sideline to sideline. When the defense adjusted to shut down the passing game, Dorsett would run wild.

The Cowboys barreled through the 1977 playoffs. Dorsett ran for 156 yards and three touchdowns on the way to Super Bowl XII. It would be played in the same stadium that Pitt won its national championship just a year before—the Superdome in New Orleans. Like Super Bowl VI, the Cowboys defense dominated the AFC champions (the Denver Broncos), and after a jittery start, the offense performed with Landry precision. Dorsett ran for the first touchdown of the game and then settled into a steady rhythm, finishing with sixty-six yards on fifteen carries. The Cowboys won their second championship with ease, 27–10.

A jubilant Gil Brandt, the one who had predicted a Super Bowl win after the draft, spoke for the franchise. "We realized we were never going to win the big games without a great tailback. Tony Dorsett is the ingredient that made us champions again." Dorsett knew it, too. Even with Dallas's hate-and-now-love relationship with him, he held the cards. "The Cowboys needed me as much as I needed them. But I knew and they knew that I could not be controlled. That gave me a lot of leverage as an athlete and a person. And I liked having that leverage."

OVERTIME

1978–1979

48

STEELERS PRACTICES WERE WIDE-OPEN AFFAIRS. REPORTERS strolled the sidelines, casually making notes of a botched play, or a player who looked tired, or a new wrinkle in the game plan. Access to the locker room was just as liberal. Before practice, after practice, whenever reporters wanted to, really, they could stroll in for a chat with the players. Noll gave his one press conference on Monday and preferred not talking to reporters again until after the game on Sunday. "He was glad to give us access so we wouldn't bother him," says former *Post-Gazette* writer Vito Stellino. "Joe Gordon would hand out the home phone numbers of the players on a mimeographed sheet at the start of the year."

As camp neared in 1978, the story reporters focused on was how the NFL's new rules would impact the sticky-fingered, beat-'em-up style of Pittsburgh's defensive backs and its run-heavy offense. The dictates had been the brainchild of Tex Schramm, designed from his perch as head of the competition committee. Before the 1977 season, rules outlawing the head slap and bumping a receiver more than once during his pattern had been enacted. Then, before the 1978 season, the rules committee stipulated that a defensive back's bump could only be within five yards of the line of scrimmage. It was referred to as "the Mel Blount" rule. Everyone assumed Schramm had created it to keep the Steelers from ever winning again.

But one player saw the changes as an opportunity. "I think a quarterback will now be able to adjust to his routes and maybe get rid of the ball a little quicker," Bradshaw told the *Pittsburgh Press* that summer. "I think you'll have the same basic coverages, but I think the bump-and-run will go out the window. This is gonna stop all the people laying all over the receivers' backs. And that could definitely help me, because a lot of times what has held us up is receivers getting jammed by a cornerback who is all over him."

When Pittsburgh won its first two titles, Bradshaw knew his defense was stout enough and his running game strong enough that he didn't need to win games with his right arm. But in 1978, two seasons removed from the Steelers' last title, he decided to take control of his team. He recognized that his defense was aging—Greene and Greenwood were in their tenth seasons, Blount was in his ninth, White, Ham, and Holmes were in their eighth—and that Franco Harris had been slowed by nagging injuries. Instead of managing games, he was going to win them. "The team morphed a little bit," says Ted Petersen, the former offensive linemen. "Bradshaw started taking the reins."

And Noll, for so long his quarterback's biggest critic, understood this. The chill between them didn't quite thaw, but Noll was always a pragmatist. In the first half of the decade, NFL rules gave an advantage to defensive linemen and the running game. Now they favored more wide-open offenses and a strong-armed quarterback. As a fully formed human being, a connoisseur of wine, a pilot, a scuba diver and, once, a guest conductor of the Pittsburgh Symphony, Noll could adapt.

Which is why, on the first play in the first training-camp practice of 1978, Bradshaw threw a pass. Reporters made a note of it.

The entire vibe at camp that year was different than the year before, and not just because Bradshaw had Noll's permission to let loose. There were no holdouts, no lawsuits, no "distractions," as Dan Rooney called them. "This camp is about football, not gossip," said Joe Greene. "Everything that's happening in this camp is about football. We're going to be going about our business, what we're being paid for."

"I sensed the atmosphere being different than my rookie year," says Dungy. "After two weeks of training camp I could tell it was going to be a special year. I called my mom and told her I think we are going to the Super Bowl."

It wasn't just Bradshaw who felt emboldened by the new rules. His two receivers—Stallworth and Swann—had already shown what they could do with defensive backs draped all over them. Swann's gift of flight had been proven. And in 1977, Stallworth averaged nearly eighteen yards per catch. But in the seasons prior to that, Stallworth, the fourth-round pick out of Alabama A&M, had come along more slowly than his first-round, big-school counterpart. In their second years, Swann had forty-nine catches, eleven touchdowns, and a Super Bowl MVP award, while Stallworth had just twenty catches. In their third years, Swann had ten starts and Stallworth just three. "In the beginning they didn't get along and there was competition," says Joe Gordon. "And early on Stallworth resented that Swann got more attention and balls."

The two were opposites in nearly every way. Stallworth was 6'2", 191 pounds of lean muscle. He was faster than the compact Swann, who was barely 5'11" and weighed 180 pounds. And while Swann earned his fame by making acrobatic catches against one-on-one coverage, he earned his money by using his smaller body and pitter-patter feet to sneak through the middle of the defense. Stallworth had no qualms about stretching across the field, but with his big body and long strides, he excelled at sideline routes. "The difference [between them] was that when Stallworth caught the ball and got a step," Bradshaw wrote in *Looking Deep,* "you weren't going to catch him."

Their personalities seemed to match their games. Swann was tenacious, the guy who bounced back up and told you how great he was because he never doubted it. Off the field he dressed like a first-round pick, talked like a first-round pick, and carried himself like a first-round pick, long after he had actually been a first-round pick. He had been a public relations major at USC, and had chosen that school because the highly touted quarterback he teamed up with in high school had gone to Stanford; he wanted to be on his own, to prove to people that he was the great receiver, not just the guy catching this particular quarterback's passes. "Lynn looked at himself as a national figure," says Gordon. "He was more receptive to national media than to Pittsburgh's."

Stallworth didn't want the attention; he wanted the ball. Making catches was the only way to prove, as a kid from a small black college, that he belonged as he knew he did. He quietly seethed when Bradshaw, a right-handed quarterback, naturally looked left, the direction Swann usually lined up. One afternoon after a Steelers win, he mentioned to Noll how few passes he caught and Noll told him, "John, it's not about you catching a lot of passes, it's about the fact that we won." Stallworth replied, "I'd like to think we could achieve both."

The job of receivers is inherently lonely. They line up at the edge of the field, endure hand-to-hand combat with the man covering them, run at full capacity for ten or twenty or thirty yards or more, and can only hope the quarterback sees them in the three seconds he has to unload the ball. They lack any control over their destiny, unless they scream, jump up and down, and demand they get the ball, like a six-year-old. Which is why, in nearly every huddle, Bradshaw heard from both of his receivers that they were open and he should be looking their way. "They competed against one another," says Petersen. "They liked each other, but they both wanted to be the go-to guy. Bradshaw used to say how much he loved throwing to Jim Smith, who was the third guy in passing situations. He was just getting their goat and keeping the rivalry going. 'I just love throwing to Smitty,' he'd say, to keep that fire burning."

Their early rivalry, at least the one Stallworth had with Swann, grew into grudging respect and then outright friendship as both receivers developed distinctive roles. It helped that, in 1978, it became clear early on there would be plenty of balls to pass around. Bradshaw threw a pair of touchdowns in each of the Steelers' first three games, all wins. The Steelers went six games before they had more rushing yards than passing yards. And in that seventh game, the difference in yardage was only fifteen. It wasn't until the eighth week of the season, after a franchise-best 7-0 start, that the retooled, pass-happy, Bradshaw-led Steelers finally lost. "I think Bradshaw's more confident that he's ever been before," Noll said about Bradshaw that September. "That makes a difference."

Everyone got a turn in this system. When starting tight end Bennie Cunningham was lost for the season because of a knee injury, another class of 1974 stalwart, Randy Grossman, stepped in. He'd finish the year setting a team record for catches by a tight end with thirty-seven, in just ten starts. Stallworth caught forty-one balls, nine touchdown passes, and averaged 19.5 yards per catch. Swann had sixty-one catches and eleven touchdowns. And Bradshaw threw for a career-high 2,915 yards and twenty-eight touchdowns, and completed more than 56 percent of his passes. All of this earned him the league's MVP award.

Because of Bradshaw, because of his offensive fireworks, the Steelers beat regular-season opponents by an average of more than ten points per game that season.

But, despite winning fourteen games, they weren't perfect. They led the league with thirty-nine turnovers, twenty of them coming off of Bradshaw interceptions. And when the quarterback slumped, it didn't take much for him to find those dark places. "I doubt I'll ever be able to look in the mirror and say I'm the best quarterback in football," Bradshaw said one afternoon. "Maybe it's because of my personality. I think I have charisma, but I don't think I'll get the recognition. First mistake I make, I'll be battered for it. I lose my greatness when I have a bad game. I go back to being a dummy."

The Steel Curtain, meanwhile, was starting to show some wear late in games. The front four no longer had the power to penetrate the offensive line on its own, so coaches called more blitzes. That made the Steelers vulnerable on the edges and in the middle of the field. As they never had before, teams found soft spots in the defense and exploited them. The

Oilers scored fourteen second-half points to hand them their first loss. Kansas City scored twenty-one second-half points in a mid-season game, nearly pulling off an upset. The week after that, the Saints took a fourth-quarter lead against a sputtering Steeler D, which had to be bailed out by a late Bradshaw touchdown pass. "Our defense just wasn't as good," says Ham. "We were a little bit older. One game, after Bradshaw had won it for us and there were about three seconds left, he came off the field and said to me, 'Do you think you can hold them?' He was laughing."

The inability to close out games was a concern, but the panic was relative. The Steelers D gave up the fewest points in the league that year and didn't allow a first-quarter touchdown. Noll, however, wasn't amused by any slumps, perceived or otherwise. And after a 10–7 loss to the Rams—in which Bradshaw threw three picks and Franco Harris was limited to fifty yards—dropped his team to 9-2, he decided something had to be said.

Noll had a habit of laying into the team after wins and praising them after losses. It was his way of making sure that no one became complacent with success or too overcome by failure. It was also how he avoided having to divine inspiration from defeat. But after the Rams loss, he felt he had no choice. While meeting with the team, he began a story: "Gentlemen, I want to tell you a story about two monks who go for a walk by a stream. Sometime down the stream there is a fair maiden who wants to come across. The first monk goes across, brings her to the edge, and sets her down. The two monks continue down the stream in silence, and sometime further down they stop again. The second monk says to the first, 'You know, it's against our belief and our religion to come into contact with a person of opposite sex, and you disregarded that.' The first monk responded, 'I set her down back there, but you carried her all the way here.'

"Okay, I'll see you guys tomorrow at ten o'clock."

There was total silence in the room as the Steelers looked at one another in bewilderment.

But it worked. The Steelers finished the season on a five-game win streak. "I can remember, with a couple of weeks left in the season, Joe Greene said to one of the writers, 'I'll see you at the summit,'" says Petersen. "I asked one of my teammates what Greene meant by the summit. He just looked at me and said, 'The Super Bowl.' I thought, if Joe Greene thinks we're going to the Super Bowl, we must be going to the Super Bowl."

49

"HOLLYWOOD" HENDERSON WAS DOING WHAT HE LOVED best. Talking, boasting, grabbing attention by the mouthful. Super Bowl XIII, once again in Miami and a rematch between the Cowboys and the Steelers, was just days away. And the brashest, biggest mouth on the Cowboys had an audience of reporters hanging on his every word. He had to deliver.

In the three seasons since Henderson had opened Super Bowl X with a record-setting kickoff return, he had become one of the most dynamic players in football. The speed he displayed as a rookie that sunny afternoon in Miami, sprinting up the field as fast as a man half his size, had been put to use as a pass-rushing linebacker. In 1977, his first year starting every game, Henderson destroyed quarterbacks and made three interceptions—one of which he returned seventy-nine yards for a touchdown—and was voted to the Pro Bowl. Oh yeah, the Cowboys won the Super Bowl, too.

It was the perfect storm of accolades and accomplishment for a player who believed he had become bigger than the star on his helmet. When Schramm told Henderson a business associate of the linebacker's was reportedly shady, Henderson screamed, telling Schramm he had no business deciding who he hung out with. When Giants fans cheered as he was carted off the field early in the 1978 season because of a sprained ankle, he flipped them the bird. One finger for seventy-five thousand fans. After the 1977 season, the Cowboys were one of the pro teams asked to compete in ABC's *The Superstars* competition. Landry and Schramm decided to send ten players—and Henderson, a Pro Bowler and the best athlete on the team, wasn't invited. So he bought himself a ticket and spent a few days taunting his teammates. One afternoon he challenged Staubach to a swim race. Another day he bought a bikini bottom on the beach and spent the afternoon sunbathing. "It seemed like every two hours I was on my way to my room with a different gal," he wrote in his autobiography, *Out of Control*. "I was watching the guys watch me as I go."

It was hard not to watch Henderson, no matter what he did. He played with complete abandon on kickoffs, punts, and every down on defense, laying waste to opponents with a well-placed helmet to the bottom of their chin. He darted around like a squirrel in traffic, at angles that seemed impossible to achieve for a man who was 6'2", 221 pounds. But he lived just as recklessly.

Being in big-money Dallas, a place every bit as glamorous as the TV show it inspired, encouraged Henderson to party as hard as he played. And he developed a cocaine habit. Not just a social one. He would do a line in the morning to kill the pain of all the sniffing he did the night before. He's wake up with clots of blood stuffing up his nose, injuries from the previous night's bash. He'd blow them out, feel the sting, and then snort more coke to make everything numb again. He did coke before practice, spent $1,000 a week on the drug, and carried around a roll of toilet paper to tend to his incessant runny noses. His pregame routine included packing his nose full of powder, popping amphetamines, Percodan, and some codeine pills.

None of it seemed to impact his performance. And it only amped-up his attitude. Nearly every week he was making claims to reporters about the team the Cowboys were about to play, then backing up his braggadocio on the field. Before Dallas met the Redskins on Thanksgiving, with both teams at 8-4, Henderson called his opponents turkeys and said, "We're gonna pluck 'em and cook 'em." Then the Cowboys beat 'em, 37–10.

Henderson had missed several games early in 1978 due to the ankle injury he suffered against the Giants, and the Cowboys struggled, starting just 6-4. But with Hollywood back in the lineup and fully recovered for the second half of the season, Dallas's Doomsday Defense stiffened up. The Cowboys finished the year with a six-game winning streak, leading the league in sacks and rushing yards allowed. Staubach, meanwhile, tossed an NFC-best twenty-five touchdown passes, led the league in passing efficiency, and captained an offense that scored more points than any team in the NFL, including the Steelers.

They played with the swagger of the NFL champs they were, something that Henderson never tired of reminding people about. He'd taken to planning out what he was going to say before big games, knowing reporters were waiting on him. And as the Cowboys prepped to leave for Los Angeles and the NFC title game against the Rams, Henderson's headlines were: "The Rams don't have enough class to go to the Super Bowl." He repeated it all week long and even added, "If they don't choke, I will choke them."

The morning of the game he snorted a pile of coke, climbed into a limo he'd rented for the day, threw on a fur coat, and went to the stadium. That afternoon, after a scoreless first half, the Cowboys blew out the Rams, leading 21–0 late in the fourth. The TV cameras were always looking for Henderson now, and they found him on the sideline. The microphone picked him up when he said, "It's 21–0, the Rams are choking, and I ain't through yet." On the next series, he intercepted a pass, returned it sixty-nine yards for a touchdown, and then, to celebrate, gently flipped the ball over the goalpost crossbar with a sublime finger roll.

He would have dunked it, but "My legs were dead. My cocaine use was starting to age me."

50

THE STEELERS EASILY DISPATCHED THE BRONCOS AND THE Oilers by a combined score of 67–15 in the playoffs. Super Bowl XIII would be what championships are supposed to be but rarely are: The two best teams playing at the highest levels and with a hatred for each other. In the previous decade the two franchises had combined to play in five Super Bowls, winning four of them. The winner would be the first franchise with three Super Bowl titles. It also happened to be the greatest collection of talent on a single field in NFL history, then and now. The Steelers had ten Pro Bowlers, the Cowboys nine. Noll and Landry would eventually be enshrined in Canton, and so would fourteen players who started that day, including nine from the Steelers and five from the Cowboys. *Newsweek,* splitting its cover diagonally down the middle, put Bradshaw on one side and Henderson on the other, under the cover line, A REALLY SUPER BOWL.

A poll of writers taken early in the pregame hype listed Henderson as the player they most wanted to interview. And he didn't want to disappoint. That's how he found himself in his favorite spot: surrounded by reporters, ready to talk.

First, he predicted the Cowboys would shut the Steelers out, just as they had the Rams in the NFC title game. Then, he went on to insult as many Steelers as he could think of. Lambert was a "toothless chimpanzee." Grossman, who would be lined up opposite Henderson during the game, was just a backup who only played "when someone dies or breaks a leg." Finally, he finished his rant with a shot at Bradshaw, saying the quarterback "couldn't spell 'cat' if you spotted him the 'c' and the 't.'"

Bradshaw wasn't reading the papers that week. The first time he heard the slight was when reporters asked him how he felt about it. He laughed it off, pretending to struggle after spelling out the "c" and the "t." But it punctured the thin veil of confidence he'd built during the year. It was up to Greene, forever Bradshaw's booster, to remind reporters—and the Cowboys—that the game wasn't being played during the week. "We're just going to go on the field," he said "and get the job done." Noll's response was even simpler: "Empty barrels make the most noise."

But Noll and the Steelers were particularly concerned about the Cowboys' Flex defense, which had been flummoxing opponents all season. The brainchild of Landry, the Flex ran counter to everything football players instinctively try to do: seek and destroy. It was thoughtful, required patience, and asked players to react, rather than pursue. The defensive linemen didn't line up on top of players, the way the Steelers did in their Stunt 4-3, they lined up in gaps, sometimes a couple of feet off the line of scrimmage. They were responsible for reading the direction of the play, closing a gap or keeping offensive linemen occupied, so linebackers behind them could shoot into holes. Every player on the front seven had one gap responsibility, except the middle linebacker, who had two. The defense was designed to funnel plays toward that player in the middle.

As they did the Cowboys offense, the Steelers hated the Flex for its trickery and its air of superiority. "Preparing for the Flex was difficult," says Petersen. "They had an even front, no nose tackle, and that was different than most teams. Randy White might be up on the ball and Harvey Martin might be off the ball. Or vice versa. But when they lined up like that it was easy for one of them to slide down the line, which made it hard for our offensive tackles to slide down and trap them."

During practices leading up to the game, Noll and his offensive staff altered the Steeler trap they had been running for years. Normally, they'd have a guard pull by stepping behind the center and blocking the defensive linemen on his opposite side. That sealed a hole on that side of the line of scrimmage. But against the Flex, with a defensive tackle always lined up a few feet off the ball and sliding down the line to avoid flying bodies, it would be impossible to run that kind of trap. He'd see the guard coming and sidestep the block. So the Steelers improvised. The guard who normally pulled would hold his ground. And the tackle would now pull, taking on the flexing Cowboys defender. It delayed the trap, giving the Steelers players a chance to clear space while the tackle scrambled down the line for a clean shot on the roving defender. Says Petersen: "It was something we did just for them."

"I remember reading Sports Illustrated's break down of the positions," says Ray Pinney, who was the starting right tackle that day. "The Cowboys had Harvey Martin and Too Tall Jones and Randy White and were bigger and stronger and faster and they didn't give us one ounce of respect. They thought that the Cowboys D-line was going to beat up on us."

The Steelers felt—and acted—differently. In fact, Noll was so impressed with his team's final practice the Friday before the game, he cut it short. They were ready.

It rained the night before the game and deep into the morning. Palm trees swayed violently. Bradshaw, watching the green leaves whip in the wind from his room, hoped the field would be muddy, slowing down Dorsett and the 'Boys. He forgot about the tarp covering the grass. At a morning chapel service, Steelers players began bickering about whether or not it was appropriate to pray for winning. "Of course," says Petersen, "most of these guys had rings already, so I didn't think it was fair to pray for anything but winning."

After coming in from warm-ups the team had thirty minutes before it needed to be back on the field. They had already done the coin flip and the Cowboys had won. They elected to receive the ball. As the players gathered around Noll in the locker room, he did something he rarely ever did: He made a speech. It wasn't rah-rah and it wasn't a fable about squirrels in trees or monks walking by a creek. It was about football and strategy and psychology. He said, "Okay, here's the way the game is going to play out. They are going to take the opening kickoff and run the ball down our throats. But trust me, they know they can't beat you guys just playing smash-mouth football, beating you man-to-man. Eventually they will reach into their bag of tricks. That's when you know the game is over. We will have won at that moment."

The Cowboys received the kick and Dorsett proceeded to tear up his hometown team. On three of the first four plays of the game, he gained thirty-eight yards. But on the fifth, a first and ten from the Steelers' forty-seven, the Cowboys used the tricks that Noll had predicted they would and that his players so despised. Dorsett took a pitch from Staubach and then handed it to Drew Pearson, who let it slip and slide out of his fingers and onto the ground. Steelers defensive tackle John Banaszak fell on the ball right on top of the Super Bowl logo painted at midfield. "On the sideline we all looked at each other and were like, 'Oh my god, how did he know?'" says Cliff Stoudt, a second-year quarterback that season. "From an emotional point of view we thought, he's right, game's over."

Bradshaw, calling the plays, methodically moved the Steelers down the field. A short gain on the ground, followed by ten yards through the air. Then, on first and ten from the Cowboys twenty-eight, Bradshaw huddled up his team and called "43-I Takeoff."

While watching Cowboys film, Swann had noticed that the Cowboys safeties tended to bite hard when they thought the quarterback was taking a three-step drop. In "43-I Takeoff" Bradshaw takes a three-step drop and Stallworth makes a sharp cut toward the middle of the field. During practice, when the time was right in the game, Swann had suggested to Bradshaw that he fake the three-step drop and have him sprint for the end zone. That was "42-I Takeoff" which was designed to go to him, not Stallworth. Bradshaw just looked at Swann, smiled as if to say, "Thanks for the call, I'll get you next time," and called the play for Stallworth.

Then Bradshaw made a quick three-step drop, faked and lofted a wobbly, floating, ugly pass to Stallworth, who had beaten two defenders into the end zone and leapt for the pass.

Five minutes into the game, the Steelers were up 7–0.

But Bradshaw's magic didn't last. On the next drive, he threw a pick. The one after that, he fumbled, setting the Cowboys up at the Steelers' forty-one. As they had during the season, the Steelers brought the blitz all game long. Seven, eight men at the line of scrimmage, supplementing a front four that no longer devastated the pocket around the passer. It had already produced two sacks. And as the Cowboys faced third and eight from the Steelers thirty-nine, Pittsburgh brought it again. Staubach dropped back and, just as Lambert jumped with his arms in the air, like the Grim Reaper ready to smother another victim, he unloaded a pass to Tony Hill, who was cutting toward the sideline.

The Steelers' defensive backs were locked in one-on-one coverage. Mel Blount chased Drew Pearson down the field, with his back to Staubach and the rest of the field. Hill cut underneath him, caught Staubach's pass and raced down the sideline past Blount, who didn't see him until Hill was already on his way to the end zone, tying the game at seven.

It didn't take long for the Cowboys to take the lead. On the next series, the first of the second quarter, Bradshaw had his team driving. As he dropped back to pass near midfield, the ball squirted out of his hand. He shuffled right, picked it up on one bounce, sprinted right and was sandwiched by Henderson and linebacker Mike Hegman. As Henderson wrapped Bradshaw up and threw him onto the ground, Hegman pulled the ball from the quarterback's grasp. He ran untouched thirty-seven yards to the end zone. Cowboys 14, Steelers 7.

Three minutes into the second quarter there had been three fumbles (two by Bradshaw), one interception (Bradshaw again) and three touchdowns. "Terry never got shaken by those mistakes, though," says Stoudt. "He never got shaken by anything. He would just come to the sideline. Of course, I was going to make more if we won that game than I did the entire season. So I was thinking, come on man, you're costing me money. I was just like a fan."

That's when things got really wacky.

After the tackle by Henderson, Bradshaw walked to the sidelines with his non-throwing left arm hanging limply by his side. Doctors told him that his left shoulder might be separated. No time to tape him up, let alone take a painkilling injection. Instead Bradshaw went back on the field, called two straight handoffs and then a ten-yard pass to Stallworth, who broke one tackle, spun outside, and sprinted seventy yards, with his sleeves flapping against his spindly arms as he ran, tying the record for the longest Super Bowl score in history. Cowboys 14, Steelers 14.

Eighteen minutes into the game and there were already four touchdowns on the scoreboard, all of them on long plays, one of them record-tying, and one of them a fumble returned for a score. The second quarter wasn't even half over. "No one," Noll said after the game, "could deliver a knockout punch."

Although Bradshaw tried. With twenty-six seconds left in the first half and the game still tied, he called a run-pass option from the Cowboys' seven-yard line. Sprinting right he found Bleier alone in the end zone and lofted a ball high into the air. Leaping over a Cowboy, Bleier snatched the ball from the sky with both hands and fell onto his back. On the Steelers radio broadcast, Cope screamed, "Would you have expected Rocky Bleier to turn into Nijinsky?"

His partner wondered aloud, "Who is Nijinsky?"

Cope, exasperated, answered, "He was a great ballet dancer."

At the end of the half, the Steelers led 21–14 and had gained 271 yards to the Cowboys' 102. But Stallworth, who had more than a hundred yards receiving and two touchdowns in the first half, had cramps that kept him on the bench as the third quarter got under way. And without him, the Steelers' offense made as much noise as a bag of cotton. The Flex limited Harris to just forty-four yards on fourteen carries. Bradshaw's only viable weapon was Swann. "I couldn't do anything," Bradshaw said years later.

The Cowboys came out inspired in the third. The Steelers' first drive went three plays and lost four yards. Their second went four plays (including a false-start penalty) and lost six yards. After that, midway through the third quarter, Dallas got the ball back at the Steelers' forty-two. After an incomplete pass, Dorsett ran for four yards and Staubach completed a pass for eight. First down. Three plays later, Dorsett picked up another five, for another first down. Two plays later it was seven yards from Dorsett, setting up a third and three from the Steelers' ten.

As Staubach dropped back to pass he spotted tight end Jackie Smith wide open in the back of the end zone. Smith was thirty-eight years old and had retired the previous season after fifteen years with the St. Louis Cardinals. He was as sure-handed a tight end who ever played, one of the fourteen future Hall of Famers playing that day. That September, needing one more tight end, Landry had coaxed Smith out of retirement, with the bait of one more chance to play in the Super Bowl. Now he was about to score a game-tying touchdown to keep his team alive.

Except that as the ball sailed gently toward him, Smith purposely slid to get his body underneath it. The pass, which was wobbling, hit him square in the numbers before he could get his hands to his chest. It bounced off his pads, off his fingers, and onto the end-zone turf. "Bless his heart," said the Cowboys radio announcer. "He's got to be the sickest man in America."

The Cowboys had to settle for a field goal.

Heading into the fourth quarter, the Steelers clung to a four-point lead, 21–17, and they'd get the ball back with 12:08 remaining in the game. Bradshaw, as he had done all season, took over. On a third and eight from the Steelers seventeen, he completed a nine-yard pass for a first down. On the next play, he connected with Lynn Swann for thirteen more yards. Two plays later, a long bomb to Swann led to a thirty-three-yard pass interference call against Dallas, giving the Steelers the ball at the Cowboys' twenty-three. "I remember the ball was in the air and I was looking right into Randy White's face," says Ray Pinney. "I saw disappointment. I couldn't see the play but I knew from his expression that it was bad for them and good for us. He was crushed."

Three plays later, on a third and four from the seventeen, Bradshaw dropped back to pass. Henderson came blitzing untouched up the middle and pulled him down by the sleeve of his left arm. Afterward, as a ref stood over them, Henderson took his time climbing off Bradshaw, taunting him until Bradshaw could get himself up. The play didn't count, as the refs had blown it dead before the snap because of a delay-of-game penalty, only it was too loud for anyone to hear. But Harris, the mellowest man on the Steelers, took issue with Henderson's attitude. As the linebacker stood up, Harris confronted him. "Even before that Super Bowl he was trying to get into the psyche of the Steelers," says Harris. "And when he did that I thought he crossed the line and I had to go over there, you know what I mean, and I was ready for whatever happened."

Really, anything could have happened. Before the game Henderson had mixed powder and water and poured it into an empty nasal spray bottle. He hid the inhaler in a small hip pocket in his uniform and then, on the sideline before that series, sprayed the drug up his nose. When Harris got in his face, they jawed at each other for close to twenty seconds, with Henderson finally replying, "Fuck you in your ass, and your mama, too."

Henderson had been shadowing Harris all game, keeping the running back from making the quick cutbacks he relied on. But in the huddle, Harris commanded, "Give me the ball." As Bradshaw surveyed the line of scrimmage, he saw the middle of the field wide open and called the trap the Steelers had worked on all week. As Harris took the ball, the line parted, and he ran untouched twenty-two yards into the end zone. "I just said, 'Get in the end zone, get in the end zone,'" Harris says. The score, with a little more than seven minutes left in the game, was Steelers 28, Cowboys 17.

It stayed that way for nineteen seconds.

Before the kickoff, Noll specifically instructed Gerela to boot it deep. But as he approached the tee, Gerela slipped and the ball sputtered in a slow, awkward bounce to Randy White, on the field to be the lead blocker and wearing a cast on his left hand. As he scooped up the ball and ran, cradling the ball against his cast, Dungy hit him on his side, and the ball squirted into the air. It bounced around on the ground before a tangled pile of Steelers and Cowboys could tame it. Off to the side was Steelers linebacker Dennis Winston, who had been trailing on the play. "All of a sudden he drops to a knee and starts to dig through the pile," remembers Stoudt.

"And he's digging and digging," says Petersen. "He was really out of the play. But then the refs pull everyone apart and the guy who comes out with the ball is Dennis. I once roomed with him. He could be very strong-willed."

The Steelers had the ball at the Cowboys' nineteen-yard line.

On the next play, Bradshaw looked at Swann in the huddle and called "42-I Takeoff." Bradshaw dropped back, pump-faked, and unleashed a rising rope down the middle of the field. Flashing through the end zone, Swann leaped, kicking his legs as though they were propelling him higher, snared the pass, came down on his knees, and slid out of the back of the end zone. The Steelers had opened up an eighteen-point lead.

The Cowboys didn't quit. On the next drive, Staubach threw for seven yards, then ran for eighteen, then threw for seventeen more. He handed off to Dorsett, who scampered for twenty-nine. Then Staubach completed three straight passes, including a seven-yard touchdown pass, making the score 35–24, Steelers. In a little more than four minutes he had driven Dallas eighty-nine yards. They lined up for an onside kick and the Steelers put Dungy on the front line of their "hands" team—the players who are expected to recover any bouncing balls. "I wanted them to kick it to me," Dungy says. "I had good hands. I was thinking about the Randy White fumble I had caused and how this was going to be my day and I was going to ice this game and be the hero. Then they kicked it to me, and I fumbled it."

When the Cowboys recovered the ensuing onside kick, several Steelers could be heard on the sideline having flashbacks to the defense's season long late game collapses. "We're doing it again!" they yelled.

It looked like it. Over the next two minutes Staubach surgically picked Pittsburgh apart. A twenty-two-yard pass to Pearson down the right side; a twenty-five-yard pass to Pearson down the middle. Nine more to Dorsett. And then four yards for a touchdown to Butch Johnson. Twenty-two seconds remained and both teams lined up for an onside kick. Again.

This time, Bleier stood in the middle of the field, just across from the Cowboys kicker. "I was thinking about Dungy and how he had flubbed the last kick and I was saying to myself, 'please don't kick it to me,'" says Bleier. Nearby, Dungy says he was thinking the exact same thing. The slow roller bounced gently into Bleier's arms. He cradled the ball, and the Steelers were Super Bowl champs. Again. Bradshaw, with his finger wagging in the air while Steelers celebrated all around him, was named the game's MVP, thanks to Super Bowl records of 318 passing yards and four touchdowns.

As the players walked off the field, the Cowboys' radio broadcaster said, "It was the triumph of the blue collar over the white collar."

That night, the Rooneys held a party at the Fort Lauderdale resort where the team had stayed. And when the players returned to Pittsburgh, the city celebrated with a party at Point State Park. It was five below zero that day, but fans began staking out their places before sunrise. By noon, when the first of the Steelers stood on a makeshift stage to thank them for their support, 120,000 Steelers backers had packed the park. "It was like family," says Stoudt. "They were just as much a part of it all as we were."

Says Dungy: "Everyone in Pittsburgh felt the team was theirs."

The players all felt the warmth from their fans, the elation that comes from winning. Their legacies were secure. For the rest of their lives every player on that team, from Cliff Stoudt to Joe Greene, would be treated like a Carnegie once they crossed into town over the Hot Metal Bridge. At a time when the city's industry was crumbling, when people were fleeing Pittsburgh in search of a town with a future, the players made being from Aliquippa and the North Side and everywhere else in Iron City worth bragging about. And not just for three hours on Sunday or from September to January, but for years. Over an entire decade they had played the way the city worked and lived—or at least the way it once had. That reminded everyone who lived between the Monongahela, Allegheny, and Ohio Rivers that what they believed, their way of life, wasn't completely disappearing and hadn't been discarded, like scrap iron. To work hard, to work together, to play for team above self could still lead to greatness. If not immediately, then one day soon. Again.

But as they listened to those speeches on that bitterly cold day in Pittsburgh, and they cheered for their heroes, most people there had already heard everything they needed to. It happened after the game, when the Steelers had been World Champions for less than twenty minutes. Players, coaches, owners, reporters, cameramen—all of them were gathered in the locker room, crowding around a makeshift podium for the televised Super Bowl trophy presentation. The Chief was up there. So were Dan Rooney and Pete Rozelle and Chuck Noll. The players stood at their lockers in various states of undress, some in just their grass-stained football pants, others with their shoulder pads on, loosely shifting as they hugged and laughed and waited for the trophy to be handed from the commissioner to the owner. They yelled "Chief" as Art Rooney spoke, thanking them, thanking Noll. And then it was their coach's turn to talk. The room grew silent. "You know, I said one thing to our football team after the game, and I sincerely believe it," Noll said. "I don't think we've peaked yet. And we're looking forward to even bigger and better things."

Then the room—and an entire city watching on TV—erupted in cheers.

ACKNOWLEDGMENTS

Thanking people who helped you put together a book is an impossible task. But it would be ungracious not to try.

First, we owe a debt of gratitude to our agent, Richard Abate, who not only thought of the idea that became the book you're now holding, but had the genius idea of putting us together to write it. We're also grateful to Bill Shinker of Gotham, who was not only kind enough to publish our work, but also put us under the steady guidance of Patrick Mulligan, our editor. Both Patrick and editorial assistant Travers Johnson provided expert advice—and friendly reminders to keep moving forward.

Chad would also like to thank his pals at *ESPN The Magazine*, especially his bosses, GM, Gary Hoenig, and editor in chief, Gary Belsky, who were both understanding and encouraging about the project. Chris Berend, Neil Fine, and Sue Hovey also tried their best not to constantly remind Chad that his deadline was looming. Charles Rosen and Douglas Cameron, the brilliant minds behind the New York ad agency Amalgamated, helped us shape the culture wars between the Steelers and the Cowboys. At espn.com, editor extraordinaire and Pittsburgh native John Banks let Chad bend his ear constantly and filled his notebooks with good stories and great leads from the old days. As did Ed Bouchette from the *Pittsburgh Post-Gazette*, Vito Stellino, an old *PG* scribe now at the *Times-Union* in Jacksonville, Joe Gordon, the former Steelers PR man, and Art Rooney Jr. It's easy to see why the teams from that era not only achieved greatness, but remained close for decades afterward. The Rooney clan set a fine example.

Shawn thanks all of the steelworkers from Aliquippa, Beaver Falls,

Braddock, Homestead, McKeesport, the South Side, Youngstown, Chicago, Baltimore, Gary, Indiana, and Bethlehem, Pennsylvania, from the 1970s who were a part of Steelworkers Fight Back!; his mother, Mary Jo; his sisters, Tami and Teri, and his brother, Patrick. Art Louderback at the Heinz History Center in Pittsburgh provided access to the J&L Steel company archives and Craig Britcher and Robert Stakeley from the Heinz History Center's Sports Museum for their help detailing the history of football in western Pennsylvania. Ed Sadlowski, Bob Gumpert, Steve Early, Clem Balanoff, Jim Balanoff, Andy Kmec, Oliver Montgomery, Tony Franchini, Joey Diven, Ronnie Demarski, Ed James, Ronnie Weisen, Father Jack O'Malley, Monsignor Charles Rice, Peter Mamula, Ronnie Mamula, I. W. Abel, Ed Ayoub, Joe Rauh, Walter Burke, and scores of others passed through the Coyne household. Patrick Coyne Sr. touched the lives of every one of them and like the city that forged him, he hit with everything he had until the very end.

NOTES

The bulk of the material about the Steelers for this book was culled from thirty interviews with former players, coaches, scouts, and team executives who played a role on those 1970 teams. We owe a special debt to Andy Russell, Rocky Bleier, Dick Hoak, Joe Gordon, Gerry Mullins, Dan Radakovich, Franco Harris, Ted Petersen, Tony Dungy, Mike Wagner, Bill Nunn, Randy Grossman, Art Rooney Jr., and Joe Greene, who were especially generous with their time and stories. They never deflected a question and never gave anything less than an honest answer.

Additionally, the authors read more than two dozen books about the era of the Super 70s. These were especially helpful: *About Three Bricks Shy . . . And the Load Filled Up* by Roy Blount Jr., *Steel Dynasty* by Bill Chastain, *Ruanaidh* by Art Rooney Jr., and *My 75 Years with the Steelers* by Dan Rooney, Andrew E. Maisch, and David F. Halaas, *The Murchisons* by Jane Wolfe, *Running Tough* by Tony Dorsett and Harry Frommer, *Duane Thomas and the Fall of America's Team* by Duane Thomas and Paul Zimmerman, *The League* by David Harris, *Brand NFL* by Michael Oriard, *Steelworkers in America* by David Brody, *Which Side Are You On?* by Thomas Geoghegan, *And the Wolf Finally Came* by John P. Hoerr, *Portraits in Steel* by David H. Wollman and Donald R. Inman and, *Making Steel* by Mark Reutter.

One note about the sourcing for this book: Because the stories for so many of the people told in this book have been widely told before, generally accepted facts and well-known information gathered from multiple sources were not cited. Also, game stats, season records, and play-by-play pulled from media guides were also excluded.

Prologue

Page 1 *Because of what Joe Namath* "Super Bowl's Status; Game Rated in Class With World Series After American League's Major Upset," *The New York Times*, Jan. 14, 1969.

Page 2 *"They give steel to"* Address Accepting the Presidential Nomination at the Republican National Convention in Miami Beach, Florida, Richard Nixon, Aug. 8, 1968.

Chapter 1

Page 9 *These were the* "The Winning Ways of a Thirty Year Loser," *Sports Illustrated*, Nov. 23, 1964.

Page 9 *Friends who hung* Ibid.

Page 9 *One of his top players* Ibid.

Page 10 *Once, when he was trying* Art Rooney Jr., *Ruanaidh* (Pittsburgh: Art Rooney Jr., 2008), p. 88.

Page 11 *The old pros* Ibid., p. 62.

Page 12 *"I like John"* Ibid., p. 63.

Page 12 *And Dan Rooney* Bill Chastain, *Steel Dynasty* (Chicago: Triumph Books, 2005), p. 7.

Page 12 *"The Rooneys were"* Rooney Jr., *Ruanaidh,* p. 241.

Page 12 *In high school* Chastain, *Steel Dynasty*, p. 7.

Page 13 *"We met for"* Dan Rooney, Andrew E. Maisch and David F. Halaas, *My 75 Years With the Pittsburgh Steelers and the NFL* (Cambridge, MA.: Da Capo Press, 2007), p. 125.

Page 14 *He'd end up* "Steelers Winning Ticket," *Pittsburgh Post-Gazette*, Jan. 18, 1969.

Page 14 *Several days after* Rooney, Maisch, Halaas, *My 75 Years* . . .

Page 14 *"When I first"* "Steelers Winning Ticket," Pittsburgh Post-Gazette, Jan. 18, 1969.

Chapter 2

Page 16 *"hell with the lid off"* "Pittsburg," Atlantic Monthly, Jan. 1868.

Page 16 *Pittsburgh, without exception* Anthony Trollope, *North America* (Philadelphia, PA.: J.B. Lippincott and Company, 1863), p. 75.

Page 18 *"Gorilla Men"* David Brody, *Steelworkers in America, the Nonunion Era* (Cambridge, MA.: Harvard University Press, 1960), p. 33.

Chapter 3

Page 20 *"First I've got"* Roy Blount Jr., *About Three Bricks Shy of a Load And The Load Filled Up* (Pittsburgh: Univ. of Pittsburgh Press, 2004), p. 121.

Page 20 *Because Brown's teams* Chastain, *Steel Dynasty*, p. 9.

Page 21 *Noll was always* Rooney Jr., *Ruanaidh*, p. 241.

Page 22 *Fellow assistants called* Ibid., p. 241; Blount Jr., *About Three Bricks . . .* , p. 121.

Page 22 *Heated arguments could* Blount Jr., *About Three Bricks . . .* , p. 121.

Chapter 4

Page 23 *"no murder or manslaughter"* http://en.wikipedia.org/wiki/Mob_ football.

Page 23 *"Mob Football"* Ibid.

Page 23 *"hustling over large balls"* Ibid.

Page 24 *The Monaca Scholastics* "Cradle of Pro Football," Senator John Heinz History Center, Pittsburgh, Sports Museum Exhibit.

Chapter 5

Page 27 *"We'll change history"* Rooney, Maisch, Halaas, *My 75 Years . . .* , p. 128.

Page 28 *He told the* Wikipedia, http://en.wikipedia.org/wiki/Buddy_Parker.

Page 28 *"He pointed out"* Rooney, Maisch, Halaas, *My 75 Years . . .* , p. 125.

Chapter 6

Page 30 *The origin of U.S. trade unions* Archie Green, *Wobblies, Pile Butts, and Other Heroes*, (Champaign, IL.: Univ. of Illinois Press, 1993), pp. 230–31.

Page 30 *"Iron City Forge of the Sons"* Ibid.

Page 30 *"Three giant caldrons"* Upton Sinclair, *The Jungle* (Pasadena, CA.: Upton Sinclair, 1920), p. 246.

Chapter 7

Page 34 *"Well, that's it"* Full Color Football: The History of the American Football League (Showtime: The New Frontier), Episode 1.

Page 36 *"Bell tells"* Bell Tells Congressional Hearing New Pro Football League is Being Formed," *The New York Times*, Jul. 29, 1959.

Page 36 *"There's a new league"* Full Color Football: The History of the American Football League (Showtime: The New Frontier), Episode 1.

Chapter 8

Page 38 *"I knew what"* Chastain, *Steel Dynasty*, p. 17.

Page 39 *"At the time"* Ibid.

Page 39 *For three springs* Larry Fox, *Mean Joe Greene and The Steelers Front Four* (New York: Dodd, Mead & Company, 1975), p. 19.

Page 39 *Noll sat with* Ibid., pp. 19–20.

Page 40 *He had led* "New Legend at Notre Dame," *Sports Illustrated*, Nov. 7, 1966.

Page 40 *"I feel like"* Rooney Jr., *Ruanaidh*, p. 247.

Page 40 *Remembered Rooney Jr.* Ibid.

Page 41 *Their scouting reports* Blount Jr., *About Three Bricks*, pp. 276–77.

Page 41 *"But that was"* Ibid., p. 277.

Page 41 *He called Art* Ibid., p. 45.

Page 42 *Rather than work* Rooney Jr., *Ruanaidh*, p. 145.

Page 42 *He had begged* Ibid., p. 238.

Page 43 *"Well . . . when I"* Ibid., pp. 239–40.

Page 43 *The night before* Ibid., p. 242.

Page 43 *"We need too"* Fox, *Mean Joe Greene . . .* , p. 20.

Page 44 *He ordered coffee* Rooney Jr., *Ruanaidh*, p. 245.

Page 44 *Art Jr. looked* Ibid., p. 246.

Page 45 *After he got* Fox, *Mean Joe Greene . . .* , p. 24.; Interview, Joe Greene, June 1, 2009.

Page 45 *"Joe Who?"* Fox, *Mean Joe Greene . . .* , p. 20.

Page 45 *Teammates suffered in* Interview, Joe Greene, June 1, 2009.

Page 45 *When he was embarrassed* Fox, *Mean Joe Greene . . .* , p. 30.

Page 45 *When he was ten* Blount Jr., *About Three Bricks . . .* , p. 283.

Page 46 *"I had a"* Ibid.

Page 46 *Years later, after* Ibid.

Page 46 *"When I started playing in high school . . . ,"* Interview, Joe Greene, June 1, 2009.

Page 47 *So he ran* Ibid., p. 284; Interview, Joe Greene, June 1, 2009.

Chapter 9

Page 48 *Like Hunt* Jane Wolfe, *The Murchisons, The Rise and Fall of a Texas Dynasty* (New York: St. Martin's Press, 1989).

Page 48 *Red Smith wrote* Red Smith, *To Absent Friends* (New York: Atheneum, 1982), p. 374.

Page 49 *"This is the last"* Michael MacCambridge, *America's Game* (New York: Random House, 2004), p. 128.

Chapter 10

Page 53 *"tuxedo unionism"* "Abel's Issue: 'Tuxedo Unionism' in the Steelworkers," *The New York Times*, Jan. 12, 1965.

Chapter 11

Page 54 *"Sonny, look at the schedule"* Mark Kriegel, *Namath: A Biography*, (New York: Viking Penguin, 2004), p. 126.

Page 55 *"You know you're not"* Bernie Parrish, *They Call It a Game* (New York: The Dial Press, 1971), p. 135.

Page 55 *"A million dollar set"* "Sonny Werblin, an Impresario of New York's Sports Extravaganza, Is Dead at 81," *The New York Times*, Nov. 23, 1993.

Page 56 *"There was one set"* *America's Game Super Bowl III* (NFL Films).

Chapter 12

Page 57 *He had learned* Interview, Dick Hoak, March 13, 2009.

Page 57 *The Hoaks were* Ibid.

Page 58 *Those uniforms? Well* Blount Jr., *About Three Bricks . . .* , p. 55.

Page 58 *When it rained* Interview, Dick Hoak, March 13, 2009.

Page 58 *They'd smoke some cigarettes* Blount Jr., *About Three Bricks . . .* , p. 55.

Page 58 *Each player got* Ibid.; Interview, Dick Hoak, March 13, 2009, Interview, Andy Russell, March 12, 2009.

Page 59 *"I'd rather play"* Fox, *Mean Joe Greene . . .* , p. 24.

Page 59 *But once he* Ibid.

Page 60 *"And you are at a disadvantage . . ."* Interview, Andy Russell, March 12, 2009.

Page 60 *He was the* Blount Jr., *About Three Bricks . . .* , p. 287.

Page 60 *If a player* Interview, Andy Russell, March 12, 2009.

Page 60 *"So Ray was"* Rooney, Maisch, Halaas, *My 75 Years . . .* , p. 130.

Page 60 *Years later, Russell* Interview, Andy Russell, March 12, 2009.

Page 61 *Practice jerseys didn't* Interview, Tony Dungy, Sept. 23, 2009.

Page 62 *Noll looked the* Interview, Andy Russell, March 12, 2009.

Page 63 *He ran after* Ibid., Interview, Joe Greene, June 1, 2009.

Page 63 *Greene was in* Andy Russell, *A Steeler Odyssey* (Champaign, IL.: Segamore Publishing, 1998), p. 105.

Page 63 *Greene didn't bother* Ibid., pp. 104–5.

Page 64 *Only once that* Interviews, Joe Greene, June 1, 2009; Andy Russell, March 12, 2009; Dick Hoak, March 13, 2009.

Chapter 13

Page 67 *"If you have to get"* Jane Wolfe, *The Murchisons, The Rise and Fall of a Texas Dynasty* (New York: St. Martin's Press, 1989), p. 24.

Page 68 *"We're out . . ."* Ron Chernow, *Titan, The Life of John D. Rockefeller,* Sr. (New York: Random House, 1998), p. 431.

Page 69 *"money was like manure"* Bryan Burrough, *The Big Rich: The Rise and Fall of the Greatest Texas Oil Fortunes* (New York: Penguin Press, 2009), p. 159.

Page 69 *"Vice and Versa"* Ibid., p. 282.

Chapter 14

Page 71 *On January 9* Chastain, *Steeler Dynasty,* p. 31.

Page 71 *He'd get a* Terry Bradshaw, David Fisher, *It's Only a Game* (New York: Pocket Books, May 2001), p. 4.

Page 71 *Lying on his* Ibid.

Page 71 *Bradshaw played with* Ibid.

Page 72 *He learned how* Ibid., p. 6.

Page 72 *Dresses were made* Ibid., p. 7.

Page 73 *Europe who wanted him* Ibid., p. 23.

Page 73 *So instead of* Ibid., pp. 24–25.

Page 74 *"And everything I"* Rooney Jr., *Ruanaidh,* p. 264.

Page 74 *The scouting service* Ibid.

Page 75 *"He was a"* Ibid.

Page 75 *Noll was impressed* Ibid.

Page 75 *He might have* "Everyone's No. 1 Pick," *Sports Illustrated,* February 9, 1970.

Page 75 *And Art never* Chastain, *Dynasty,* p. 31.

Page 76 *Don Shula said* Bradshaw, Fisher, *It's Only a Game,* p. 29.

Page 76 *"Thrilled. I wanted"* "Everyone's No. 1 Pick," *Sports Illustrated,* February 9, 1970.

Chapter 15

Page 77 *Texas Schramm Jr.* David Harris, *The League: The Rise and Decline of the NFL* (New York: Bantam, 1986), p. 27.

Page 78 *"The only person"* Ibid.

Page 79 *Winter Olympics* Michael MacCambridge, *America's Game* (New York: Random House, 2004), p. 204.

Page 81 *"Mr. Vice-Commissioner"* David Harris, *The League: The Rise and Decline of the NFL* (New York: Bantam, 1986), p. 30.

Page 82 *"If I try"* Michael MacCambridge, *America's Game* (New York: Random House, 2004), p. 224.

Page 85 *"'It's a lack of character'"* Duane Thomas and Paul Zimmerman, *Duane Thomas and the Fall of America's Team* (New York: Warner Books, 1988), p. 50.

Chapter 16

Page 86 *"Collective bargaining"* "I.W. Abel of Steelworkers Dies at 78" *The New York Times*, Aug. 11, 1987.

Page 87 *A former star running back* "Right to Challenge; People and Power in the Steelworkers Union," *The New York Times*, Feb. 20, 1972.

Page 87 *"You've got the younger element"* "I.W. Abel of Steelworkers Dies at 78" *The New York Times*, Aug. 11, 1987.

Page 87 *"a buck for Emil"* "Steel Union Vote is Set for Today," *The New York Times*, Feb. 10, 1969.

Chapter 17

Page 89 *Noll arranged the* Interview, Rocky Bleier, May 22, 2009.

Page 89 *"This guy is"* Bradshaw, Fisher, *It's Only a Game*, p. 39.

Page 89 *The weekend of* Russell, *A Steeler Odyssey*, p. 128.

Page 90 *Nights were spent* Ibid.; Interview, Gerry Mullins, June 2, 2009.

Page 90 *That night, Russell* Russell, *A Steeler Odyssey*, p. 128.

Page 90 *Bradshaw made his* Ibid., p. 129.

Page 91 *"Nobody at Tech"* Bradshaw, Harris, *It's Only a Game*, p. 39.

Page 91 *He underestimated the* Ibid., p. 40.

Page 92 *"I couldn't believe"* NFL Films, *Steelers: The Complete History*.

Page 92 *After the game* Bradshaw, Harris, *It's Only a Game*, p. 42.

Page 92 *One night he* Ibid., p. 43.

Page 93 *"The only thing"* Ibid.

Page 93 The *punt was* Ibid.

Page 94 *Late in the* Russell, *A Steeler Odyssey,* p. 106; Interview, Joe Greene, June 1, 2009.

Page 94 *As the official* Ibid.

Page 94 *Only this time* Ibid.

Page 95 *"No one ever said"* Ibid.

Chapter 18

Page 96 *Murchison had been hoping* Jane Wolfe, *The Murchisons, The Rise and Fall of a Texas Dynasty* (New York: St. Martin's Press, 1989), pp. 305–10.

Page 96 *"the finest football stadium"* Ibid.

Page 97 *"The problem with"* Ibid.

Page 97 *"Circle Suites"* Ibid.

Chapter 19

Page 99 *"couldn't get over"* Duane Thomas and Paul Zimmerman, *Duane Thomas and the Fall of America's Team* (New York: Warner Books, 1988), p. 18.

Page 100 *"The first thing"* Ibid., p. 21.

Page 101 *"My day would start"* Ibid., p. 61.

Page 101 *"He said he'd"* Ibid., p. 48.

Page 103 *"He was perfect"* Ibid., p. 101.

Page 104 *"Nope. But I've"* Deane H Freeman and Jaime Aron, *I Remember Tom Landry* (Sports Publishing, LLC, 2001), p. 17.

Page 105 *"After that game"* Duane Thomas and Paul Zimmerman, *Duane Thomas and the Fall of America's Team* (New York: Warner Books, 1988), p. 74.

Chapter 20

Page 106 *Born and raised* Stanley H. Brown, *Ling: The Rise, Fall, and Return of a Texas Titan* (New York: Atheneum, 1972).

Page 106 *"two plus two"* "The Urge to Merge," *The New York Times,* Oct. 27, 1968.

Page 108 *"You wear two"* "Young Workers Are Raising Voices to Demand Factory and Union Changes," *The New York Times,* Jun. 1, 1970.

Chapter 21

Page 109 *"Tom never once"* Duane Thomas and Paul Zimmerman, *Duane Thomas and the Fall of America's Team* (New York: Warner Books, 1988), p. 87.

Page 110 *"The day that"* Ibid., p. 85.

Page 110 *"He came in"* Ibid., p. 80.

Page 110 *"From the first"* Ibid.

Page 110 *"I told him"* Ibid., p. 82.

Page 112 *"We had to"* Ibid., p. 87.

Page 112 *"A lot of players"* Ibid.

Page 113 *"dishonest, sick"* Ibid., p. 90.

Page 113 *"plastic man"* Ibid.

Page 114 *"shadowed by a"* Ibid., p. 92.

Page 114 *"I told him"* Ibid., p. 93.

Page 115 *"I suppose that"* Ibid., p. 110.

Page 116 *"I still have"* Ibid., p. 103.

Page 116 *"Duane represented"* Ibid., p. 104.

Chapter 22

Page 118 *Noll had a* Interviews, Dick Hoak, March 13, 2009; Dan Radakovich, May 15, 2009.

Page 118 *But after getting* Interview, Dan Radakovich, May 15, 2009.

Page 119 *Radakovich showed up* Ibid.

Page 119 *But Noll wanted* Interviews, Dick Hoak, March 13, 2009; Dan Radakovich, May 15, 2009.

Page 120 *When Joe Gordon* Fox, *Mean Joe Greene . . .* , p. 84.

Page 120 *"Some tried," he* Ibid.

Page 120 *At home, as* Ibid., p. 85.

Page 120 *He had gone* Ibid, p. 89.

Page 120 *Through those first* Interview, Dan Radakovich, May 15, 2009.

Page 120 *He didn't trust* Fox, *Mean Joe Greene . . .* , p. 82.

Page 121 *So Radakovich trained* Interview, Dan Radakovich, May 15, 2009.

Page 122 *We all came* Fox, *Mean Joe Greene . . .* , pp. 4–5.

Chapter 23

Page 123 *As the 1972* Interviews, Dan Radakovich, May 15, 2009; Art Rooney Jr., April 16, 2009.

Page 124 *All Penn State* Interview, Dan Radakovich, May 15, 2009.

Page 124 *During their senior* Blount Jr., *About Three Bricks . . .* , p. 332.

Page 125 *The next day* Ibid.

Page 125 *It was an* Interview, Dan Radakovich, May 15, 2009.

Page 126 *His agent stopped* Blount Jr., *About Three Bricks . . .* , pp. 332.

Chapter 24

Page 127 *Abel's biggest concerns* John P. Hoerr, *And the Wolf Finally Came* (Pittsburgh: University of Pittsburgh Press, 1988), pp. 109–13.

Chapter 25

Page 130 *He had taken* Interview, Dick Hoak, February 19, 2009.

Page 130 *those first few* Ibid; Interview, Andy Russell, March 12, 2009.

Page 131 *"Dick, don't overcoach'"* Interview, Dick Hoak.

Page 132 *In a trap* Interviews, Dan Radakovich, May 15, 2009; Gerry Mullins, June 2, 2009.

Page 132 *Harris not only* Interview, Joe Greene, June 1, 2009.

Page 133 *Their dominance was* Blount Jr., *About Three Bricks . . .* , p. 88.

Page 133 *On one play* Ibid.

Page 133 *A fourth starting* Matt Fulks, *The Good, The Bad and the Ugly: Pittsburgh Steelers* (Chicago: Triumph Books, Sept. 2008), p. 11.

Chapter 26

Page 135 *They wore green* NFL Films, *Steelers: The Complete History.*

Page 136 *"They just approached"* Interview, Franco Harris, May 22, 2009.

Page 136 *There was an* NFL Films, *Steelers: The Complete History.*

Page 137 *They begged Steelers* Ibid.

Page 137 *After a couple* "The Immaculate Reception," *Sports Illustrated,* August 20, 1973.

Page 137 *"Dear Frank:* We": Ibid.

Page 138 *It was the* Ibid.

Page 138 *They had an* NFL Films, *Steelers: The Complete History.*

Page 138 *"Franco, get over"* Ibid.

Page 138 *"It was like"* "The Immaculate Reception," *Sports Illustrated*, August 20, 1973.

Page 139 *Before the night* Fox, Mean Joe Greene . . . , p. 124.

Page 139 *Once, as an* Interview, Harold Siegel, March 20, 2009.

Page 140 *"He wanted nothing"* Rooney, Maisch, Halaas, *My 75 Years* . . . , p. 109.

Page 140 *"Not only by"* Ibid.

Page 140 *"Treating NFL teams"* Ibid.

Page 141 *"Yeah," Noll said* Chastain, *Steel Dynasty*, p. 60.

Page 141 *It was a* Bradshaw, Fisher, *It's Only a Game*, p. 110.

Page 141 *Meanwhile, Stagno dropped* NFL Films, *Steelers: The Complete History.*

Page 142 At that moment: Chastain, *Steel Dynasty*, p. 60.

Page 142 *Just then, Vento* NFL Films, *Steelers: The Complete History.*

Page 142 *As the ball* Fox, *Mean Joe Greene* . . . , p. 128.

Page 142 *He'd missed what* NFL Films, *Steelers: The Complete History.*

Page 142 *Forty-five minutes* Steelergridiron.com; http://www.steelergridiron .com/history/reception.html.

Page 143 *Then Cope said* Ibid.

Chapter 27

Page 147 *"He's in trouble"* Fox, *Mean Joe Greene* . . . , p. 148.

Page 147 *The Steelers cut* Ibid., p. 99.

Page 148 *"Yeah, fat boy"* Ibid., p. 97.

Page 148 *The Steelers brought* Ibid., p. 106.

Page 148 *Holmes had decided* Ibid.

Page 149 *"I don't know"* "Half a Ton of Trouble," *Time*, December 8, 1975.

Page 149 *Occasionally he'd stop* Rooney, Maisch, Halaas, *My 75 Years* . . . , p. 187.

Page 149 *During practices veteran* Interview, Mike Wagner, June 6, 2009.

Page 150 *But in March* Fox, *Mean Joe Greene* . . . , p. 149; "Dodging a Silver Bullet," *Sports Illustrated*, March 7, 1977; "Half a Ton of Trouble," *Time*, December 8, 1975.

Page 150 *He was overextended* Ibid.

Page 150 *Without promising anything* Ibid.

Page 150 *He arrived after* Fox, *Mean Joe Greene* . . . , p. 150.

Page 150 *At the scene* "Half a Ton of Trouble," *Time*, December 8, 1975.

Page 150 *The state police* Fox, *Mean Joe Greene* . . . , p. 151.

Page 150 *He carried his* Fox, *Mean Joe Greene* . . . , p. 151; "Dodging a Silver Bullet," *Sports Illustrated*, March 7, 1977; "Half a Ton of Trouble," *Time*, December 8, 1975.

Page 150 *We could have* Fox, *Mean Joe Greene* . . . , p. 151.

Page 150 *"We'll do everything* Ibid., p. 152.

Page 151 *At sentencing, a* Fox, *Mean Joe Greene* . . . , p. 157; "Dodging a Silver Bullet," *Sports Illustrated*, March 7, 1977; "Half a Ton of Trouble," *Time*, December 8, 1975.

Page 151 *Holmes had three* Blount Jr., *About Three Bricks* . . . , p. 130.

Page 152 *"I don't watch"* Ibid.

Page 154 *Hanratty, meanwhile, was* Interview, Terry Hanratty, June 4, 2009.

Page 154 *The next week* Fox, *Mean Joe Greene* . . . , p. 166.

Chapter 28

Page 156 *"You go in there"* James B. Lane and Mike Olszanski, *Steel Shavings: Steelworkers Fight Back* (Gary, Indiana: Indiana University Northwest, 2000), p. 80.

Page 159 *"I went on"* Ibid., p. 75.

Page 159 *Pittsburgh-based USWA* "USW Rebel Sadlowski Has Rebel Backer Here," *Pittsburgh Press*, Nov. 28, 1976.

Page 160 *"Really, I'm Irish"* "The Boxer and the Blonde," *Sports Illustrated*, Jun. 17, 1985.

Page 161 *"All the union bosses"* "Oilcan Eddie Takes on the Old Guard," *The New York Times*, Dec. 19, 1976.

Chapter 29

Page 163 *Every year, Nunn* Interview, Bill Nunn, May 28, 2009.

Page 164 *He went to* Ibid.

Page 164 *He helped the* Rooney Jr., *Ruanaidh*, p. 135.

Page 164 *His times were* Interview, Bill Nunn, May 28, 2009.

Page 165 *He kept it* Chastain, *Steel Dynasty*, p. 83.

Page 165 *But he was* Rooney Jr., *Ruanaidh*, p. 151.

Page 165 *It wasn't his* Interview, Art Rooney Jr., April 16, 2009.

Page 166 *When he exploded* Interview, Andy Russell, March 12, 2009.

Page 166 *"He was just"* Chastain, *Steel Dynasty*, p. 83.

Chapter 30

Page 167 *For more than a century* David H. Wollman and Donald R. Inman, *Portraits in Steel* (Kent, Ohio: The Kent State University Press, 1999).

Page 169 *"the best possible"* Ibid p. 59.

Page 171 *"Little Siberia"* "Aliquippa: The Company Town and the Contested Power in the Construction of Law," *Buffalo Law Review*, Winter 1995.

Page 171 *Wesley and Myrtle* Tony Dorsett & Harvey Frommer, *Running Tough* (New York: Doubleday, 1989), p. 3.

Page 172 *"The name Dorsett"* Ibid., p. 8.

Page 173 *"Hey, man"* Ibid., p. 9.

Page 173 *Midget Football League* Ibid.

Page 173 *"You can't even"* Ibid.

Page 173 *"I remember"* Ibid., p. 10.

Page 174 *"flashes of color"* Ibid., p. 88.

Page 174 *"Do something better"* Ibid., p. 6.

Page 174 *"Once I was sent"* Ibid.

Chapter 31

Page 175 *"No freedom, no"* Interview, Gerry Mullins, June 2, 2009.

Page 175 *Some people thought* Blount Jr., *About Three Bricks ...*, p. 99.

Page 176 *With both legs:* Ibid Chastain, *Steel Dynasty*, p. 93; Interview, Rocky Bleier, May 22, 2009.

Page 176 *Hanratty, his buddy* Chastain, *Steel Dynasty*, p. 94.

Page 176 *Bleier went through* Interview, Rocky Bleier, May 22, 2009.

Page 176 *The next day* Ibid.

Page 177 *After visiting his* Ibid.

Page 177 *Occasionally, he used* Interview, Rocky Bleier, February 11, 2010.

Page 177 *They had become* "Pumped up Pioneers: The '63 Chargers," ESPN .com, February 1, 2009, http://sports.espn.go.com/espn/otl/news/story?id=3866837.

Page 178 *By 1973, Bleier* Blount Jr., *About Three Bricks ...*, p. 99.

Page 178 *But in the* Interview, Rocky Bleier, July 16, 2009.

Page 178 *Dan negotiated with* Fox, *Mean Joe Greene* . . . , p. 159.

Page 179 *Then he left* Interview, Gerry Mullins, January 18, 2010.

Page 179 *Against the advice* Rooney, Maisch, Halaas, *My 75 Years* . . . , p. 154.

Page 179 *He had a* Blount Jr., *About Three Bricks* . . . , p. 190.

Chapter 32

Page 180 *And then a* Tony Dorsett & Harvey Frommer, *Running Tough*, p. 9.

Page 180 *"When Melvin died"* Ibid.

Page 181 *"That kid will"* Ibid., p.13.

Page 181 *"That Dorsett's just"* Ibid., p.16.

Page 183 *"If this is"* Ibid., p.21.

Page 183 *"We've got an"* Ibid.

Page 184 *"Even with my"* Ibid., p. 23.

Page 184 *"If you quit"* Ibid., p. 24.

Page 185 *"I had outrushed"* Ibid., p. 33.

Page 185 *"The media made"* Ibid., p.36.

Page 186 *"As far as"* http://www.youtube.com/watch?v=y6rlq_Sp6Mg.

Chapter 33

Page 187 *After he was* "A Living Legend Called Mean Smilin' Jack," *Sports Illustrated*, July 12, 1976.

Page 187 *"First set of"* Tom Danyluk, The Super 70s (Mad Uke Publishing, 2005), p. 15.

Page 188 *Lambert had blond* Russell, *A Steeler Odyssey*, p. 212.

Page 188 *"Kiss my ass"* Terry Bradshaw, Buddy Martin, *Looking Deep* (New York: Berkley, 1991), p. 79.

Page 188 *They played poker* Interviews, Joe Greene, Franco Harris, Gerry Mullins.

Page 189 *After games, Three* Interview, Rocky Bleier, May 22, 2009.

Page 189 *One year Bradshaw* Blount Jr., *About Three Bricks* . . . , p. 81.

Page 190 *If a guy* Interviews, Joe Greene, Franco Harris, Gerry Mullins, Rocky Bleier.

Page 190 *A lack of* Interview, Joe Greene, June 1, 2009.

Chapter 34

Page 191 *Noll, who let* Rooney, Maisch, Halaas, *My 75 Years . . .* , p. *155.*

Page 192 *But Gilliam consistently* Ibid., p. 156.

Page 192 *Several times on* Ibid.

Page 192 *At one point* Fox, *Mean Joe Greene . . .* , p. 172.

Page 192 *He was "Pittsburgh's"* "Pittsburgh's Black Quarterback," *Sports Illustrated*, September 23, 1974.

Page 193 *While Noll didn't* Ibid.

Page 193 *Afterward, even Noll* Fox, *Mean Joe Greene . . .* , p. 173.

Page 194 *That week, Greene* Blount Jr., *About Three Bricks . . .* , p. 265.

Page 194 *But in the* Interview, Dick Hoak, March 13, 2009.

Page 195 *The theory for* Ibid., Fox, *Mean Joe Greene . . .* , p. 184.

Page 195 *So he had* Ibid.

Page 195 *Greene lined up* Ibid.

Page 195 *Either Greene and* Ibid.

Page 195 *It also made* Ibid.

Page 196 *"If you can"* Fox, *Mean Joe Greene . . .* , p. 194.

Chapter 35

Page 197 *Joe Chiodo's tavern* Author's recollection.

Page 197 *"mystery meat sandwich"* Ibid.

Page 198 *"When my father"* Art Rooney Jr., *Ruanaidh* (Pittsburgh, Art Rooney Jr., 2008), p. 177.

Page 198 *Owney McManus's* Ibid., p. 177.

Page 198 *"Fuck the Steelers"* Ibid., p. 177.

Chapter 36

Page 201 *"It was a"* NFL Films, *The Super Bowl Champions: Pittsburgh Steelers Collection.*

Page 201 *It showed, even* Ibid.

Page 201 *That week in* Ibid.

Page 202 *Then Stabler winked* Russell, *A Steeler Odyssey*, p. 174.

Page 202 *"You hear people"* NFL Films, *The Super Bowl Champions: Pittsburgh Steelers Collection.*

Page 203 *So with Bourbon* Interviews, Andy Russell, March 12, 2009; Jack Ham, May 15, 2009.

Page 203 *Mike Wagner learned* Interview, Mike Wagner, June 2, 2009.

Page 203 *At one point* Interview, Andy Russell, March 12, 2009.

Page 203 *The night before* Blount Jr., *About Three Bricks . . .* , p. 269.

Page 204 *Come Saturday night* Fox, *Mean Joe Greene . . .* , p. 5.

Page 204 *Before they left* Interview, Terry Hanratty, June 4, 2009.

Page 205 *At one point* Bradshaw, Martin, *Looking Deep*, p. 111.

Page 205 *Perles had told him* Fox, *Mean Joe Greene . . .* , p. 14.

Page 205 *At one point* Interview, Andy Russell, March 12, 2009.

Page 206 *At one point* Interview, Gerry Mullins, June 2, 2009.

Page 207 *The game-winning* Fox, *Mean Joe Greene . . .* , p. 217.

Page 207 *In the locker* Interview, Andy Russell, March 12, 2009.

Page 207 *With tears in* Chastain, *Steel Dynasty*, p. 119.

Chapter 37

Page 211 *Tim Rooney, one* Interview, Mike Wagner, June 2, 2009.

Page 211 *The prickly middle* NFL Films, *The Super Bowl Champions: Pittsburgh Steelers Collection.*

Page 211 *Sports Illustrated wrote* "For Openers, Super Bowl VIII1/2," *Sports Illustrated*, December 23, 1974.

Page 212 *It didn't matter* Ibid.

Page 212 *Or that his* Ibid.

Page 212 *Lambert was so* Ibid.

Page 213 *Grossman, a nice* Interview, Randy Grossman, June 2, 2009.

Page 213 *Bleier's constant talking* Interview, Rocky Bleier, May 22, 2009.

Page 213 *Bradshaw's acting* Interview, Andy Russell, March 12, 2009.

Page 213 *The merry prankster* Interviews, Russell, March 12, 2009; Bleier, May 22, 2009; Wagner, June 2, 2009.

Page 213 *Once, he started* Interview, Terry Hanratty, June 4, 2009.

Page 213 *He'd fill a* Ibid; Interview, Rocky Bleier, May 22, 2009.

Page 213 *During practice one* Ibid.

Page 214 *During the end* Russell, *A Steeler Odyssey*, p. 169.

Page 215 *Then Bradshaw threw* Ibid.

Page 215 *The Steel Curtain* "Half a Ton of Trouble," *Time*, December 8, 1975.

Page 215 *Looking for a* Interview, Dan Radakovich, May 19, 2009.

Page 216 *One day during* Ibid.

Page 216 *Another innovation* Ibid. Interview, Gerry Mullins, June 2, 2009.

Page 217 *And with less* "A Steel Bit Drills the Oilers," *Sports Illustrated*, November 17, 1975.

Page 217 *Players often heard* Blount Jr., *About Three Bricks* . . . , p. 122.

Page 217 *The Steeler huddles* Interview, Gerry Mullins, June 2, 2009.

Page 217 *For the season* "A Steel Bit Drills the Oilers," *Sports Illustrated*, November 17, 1975.

Chapter 38

Page 218 *Edward Ayoub* John P. Hoerr, *And the Wolf Finally Came*, p. 72.

Page 219 *"The second afternoon"* James B. Lane and Mike Olszanski, *Steel Shavings: Steelworkers Fight Back* (Gary, Indiana: Indiana University Northwest, 2000), p. 75.

Page 220 *"I've listened"* Ibid.

Page 220 *"It's obvious, Sadlowski"* Ibid.

Chapter 39

Page 221 *Eight of eleven* Rooney, Maisch, Halaas, *My 75 Years* . . . , p. 182.

Page 221 *It was radio* "Tales of the Terrible Towel." *Sports Illustrated*, July 30, 1979.

Page 222 *On his nightly* Ibid.

Page 222 *Come Sunday, even* Rooney, Maisch, Halaas, *My 75 Years* . . . , p. 183.

Page 222 *The club had* Ibid.

Page 222 *Water seeped in* NFL Films, *1975 Steelers*.

Page 223 *"We saw Jaws"* "Two for the Super Bowl," *Sports Illustrated*, January 12, 1976.

Page 223 *"You couldn't play"* Fulks, *The Good, The Bad and The Ugly* . . . , p. 134.

Page 223 *"The hardest hitting"* "Two for the Super Bowl," *Sports Illustrated*, January 12, 1976.

Page 223 *As a receiver* "An Old Raiders Old-School Values," *The New York Times*, December 9, 2009.

Page 224 *"Thank you," Greene* NFL Films, *1975 Steelers*.

Page 224 *"We'll be bringing"* "Two for the Super Bowl," *Sports Illustrated*, January 12, 1976.

Chapter 40

Page 225 *Swann hadn't been* NFL Films, *The Super Bowl Champions: Pittsburgh Steelers Collection*.

Page 225 *Cowboys players had* Wikipedia http://en.wikipedia.org/wiki/Cliff_Harris.

Page 225 *"I read what"* NFL Films, *The Super Bowl Champions: Pittsburgh Steelers Collection*.

Page 225 *Doctors had told* Ibid.

Page 227 *"They mess up"* "Two for the Super Bowl," *Sports Illustrated,* January 26, 1976.

Page 227 *"I hope Staubach"* Ibid.

Page 227 *The cost of* Wikipedia, Super Bowl X, http://en.wikipedia.org/wiki/Super_Bowl_X.

Page 227 *Someone had forgotten* Blount Jr., *About Three Bricks . . .* , p. 298.

Page 228 *Henderson stopped the* Thomas Henderson, *Out of Control* (New York: Pocket, 1990), p. 65.

Page 228 *On the play* Blount Jr., *About Three Bricks . . .* , p. 298.

Page 228 *Standing on the* Bradshaw, Martin, *Looking Deep,* p. 120.

Page 229 *Lambert was so* Blount Jr., *About Three Bricks . . .* , p. 298.

Page 230: *But in the* "Dallas Feels the Steeler Crunch," *Sports Illustrated*, January 26, 1976.

Page 231 *"I don't care"* Ibid.

Chapter 41

Page 234 *"You have a"* Chastain, *Steel Dynasty,* p. 144; Rooney, Maisch, Halaas, *My 75 Years . . .* , p. 188.

Page 234 *For his hit* Rooney, Maisch, Halaas, *My 75 Years . . .* , p. 191.

Page 235 *Passes were so* Chastain, *Steel Dynasty,* p. 151.

Page 235 *Lambert called it* NFL Films, *Steelers: The Complete History*.

Chapter 42

Page 236 *For a few days* Author's recollection.

Chapter 43

Page 239 *"Don't let me go" Running Tough.*

Page 240 *"We realized we"* Ibid., p. 47.

Page 240 *"My mom and"* Ibid.

Page 241 *"nigger son of a"* Ibid., p.51.

Page 241 *"Whenever a fight"* Ibid.

Page 241 *"being and outspoken"* Ibid., p. 52.

Page 241 *"All through high"* Ibid.

Page 242 *"In a game"* Ibid., p. 55.

Page 243 *"Tony, I hear"* Ibid., p. 62.

Page 243 *"If you showed"* Ibid., p. 65.

Page 244 *"One night I was"* Ibid., p. 75.

Chapter 44

Page 245 *Edward Sadlowski's USWA* James B. Lane and Mike Olszanski, *Steel Shavings: Steelworkers Fight Back*, p. 80.

Page 246 *"a rebel candidate"* "Oilcan Eddie Takes on the Old Guard," *The New York Times*, Dec. 19, 1976.

Page 246 *"the beginning of"* Archie Green, *Wobblies, Pile Butts, and Other Heroes*, p. 269.

Page 248 *"First of all"* Penthouse Interview, Ed Sadlowski, *Penthouse*, January 1977.

Page 248 *"The poor motherfucker"* Ibid.

Page 249 *"You know, I"* James B. Lane and Mike Olszanski, *Steel Shavings: Steelworkers Fight Back*, p. 80.

Page 249 *Coyne pushed hard* Author's recollection.

Chapter 45

Page 250 *Depositions were taken* Rooney, Maisch, Halaas, *My 75 Years . . .* , p. 193.

Page 250 *Upon hearing that* Steelers website http://news.steelers.com/article/78767.

Page 251 *The capricious middle* Ibid.

Page 251 *"This isn't like"* Ibid.

Page 251 *In December, the* Ibid.

Page 252 *Noll knew his* Interviews, Dan Radakovich, January 7, 2010; Art Rooney Jr., January 18, 2010.

Page 252 *He had been* "Pumped up Pioneers: The '63 Chargers," ESPN.com, February 1, 2009, http://sports.espn.go.com/espn/otl/news/story?id=3866837.

Page 252 *In the mid* "Big Night," *ESPN The Magazine*, January 21, 2003.

Page 253 *While they had* Ibid.; Interview, Ted Petersen, January 7, 2010.

Page 253 *Growing up on* "Blood and Guts," ESPN.com, January 25, 2005, http://sports.espn.go.com/nfl/news/story?id=1972286

Page 253 *Years later, espn.com* Ibid.

Page 254 *He had heard* Steve Courson, *False Glory* (Stamford, CT.: Longmeadow Press, 1991), p. 17.

Page 254 *Within a month* Ibid.

Page 254 *On drive block* Interviews, Ted Petersen, June 15, 2009; Dan Radakovich, January 7, 2010.

Page 255 *His successor in* "A Detailed History," *San Diego Union-Tribune*, September 21, 2008.

Page 255 *Bob Young, an* "Big Night," *ESPN The Magazine*, January 21, 2003.

Page 255 *Courson, who bench* Courson, *False Glory*, p. 18.

Page 255 *Right up until* Obituary, *Boston Globe*, November 11, 2005.

Page 255 *The day he* Interview, Tony Dungy, September 23, 2009.

Page 255 *Dungy backed up* Ibid.

Page 256 *Then he threw* Ibid.

Chapter 46

Page 257 *On Christmas Eve* Author's recollection.

Page 257 *"Our union has"* "Steelworkers Seek U.S. Aid for Industry," *The New York Times*, Oct. 12, 1977.

Page 258 *"We're all sitting"* Interview, Peter Mamula, April 17, 2009.

Chapter 47

Page 260 *"We realized we"* Tony Dorsett and Harvey Frommer, *Running Tough*, p. 47.

Page 260 *"The Cowboys needed"* Ibid., p. 71.

Chapter 48

Page 263 *Noll gave his* Interview, Vito Stellino, October 5, 2009.

Page 263 *But one player* Steelers website, http://news.steelers.com/article/81099.

Page 264 *Which is why* Ibid.

Page 264 *"This camp is"* Ibid.

Page 265 *Stallworth had no* Bradshaw, Martin, *Looking Deep*, p. 76.

Page 265 *He had been* Blount Jr., *About Three Bricks . . .* , p. 312.

Page 267 *"I think Bradshaw's"* Steelers website, http://news.steelers.com/article/81099.

Page 267 *"I doubt I'll"* Ibid.

Page 267 *The front four* Interview, Jack Ham, May 15, 2009.

Page 268 *Noll had a* Interview, Tony Dungy, September 23, 2009.

Page 268 *"Gentlemen, I want"* Interviews, Rocky Bleier, July 16, 2009; Randy Grossman, June 26, 2009.

Chapter 49

Page 270 *When Schramm told* Henderson, *Out of Control*, p. 218.

Page 271 *"It seemed like"* Ibid.

Page 271 *He'd blow them* Ibid., p. 206.

Page 271 *He did coke* Ibid., p. 213.

Page 271 *His pregame routine* Ibid., p. 237.

Page 272 *And as the* Ibid., pp. 235–36.

Page 272 *He would have* Ibid., p. 250.

Chapter 50

Page 273 *The Steelers had* Chastain, *Steel Dynasty*, p. 176.

Page 273 *A Really Super* "A Really Super Bowl," *Newsweek*, January 22, 1979.

Page 273 *Finally, he finished* Chastain, *Steel Dynasty*, p. 176.

Page 274 *But it punctured* Bradshaw, Martin, *Looking Deep*, p. 124.

Page 274 *Noll's response was* Chastain, *Steel Dynasty*, p. 176.

Page 274 *During practices leading* Interview, Gerry Mullins, June 2, 2009.

Page 275 *At a morning* Interview, Ted Petersen, June 15, 2009.

Page 275 *It was about* Interview, Cliff Stoudt, January 8, 2010.

Page 276 *Then, on first* NFL Films, *The Super Bowl Champions: Pittsburgh Steelers Collection.*

Page 276 *While watching Cowboys* Ibid.

Page 276 *During practice, when* Ibid.

Page 278 *Doctors told him* Interview, Cliff Stoudt, January 8, 2010.

Page 279 *That September, needing* NFL Films, *The Super Bowl Champions: Pittsburgh Steelers Collection.*

Page 280 *Before the game* Henderson, *Out of Control*, p. 253.

Page 280 *But in the* Bradshaw, Fisher, It's Only a Game, p. 78.

Page 281 *On the next* NFL Films, *The Super Bowl Champions: Pittsburgh Steelers Collection.*

Page 281 *They lined up* Interview, Tony Dungy, January 7, 2010.

Page 281 *When the Cowboys* NFL Films, *The Super Bowl Champions: Pittsburgh Steelers Collection.*

Page 282 *Nearby, Dungy was* Interview, Tony Dungy, January 7, 2010.

Page 282 *That night, the* Interview, Cliff Stoudt, January 8, 2010.

Page 282 *It was five* Ibid.

Page 283 *Players, coaches, owners* NFL Films, *The Super Bowl Champions: Pittsburgh Steelers Collection.*

Page 283 *They yelled "Chief"* Ibid.

Page 283 *Then the room* Ibid.

INDEX